JUST FOR ONE HOUR

JUST FOR ONE HOUR

MOMENTS I PINCHED MYSELF IN THE MUSIC INDUSTRY

JOHN KENNEDY

First published in Great Britain in 2024.

Copyright © John Kennedy 2024.

Thanks to Wikipedia.

ISBN 978-1-0685184-0-9 (Print hardback version)
ISBN 978-1-0685184-2-3 (Print paperback version)
ISBN 978-1-0685184-1-6 (eBook)

Published by John Kennedy 2024
Cover Concept – Sam Barclay

Design and Artwork – Martin Lewis
www.martinlewisdesign.com

Picture credits;
All photos; © John Kennedy.
Except;
Page 252; Nick Stern, PA Images / Alamy Stock Photo.
Page 304; Top left; NDK / Alamy Stock Photo.
Page 304; Top right; Joe Sohm, Visions of America, LLC / Alamy Stock Photo.
Page 304; Bottom left; Tim Graham / Alamy Stock Photo.
Page 304; Bottom right; Fabio Diena / Alamy Stock Photo

With thanks to:

MY WIFE CAROLINE
Still the most beautiful woman in any room.

ELLIE, CONOR, AND GRACE
Our three wonderful children
who are very nervous about
what faux pas I will make
in this book.

MY LONG DEPARTED MUM AND DAD,
ELLIE AND MICHAEL
Who gave us our Irish heritage and the spirit,
strength, determination, and stubbornness
that comes with that.

MY SIBLINGS
JIM, MICHAEL, PAT, MAURICE, AND ANNE
For love and support.

LESLEY SPINKS
For going so far beyond the call
of duty with her help and advice.

TINA HUGHES AND JILL SINCLAIR
For chiding me for talking about a book
but not doing anything about it – that
chiding was very important,
thank you!

CONTENTS

INTRODUCTION

Why have I had the cheek to write a book and the bigger cheek of expecting you to read it?

Well I could point out I have worked in the music industry for more than 45 years and dealt with and been friends with many superstars, but you know that would not be enough to justify this book.

I can justify this book because of one single minute on a Monday in November 1984.

At the time I was a music business lawyer plying my trade by charging for my time by the hour.

My office door slammed open! And there was the man I saw on the evening news the night before. You know him as Sir Bob Geldof or 'Saint Bob' or for some 'that scruffy Irishman'.

I didn't really know him personally – I didn't think he knew me but he was looking for me.

He told me he needed my help – he needed just one hour of my time to negotiate a record deal for his charity record.

It wasn't a request it was a demand. Of course I said 'yes' and the lanky, impetuous domineering Irishman charged off down the corridor shouting at someone else.

At the time he was famous for being the lead singer in The Boomtown Rats. He was about to become the most famous person in the world telling presidents and prime ministers what to do about the terrible famine in Africa.

He (we) would put on the greatest concert in the world.

He would transform individual and politicians' thoughts on overseas aid and he would change and save many lives.

And for all of this I would have a ringside seat – that's why I hope you will find this book worth reading.

I promised an hour of my time, and in the end it was a lifetime's commitment, but I would not have swapped for anything and certainly not for fees.

That 'hour' turned into 40 years of the maddest, wildest, most terrifying, most gratifying, and finally along with my family the most wonderful part of my life.

It's been an honour and a privilege to be part of the Band Aid, Live Aid and Live 8 journey, but during it I had various day jobs, and stories from the day jobs also pepper the pages of this book.

John Kennedy OBE
August 2024

FOREWORD by Bob Geldof

There is not, never was, and never can be Band Aid without John Kennedy.

Although since 1985 we are the same small group of trustees guiding the good ship Band Aid, it is Kennedy who is in effect the CEO. The enabler. The protector. The inexhaustible small print and document reader who ensures that all the tens of millions we received is not only safe but well spent, accounted for and has resulted in the best possible outcomes we would have wished for. And for 40 years all of this monstrous responsibility and workload done for free. All the studying and necessary knowledge of shipping laws, commercial law, purchase and trans-national law etc etc etc.

Nothing. Not a cup of coffee or a phone call has been charged for. Why? Because he believes through a long career with the greatest artists in rock 'n' roll that this is what's right. The pop singers could write or play their songs for the starving but John is a lawyer/manager/executive and this is what he felt he could turn his talents to. He would contribute himself. If I felt at the time, and still today, that the disastrous, sickening and shameful African famine of '84 -'86 then and now demanded something other than a quid in the charity box, that there needed to be given something of the self to almost expunge the shame and grief, and yes guilt and rage, then so too did he.

I'm not sure how, or why, but a strange ragtag of people seemed to just gather around me back in those days as I railed and ranted and rashly promised but had no real idea how precisely I could ever fulfil that promise, that cheque my mouth wrote but my brain couldn't cash. John was probably the first person to say "you're going to need to do this…" and I blithely said "could you just take care of that for me please." And he did. And 40 years on is still taking care of it.

There were two groups. The trustees, the suits – but not really – showbiz types don't really do suits and if they do they're usually f*cking horrible things, those who protected me from my more intemperate urgings and more importantly the gathering of the monies, its safety and its expenditure.

And then there were the enablers, another group who understood the "suits" hadn't a single clue as to how to spend that money, and on what, but they did, and could organise the actual aid effort into coherence and effect as the "movement" (I suppose that's what it was) and our financial and political clout grew exponentially. That was and that is Band Aid.

And as I continued to rant and rail and at each step announcing some new improbability these poor, long-suffering fellow travellers would clutch their heads, watch my back and then help me realise the shared and ludicrous dream of keeping as many people alive as possible.

He's a very wise person is Kennedy. An odd cove to be sure. He's a ferociously hard deal maker. He speaks in a peremptory blunt, often monosyllabic, manner that some might take for rudeness. And some times it is! He gets outraged at perceived unfairness. He often finds the law faulty or over-blunt and lacking nuance or sensibility so that Justice can be simply too cruel when what is needed is understanding. But he is at the same time a fiercely competitive lawyer/talent manager or whatever role he decides to take on in the rock recording industry. And he has done it all and with all of them. He is also a fabulous and hilarious storyteller and those wildly improbable stories and characters are all here in this book. What a life!

He is a lovely man, he is my great friend whom I depend upon and lean on almost unconsciously but never without relief and gratitude and if I ever listen to anyone's advice - it's his. Poor bugger. Such is his burden and my complete confidence in his knowledge, sagacity and wisdom and I mean it quite literally when I tell you that none of us, and definitely not myself, could have even begun Live Aid and Live 8 or any of everything we've done without this man. Nothing. None of it. It would all have been a disaster. I and we all owe him.

He walks bent foreword into the headwinds of his life, determined, aggressive, blunt, peremptory, funny but ... the kindest of men, the most empathetic of souls, one of the loveliest of people. A good man to his marrow. I have met many great men in my life and he, for me, stands square amongst them.

CHAPTER 1

EARLY LIFE

I have joked for a long time that I would write a book – so do many people. If like me you are not a celebrity and if like me you do not have a publisher then you should write as if you will be the only person who would read it, maybe my wife – maybe – certainly not my children. Anyone who has children will know if you can't get the attention of a publisher then you have absolutely no hope of getting your kids interested, but that's fine. I suspect one day they will read it maybe six months after my funeral.

I don't know what this is – is it an autobiography – a memoir? I suppose of sorts – anyhow whatever it is I know when I read such a book I struggle through the writer's childhood so I will try and fly through the first quarter of a century of my life.

I was born in February 1953 – I will omit the day for reasons which will become clear later – one of six kids of Irish immigrants.

London in the 1950s you could play football in the streets but some days the smog made it dark before sunset, you didn't go inside but you knew it wasn't normal. I was born in our front room, nothing extraordinary about that but the house had three different groups of occupants. The owner of the house was a German lady – Miss Homberger – she had two rooms on the first floor and there was an air of mystery about her.

I was born less than a decade after the Second World War and as I grew up almost every film on TV, (when we got a TV), was a war film – and they left you in no doubt that the Germans were baddies. The strange thing is we didn't see her much. In fact I don't really ever remember seeing her more than once even though I shared a house with her for at least 10 years. On the top floor was an elderly couple Mr and Mrs de Pavia and they had just two rooms.

What seems extraordinary is that Miss Homberger was prepared to let the house to my mum and dad and their four children – this was the era of the signs 'No dogs, No blacks, No Irish, No Jews'. Fortunately we have come a long way from that and for some reason I had the impression that I must have got from my parents that our landlady was a good woman – happy to give a safe (not warm - before central heating) home to a young family. Maybe she understood that prejudiced list could easily have included 'No Germans' if any landlord thought a German would be applying, and maybe she was Jewish, and maybe a refugee – I will never know now.

So three families – one outside toilet (every autobiography needs one!) and one inside bathroom which we were only allowed to use on Saturday evenings. We were not allowed to use the inside toilet – I think that showed that Miss Homberger, as well as being a kind woman, was an astute woman – I wouldn't want to share a loo with a family of eight even if they were my family! Miss Homberger didn't collect the rent, the rent man came on Saturdays and the coal man less regularly – and would of course pour sacks of the black, dirty, toxic coal into our cellar. What would Greta have made of that – especially as we would often play down there?

So I am writing about a time 60 plus years ago – tough times? Yes and no ... one of the most striking things about the time and for which I will be eternally grateful was the NHS and the education system.

We were as working class as you could possibly get. With eight mouths to feed from a carpenter's wage I am sure we were poor but I never ever felt it. We never went hungry though I suspect that sometimes my mum did put food on our plates from hers. In fact my mum used to say rich people don't eat as well as we do - I think she was right.

I got distracted, the point I was making is that as a working class family we had extraordinary access to a great education and healthcare – this was socialism at its best. There was the opportunity to keep well and in due course to become upwardly mobile because of a great education and great parents. Of course there were social inequalities but I wasn't aware of them and put them on a set of scales opposite great schooling and health care and it would be as if you put feathers on the scale.

Our community was a Catholic Irish community bound together by work – and for my father the pub – and by school for the kids. For my mum there wasn't much chance to think beyond cooking, washing and ironing and then each summer we would head back to Ireland.

Catastrophe hit when I was very young – my father fell off a high floor on a building site – he was in hospital for a long time and then unable to work for even longer. When he was released from hospital and we went to collect him I remember him shaking my hand as if I was a stranger – I realised he was out of hospital but not fully recovered.

I knew things were bad, how do you feed eight people when the bread winner isn't winning bread anymore?

I have done very stressful jobs over the years but I have never lost sight of the fact that the most stressful thing in the world is when a bill drops on you mat and you can't afford to pay it and I remember how frightening it must have been for my mother with a hospitalised husband and breadwinner and seven mouths to feed. Yes I knew things were bad but I didn't suffer the badness. I certainly never went hungry, nor was I aware of the extraordinary battle that must have been going on to make ends meet. I have no idea how she did this but my mother, as well as looking after seven people, took on night work as an untrained nurse and Jim my eldest brother curtailed his education to get a job. A real sacrifice that he never mentioned or complained of – in fact when I last discussed it he said he didn't curtail his education it was just natural timing.

From this working class background I am undoubtedly now middle class – often with a critical eye of trade unions and their leaders. However I don't know what would have happened without my father's membership of his union. No doubt he had paid a weekly membership fee and maybe at times he wondered if it was money well spent with those eight mouths to feed, but believe me it was!To be fair, the social security system kicked in as well. I remember being sent to the post office to collect two payments that as a family we were entitled to because of my father's accident. I am sure they were not big payments but they were very important payments in the scheme of things.

Of course my mother would have not known much about the circumstances of my father's accident, nor would she have had the time, energy or expertise to take on his employers – but his union 'stepped up', maybe prodded by his work colleagues. There had been a missing guard rail where my father was working – one that would have stopped him falling if it was in place.

The union hired a solicitor, of course my mother probably did not even know what one of those was (though subsequently two of her sons would qualify in that profession) and the solicitor did their job. The building company accepted liability and so then it was a question of what would the damages be? My mother had to go and see a barrister in the unfamiliar terrain of the Inns of Court in Lincoln's Inn Fields, London. It's not difficult to imagine what a daunting experience it was and funnily enough I don't ever remember hearing that my father was interviewed about the accident. Anyhow, my mother would tell the story of her going to see a very posh, serious man in an office full of books. No matter how good the barrister's bedside manner was he could not have been more removed from my mother's walk of life.

He said, "Mrs Kennedy, I need to ask you some difficult questions about your husband. I need to understand his demeanour". My mother nodded, he continued, "Can you please explain to me what your husband is like? "Well" she said, "He really doesn't say anything at all, he would not volunteer conversation, he goes out and doesn't say where he is going, he comes back and doesn't say where he has been". "Tut tut" said the barrister scribbling, "and how is he with the children?" "Well" she said, "a typical line of communication would be to tell them to go out and sweep the backyard" – "Terrible, terrible" muttered the barrister, and he asked "How is the relationship between the two of you?" "Well" my mother said "I am really a cook and a cleaner". The barrister gave a very sympathetic look and brought the meeting to an end.

As my mother left the meeting she turned to my brother who had accompanied her and said "He is obviously a very clever man – but that barrister never asked me what your dad was like before the accident !!!"

She was making the best of a terrible situation, my mother would never have lied or even misled by silence. My father was dramatically changed by the accident, before it he would sing loudly as he shaved, 'Take me home again Kathleen' was a favourite of his – I'm not sure what my mum thought of that as she was not called Kathleen – but after the accident he didn't sing any more and was very introverted.

The implication that it wasn't his head injury that made him difficult to live with but the fact he was an old fashioned Irishman certainly masked the consequences of a terrible accident that changed his personality. The system couldn't put him back together again. Through sheer determination he returned to work as a carpenter, but was never the same person as reflected by compensation award of £9,000 – a very, very substantial sum in the late 1950s. Compensation he would not have got but for his union. Throughout the accident and his recovery I was certainly shielded from any hardship.

During my father's illness and subsequently, my mother would work nights as an untrained nurse. It was my brother Maurice's job to drop her off at work at 8pm and collect her at 8am on Tuesdays and Wednesdays. Maurice was a big character – physically and personality wise – good-looking and fun. For a number of years he had two serious girlfriends – both helpfully called Anne. He would take them out on alternative nights. Fortunately, because God had the foresight to make a week have an odd number of days, they would each get a Saturday night every second week. Well, before he settled down (!!!) with the two Anne's he would, shall we say, play the field. My mother was quite a disciplinarian and there would be curfews for getting home – strict during the week, a bit more relaxed at weekends.

Now of course my mum's night work was a boon for Maurice. My saintly and dutiful brother would leave home at 7.45pm on Tuesdays and Wednesdays to drop my mum off to work. I shared a bedroom with him and I didn't need an alarm clock on Wednesdays and Thursdays. Our bedroom door would be flung open at 7.30am and he would go over and muck-up his bed to show it had been well-used the previous night. This went on for a number of years, with me sworn to secrecy and Maurice very pleased with his ruse.

Then one Sunday lunch Maurice was being admonished for what time he got home Sunday morning – given the freedom of Tuesdays and Wednesdays he found it hard to be well behaved at the weekends – he started to defend himself, even mistakenly making as part of his defence his good deed at getting up every Wednesday and Thursday to collect my mum from her work. Well she was having none of it, and took the pin out of the grenade and lobbed it in Maurice's direction ... "And don't think you fool me with that mucking up your bed malarkey, YOU ALWAYS FORGET TO DO THE PILLOW!" Game, Set and Match to Mum!

Because Maurice had a reputation as being a 'bit-of-a-lad' it could sometimes have unintended consequences. There are many benefits to being one of six children, and some minor hazards. How old do you think you are when you realise before the actual day that birthdays are a great thing? Four years old?

Anyhow, one day I am sitting with my mother and Maurice, I am just playing, and I ask my mum what date my birthday is on. She replies unhesitatingly "Feb 9th". "NO" Maurice says "It's Feb 10th". As Anne (my younger sister by two years) was a birthday present for him when she was born the day before his birthday on Feb 9th This sounded convincing to me but my mum dismissed his contribution and insisted my birthday was Feb 9th. So of course I believed her and celebrated my birthday on Feb 9th and my sister Anne celebrated hers on Feb 10th.

Fast forward, say 12 years, and I am getting a holiday job working for Barclays Bank. For that I need an insurance certificate, and for that I need a birth certificate which reveals Maurice was right – I was born on Feb 10th. Not many people celebrate their birthday on the wrong date for 12 years and the knock on effect was so did Anne. If only we had listened to Maurice.

My father worked hard and at the weekends he was a regular visitor to two pubs. On the way back home from one he would cross Archway Bridge, which was for reasons that need no explanation, known as 'Suicide Bridge'. This bridge was next to my school and one Tuesday morning our headmaster walked into school assembly looking even sterner than usual. He referred to the unfortunate incident the previous afternoon when a truly troubled soul had found his way onto the parapet of the bridge with a view to ending his life. The headmaster berated us for our response to this scenario pointing out that as pupils at a good Catholic school our response to such a scenario should not be for a hundred boys to be leaning out the window shouting JUMP - JUMP - JUMP .

As my father walked across the bridge one Saturday night, to his horror, he saw a man in a similar position on the parapet. He tried to engage with him and dissuade him from his plan and to return to the safe side of the bridge – but he wasn't getting anywhere. When he saw another man sauntering over the bridge he called him, pointed out what was happening, and asked him to engage with the man on the parapet whilst he went the two minutes to our home to call the emergency services – of course there were no mobile phones – my father hurried home and made the call. The following day the front page of the Sunday newspapers carried the headline, 'PETER SELLERS SAVES LIFE OF MAN ON BRIDGE'. The man my father had enlisted to help was one of the world's most famous comedians, who was himself a troubled soul, and had been a pupil at the misbehaving school!

The National Health Service (NHS) helped my father in his time of need, social security helped with the finances and education served the Kennedy clan of six children very well. The local primary school run by fearsome nuns delivered an outstanding education and then I went to a grammar school, less than five minutes' walk from home, that simply gave an education that money could not buy. This to my mind was a system that was not broken, but subsequently politicians decided to fix it anyhow. Hating the idea of having twin tracks for education based on ability they introduced comprehensive schools to bring the grammar school system to an end – and to my mind a mistake. By the time I had my own children, both my schools were within walking distance of where we now lived, but standards had slipped so badly that we sent our children to private school. So the fixes had created a scenario where it was money rather than ability that got you the best education. I felt sad and bad about that but my parents wanted the best for their children and would have done anything they could to achieve that. The irony of ironies was that I was now paying to send my children to a school which in my day could not get close to competing academically with my free state schools – and that's called progress! I seem to remember in Tony Blair's autobiography he regretted that the Labour Party had abolished grammar schools – not just you Tony, me too!

Free and good quality education had prepared me well for the road ahead. If there was a possibility of a working class background being a disadvantage in forging a career then that was swept aside by the background of a great and free primary, secondary and tertiary education.

Not to mention or underplay the importance of great public libraries. During school holidays I would visit our local library on a daily basis. And then the icing on the cake – I feel guilty saying this, given the huge and long lasting burden of university loans, but we were actually paid to go to university! What an astonishing notion – but I don't think it would take a great economist to work out that most of us from that era repaid many times over the wonderful investment in our free education in taxes subsequently paid.

My mother and father on their wedding day.

My wedding to Caroline, 25/8/89.
Including guests; Bob and Paula, Sinéad, her husband John Reynolds, her manager Fachtna,
Doreen Loader (the lady who told Sinéad to call me), Pat Savage (premier accountant
including for the Stone Roses and Morrissey), Dave Bates (one of the most successful A&R
executives of all time), Nikki, Jill Stean, Bob and Wendy Fisher.

The golden fruit of J P Kennedy and Co.

CHAPTER 2

BECOMING A MUSIC BUSINESS LAWYER

I didn't have a long term ambition to be a lawyer – my brother was a very successful one. He got the bug for law after watching my mum and dad have to deal with the court case I mentioned in chapter one. He qualified as a solicitor without going to university – a solicitor was a first for our Irish immigrant community – it was not only my parents who were proud, but their friends as well – he soon became the port of call for wills and property purchases.

Down the road from our family home was the Archway Tavern – at the time a pub frequented by a good regular Irish crowd – especially youngsters coming over on the ferry and looking to make friends. One of these regulars was a young David O'Leary – for those of you who don't follow football he was to become an Arsenal and Ireland footballing legend. He was living the dream playing football as an arsenal apprentice, but he didn't know many people in London so this tavern became a regular haunt for him. That would be frowned upon now as he was a top athlete, but this is now, and that was then!

Anyhow, of course he and Frank the publican became good friends. One evening Frank looks across at David and sees a troubled soul;

"What's the problem David?" Frank says.

"Well", David replies, "I have had some good news and some bad news today, the good news is Arsenal told me today I am doing really well, the bad news is that as a result they want me to sign a contract – sure Frank what do I know about contracts?"

"Don't worry David" says Frank, and he goes to the phone on the wall behind the bar and dials 272-7107 – when my brother Michael answers, Frank asks him to come down to the tavern and so begins my brother's illustrious career as a sports lawyer – all because he had helped Frank the publican with his lease on the Archway Tavern. They say 'oak trees grow from small acorns', well from that brush with destiny Michael went on to become famous and revered in the world of football – at one time he represented half of the Manchester United team, all of the Irish national team and many more.

He was particularly famous for representing Roy Keane for more than 10 years, and if you were so inclined as to watch the YouTube clip *'I don't forgive Alex Ferguson*' by Roy Keane then Michael gets a few mentions. At one time it felt like Roy Keane was the most famous person in Ireland. I holiday a lot in Ireland and I would frequently be standing in a pub and would notice people nudging each other and looking over my way – not very subtly – excitedly saying that's Michael Kennedy's brother -oh the joys of fame.

During the Gulf war I frequently heard the music come on the radio in Ireland to indicate that we were about to hear the main news bulletin and I wondered what news there would be of Saddam Hussein's latest tactics only to hear the news reader say in a sombre breaking news tone 'Today Roy Keane's agent Michael Kennedy said ... "and now, news from Kuwait and Iraq" – not a word of exaggeration, the Gulf war was the second item to Michael.

Like many people, Michael did not think practicing music business law was proper law, but on a couple of occasions I proffered advice – on one occasion he partly took it and on the other he completely rejected it.

By the time I made my suggestions I considered myself a specialist in contract law as did many in the music industry – this was not a view shared by my elder brother.

He was representing the footballer Frank Stapleton. Frank had been offered a chance in a life time move from Arsenal to Manchester United, this was a time that even though a player's contract was finished, his club could still demand a transfer fee. It seems extraordinary now – there was a transfer tribunal and if, as in this example, Manchester United and Arsenal can't agree a fee then the transfer tribunal would meet and set what they considered an appropriate fee. If Manchester United considered it too high, then they would walk away from the deal and Frank would not only lose his dream move but he would be stuck at a club, team and with supporters that he had indicated he wanted to leave – not ideal for anyone. So I heard though the media that the matter had been referred to the transfer tribunal and I was interested in what arguments Michael would put to them. To my absolute astonishment he told me that Frank was not allowed representation at the tribunal.

I was shocked, this was Frank's livelihood, this was archaic. I am sure he would have done it anyhow, but because of my music industry focus I took the view that this whole process was in 'restraint of trade', and I encouraged a two-step process. First, write asking for permission to attend to represent Frank and then when they inevitably and arrogantly refused say OK, you reserve the right to take the matter to the European Court of Justice. Well, however it played out, I believe Michael was the first person given a right to speak on behalf of his client at the tribunal. Frank got his move to United and I had the privilege of meeting him at Michael's house – I remember him telling me the old Trafford crowd instilled in you extra speed, pace, energy and stamina. I suspect Michael would have suggested, like this next tale, that I am imagining things regarding my role in his attendance at the tribunal.

I read in the papers that Roy Keane had shaken hands on a deal to go to Blackburn Rovers. Then I heard the move was off and he was being represented by the famous Michael Kennedy. I happened to be speaking to Michael about something else and I said,

"What a great client – what happened?"

I knew from the papers Man U had come in for him – I said,

"What about the handshake?"

"What about the handshake?" he replied.

I knew that football contracts were largely standard form so I said, "Doesn't the handshake and the standard form create a binding contract?'

He laughed and was dismissive, asking me if I really had studied law. I followed the Man U courtship in the press, and spoke to Michael on the phone a few times and flagging the handshake and each time Michael laughed it off. Roy completed his move to Manchester United.

Subsequently, I discovered that Michael had got a call one day from Kenny Dalglish, the manager of Blackburn.

"Michael" he said, "What do you think I have in my hand?"

"I don't know Kenny, what do you have in your hand?"

"I have a writ suing Roy for breach of contract."

"Do you now Kenny, and what are you going to do with that worthless piece of paper?"

"Well" Kenny said, "Your client is a lucky man. I have persuaded my chairman to do nothing with it because if we succeed we still won't get Roy and we will just do damage to a great young footballer with a great career ahead of him. We are going to do the decent thing, but a top barrister has advised us that that handshake was a contract."

I suspect all along Michael was keeping one eye on the significance of that handshake, but he took a calculated gamble and it paid off.

Anyhow, this chapter was supposed to be about becoming a music business lawyer when I started it – so back to that tale. There can be no doubt that I had the idea of being a lawyer because of Michael, but the music industry was lightly on my horizon because of my sister Pat.

She worked at a young age for Polydor records – a company I eventually ended up being chairman of and she had a successful career at Atlantic Records. As an aside, I should mention she ended up being Peter Stringfellow's p.a. for 30 years, but those stories are for her book!

Pat would bring home records before they were released, and sales figures, and the important USA trade magazines Billboard and Cashbox. I would listen to the music and read the magazines avidly. I remember one time noticing in Billboard the joint managing directors of RSO Records being awarded gold discs. Wow, I thought and I asked Pat,

"So it's not only artists who get gold discs record, executives can as well?"

"Yes" she said – and in crude terms I thought to myself I fancy some of that.

Of course nothing happens overnight. So I go to university and law school to qualify as a solicitor and do my in-house apprenticeship at a firm in Highgate Village where I had a fascinating work load for two years. In the morning, I would meet a female client for the first time and they would tell me how their husband had abused them and they had to leave their home, or another client would tell me their landlord had evicted them. By mid afternoon, I would have secured an injunction for them, the wife would be back in her home with her husband ejected – and the landlord would have to let the tenant back in.

This was fascinating rewarding work, legally challenging, but extraordinary experience for a 23 year old lawyer and indeed life experience for a 23 year old young man. Again social justice worked then – this service was provided on legal aid and, for a relatively small sum, got people's lives back on track – and in the majority of cases would have saved society huge sums in rent bills and benefits. I say that, not to praise myself because I was paid for it, but to show that the investment in legal aid certainly at that time could pay dividends. I was certainly not operating in an ivory tower, but in touch with life, sometimes on the breadline, but certainly on the hard line. It was about this time that Erin Pizzey was opening her women's refuge. She was based in Chiswick and I was in North London, but I could see what her refuge meant to women in desperate circumstances. I wonder what the figures for domestic abuse were in 1976 and what they are now? I wonder whether we have progressed or regressed ?

I worked for a firm called Henry Boustred and Sons – it was set up by Henry, but he had died some time ago. I loved the work, we worked hard and then partied hard at the weekend, but I would be at my desk 8.00 am Monday morning – relatively sharp!

One Monday morning I sat down at my desk to open the post from the weekend. There was a letter addressed to the long deceased Mr Henry Boustred - I smiled and opened it:

'Dear Mr Henry, I saw your name in Yellow Pages and I was wondering whether you would represent me at Highgate Magistrates Court next Monday at 10 am' and he signed his name which I can remember but won't repeat for reasons which will become apparent.

Oh no! – today is that 'next Monday'. I thought it's 8.30 am now, but OK the court is only 10 minutes away, it gives us a bit of time. I couldn't go because I was a trainee but my two colleagues were qualified and they would be in soon – or so I thought. Remember – no mobile phones.

The minutes ticked away and no sign of my colleagues – still they were ALWAYS in by 9.05/9.10am. Now I am breaking out in a sweat – so I take two copies of the letter and put it both on Brian and Gerard desks, and a note basically saying 'HELP – I will go down and meet the client but you need to be there for 10 am'. I have no right of audience – i.e. as I was not qualified I was not allowed to speak to the magistrates.

So, I head to Highgate Magistrates Court not in a panic but thinking how bad can it be – I will just have to explain to the court clerk that he has to put my client's hearing back to say noon.

I walk into the foyer of the magistrates court expecting to meet my client – there does seem to be a bit more activity than usual, even lots of policemen but then it is a magistrate's court! I am looking for someone I have never met. I know they are male, no idea how old, or what they look like. My best lead is that they are likely to be on their own, or with their wife, but everyone in the foyer seems to be with their advisers. Only one thing for it – I walk around the foyer calling out my client's name. I get some quizzical looks from the other lawyers and a policeman grabs me very forcibly by the arm and basically says 'what the f*ck do you think you are doing?' I look at him and am not sure this is how he should be talking to me – me being nearly an officer of the court or at least I will be when I qualify in 18 months. But he is big, strong and burly so I go with the flow. I say I am looking for my client – he looks me up and down with disdain and asks me to repeat to him, not the whole foyer, my client's name. I do so and he looks visibly shocked and says,

"Where is your barrister?

I say, "It's a bit early for that, this is a first hearing."

He rolls his eyes and says, "Your client is in custody, you had better go round to the back the door leading to the cells."

I go around the back and knock solidly on the door. The grill opens with a 'YES' – the YES was like a sentence – it was more like 'yes what the f*ck do you want'. I stood my ground and said,

"I have come to see my client."

And he looks at his clipboard. I name my client, he stops looking at the clipboard, and opens the door quickly and literally hauls me in by my lapels. I have the same 'officer of the court thought' but by now, I am beginning to realise something is not quite right.

He says, "You do know what is going on – don't you?"

I had to confess that my knowledge was limited. He made it clear I should stand by his side and look out the grill. I did as I was told – I wasn't sure what I was looking for, and it wasn't helped by 'what can you see'? I knew 'building' wasn't the answer he was looking for so I shrugged my shoulders.

He said "Over there, on top of that building."

I knew if this was a quiz, I wasn't faring well – but I had spotted two men and I said so, knowing that wasn't going to win me a prize.

He seemed momentarily satisfied;

"Those two men" he said "are armed police marksmen."

"What?" I exclaimed.

"Yes" he said, "Snipers – police marksmen, and in 10 minutes time 10 people will be charged in court one with one of the biggest robberies in this country … ever – and your client is one of the defendants."

"JESUS" I said – and then it got worse …

"And your client has decided to save his skin by becoming one of the most important supergrasses in the UK …EVER." Well I nearly fainted!

He continued;

"Those snipers are there just in case the bad guys try to free the other defendants with an armed attack or to try and 'take out' your client."

I had watched enough films to know 'take out' was not a good thing.

I wondered whether (and even hoped) I was on candid camera – but I soon realised I wasn't – I recovered sufficiently to say I need to see my client.

It was surprisingly easy, given the security there was supposed to be – I hadn't had to produce any I.D. Just as well, all I had was my Williams and Glyn's bank card and the 'Dear Henry' letter written in biro on flimsy paper. I was told I had five minutes and was taken to see my client. He seemed so relaxed I wondered whether he was deluded about what was going on.

I explained to him I only got his letter this morning and that there had been no time to sort out a barrister for him – and that I wasn't even qualified. I expected him to shout at me, but he was very calm, and it's an odd thing to say but we even got on during those few minutes. I suggested we weren't really a top criminal firm but he actually said something like 'I am fine with you John'.

"Anyhow, John" he said, "if you had found me the top barrister in the land they weren't going to get me out on bail were they – and actually I am probably safer in here?"

Amazingly, given the circumstances, we were able to laugh at this observation! I left him, went round to the court and explained the situation to the court clerk. He looked a bit shocked and went to tell the magistrate what the situation was so that he knew before he came into court.

My God, the court was crowded. There were many defendants, many solicitors and many barristers – a number of whom were à la mode of 'Rumpole of the Bailey'. Clearly my client was more experienced than me at this because no matter what their reputation, and no matter how much they were being paid, none of them were going to be giving their client a lift home.

Of course, I wasn't allowed to sit with the barristers – the magistrate addressed my client and said,

"I understand you don't have legal representation."

My client took offence at that and said,

"Yes I do … MR KENNEDY" and pointed at me.

There is little doubt that the only reason he remembered my name without checking my unimpressive business card was the assassination of my namesake in Dallas had given many people perfect recall of my name.

On this occasion it would have been better for me if he couldn't remember and couldn't find me in court, but there was nothing wrong with his vision and the eyes of many of the countries top villains stared at me with more focus than I would ever want.

As my client predicted, all the defendants were to be detained at Her Majesty's pleasure until the next hearing – and my client's prison would be a different one from all the other defendants for obvious reasons.

I stood outside and thought 'what a morning', and watched as the various barristers and solicitors drove off – many of them driving Rolls Royces. I headed back to the office – I was emotionally exhausted. I climbed to the top floor of our office and said to Brian and Gerard, 'Where were you?' Brian was my boss, and I was about to tell him about my morning – he said

'Tell us over lunch.' I looked at my watch, wow, it was indeed lunch time – the morning had flown.

As usual we went to the Angel pub in Highgate Village. We did this most days – also most days Graham Chapman from Monty Python was on the next table. He was there today and I thought of offering him my morning as material for a script. So as I ate my sausage chips and beans I told my story, Brian could hardly eat for laughing. I said,

"I am glad you find it amusing … well now it's all yours."

"No" he said, "it's your case, it will be unbelievable experience for you – though the truth of the matter is he will probably now hire one of the big criminal firms, but if he doesn't you should stick with it."

Well my new client stuck with us to everyone's surprise. It is quite possible that either he did not feel safe with the big firms, or they wouldn't touch him because he was breaking the criminal code of ethics in a big way. It seemed even criminal lawyers don't like 'grassers'.

And so, I carried on with an astonishing case. Of course, I hired a top barrister and made it clear to my client and the barrister that I would not be offended if it was decided that a solicitor of more experience was required – in fact even a solicitor because I was only a trainee!

But no, I stayed in place. At the time, after work I would amuse myself and wind down by watching The Bill, a TV twice-weekly police soap drama. Well, now my life was like tens of episodes of The Bill. I was sent tens of thousands of pages of statements to read. The story was much better than The Bill – in fact, if it was on the Bill I might have turned off in disgust because it was too far-fetched. My client was spilling the beans in immense detail about some of the country's biggest gangsters, and my client had two families – literally, two families! With two different names, two homes, two wives, two sets of children, two sets of in-laws, double holidays – absolutely the life of a perfect family man, but twice – and with neither having any suspicion. Yet the two families lived only 20 miles apart from each other in Kent. As I poured through these documents, for day after day, it was like being paid to watch The Bill or read a crime thriller - I loved it.

It was my job to go and visit my client in prison to ask him to comment on the statements he had given the police and to comment on what others were saying about him. The other defendants basically said my client was a complete fantasist and everything he said was made up. It was easy to see his double family was going to be pounced on by the defence barristers as great evidence that this man was an accomplished liar and you could not believe a word he said. Of course the police did have other evidence, and after a while they secured their convictions, and my client got a much lesser sentence than he would have done. I never heard whether he suffered any recriminations for his evidence breaking the underworld code of silence, whether inside of jail or outside, or even from his two families. I did wonder if either of the two families had him back when he was released, or how they divided up the limited visiting permits. As I have been writing this I smiled a lot.

My client was not the perfect father, husband, criminal colleague or even supergrass, but I was never bored in my visits to meet him. Now, he could have written a great book! Maybe I should look him up and we could collaborate ... actually maybe best to stay away from that murky world. It was a world that was to turn murkier as the Independent newspaper observed much later. Whilst at the time, armed robbery was the crime of choice for real villains, it gradually gave way to drug dealing, which would ruin many more lives. Who would ever have thought that society would have been better served if the bad guys had stuck to armed robbery!

I had the most astonishing training at Henry Boustred and Sons. I had tried to get a job in the music industry but the door had always been slammed shut because of the usual conundrum line of questioning ...

'Do you have any relevant experience? ... 'No.' ... 'Ah, well we can't hire you.' ... 'Then how do I get relevant experience?' ... 'Not our problem.' ... 'Thanks.'

So I decided to apply for a job doing shipping law. This was a niche, elite, well remunerated area of the law and responsible for more cases going to the top court in the land. I got myself a job at the best firm – I was apparently the first person they hired who hadn't been to Oxford or Cambridge.

So I gave up my 15 minute walk to work to commute to the city. It was a prestigious role – I hated it – I had no responsibility and was basically managing other people's files. I was unhappy, but I had made my bed and needed to lie in it. Like most tube commuters I would get the Evening Standard newspaper every evening, and out of sheer boredom would read it cover to cover. After three months of commuting I was apparently reading even the job ads page where there certainly weren't going to be career advancement opportunities for a young lawyer.

One evening I saw an advert from Phonogram Records for cleaners and security men. It is a strong indication of my level of boredom and frustration that I wrote them a letter saying, *'I see you are recruiting, are you by any chance looking for lawyers?'*

Neither surprisingly, nor unreasonably, I got a letter from their Human Resources department making the point that if they were looking for a lawyer they would have said so, but probably not in the Evening Standard – fair enough. I wrote another letter, expressing a passionate ambition to work in the music industry and asked them to keep my CV on file, just in case an opportunity arose. I expected to hear nothing and I was right until …

I got a letter from a real, live, record company, with a cool logo i.e. Phonogram – sensibly managing my expectations by saying 'we don't have any opportunities at the moment, but would you like to come in for a chat.'

OH YES – I CERTAINLY WOULD.

The day came and I headed off to 126 Park Street - very close to London's Marble Arch, above what is now a huge Primark. I just loved waiting in reception, music was playing, people were laughing, there was energy. I knew I should just enjoy the experience and have no expectations. After a while I was told I would be meeting David Baker, the director of Business Affairs. Apologies for the delay, but he had not yet returned from a very important meeting – no problem, I had time - I was shown to his office by his sexy secretary Cathy and offered a cup of tea. His office was out of a film – completely white with three white sofas. My cup of tea arrived in elegant China and I sat and waited for him to return – he could take as long as he wanted as far as I was concerned. There was an impressive music system and gold discs on the wall.

When David arrived, he did not disappoint. The important meeting was clearly a lunch meeting and the alcohol had not been spared - he was not drunk, just the right side of professionalism.

This was a time – as I later discovered – when a music business lunch was one or two aperitifs, then starter / bottle of white wine / main course / bottle of red / dessert plus a glass of dessert wine, and brandy and coffees to finish off.

It was called networking!

Anyhow, David had style – his shirt and jeans matched his white sofas and wonderfully he was smoking a large cigar which he inhaled and exhaled theatrically. He feigned surprise when he entered the office and saw me sitting on his sofa.

"Who the f*ck are you?" …

"John Kennedy." I replied. He again feigned surprise and then said,

"Oh yes, you are the lawyer idiot who responded to our advert for security men and cleaners." I nodded.

"What the f*ck was all that about?" he said.

I muttered something like 'nothing ventured, nothing gained' and I pointed out that it had got me into a record company and into his office which was further than I had got before. He laughed and we chatted about his job - he had an ego but he deserved to. He was smart, personable and it seemed like he did a great job for the company. It was time to wind things up i.e. our little chat and he reminded me they had no legal openings and I said I knew that, and thank you very much for your time and bear me in mind if an opening arose – he said he would. I got up to go, and considered it a success, and was going to love telling the story to my flat mates over a pint that evening. As I reached the door, he said,

"Actually, we do have something ..." but then contradicted himself and said "...no you are overqualified for it."

I said, "I will take it."

This time he looked at me as if, as previously he had suspected, I was a nutter who as a lawyer answered ads for cleaners and security men, but now he knew I was a nutter ... as he screamed,

"I HAVEN'T EVEN TOLD YOU WHAT THE F*CKING JOB IS!"

I risked riling him more by saying again, "I will take it." ....

"I HAVEN'T TOLD YOU HOW MUCH IT PAYS!"

He was shouting so loud Cathy came to see what was going on and was relieved to see me smiling. David calmed down and said,

"No, you are overqualified."

I said, "Isn't that more my problem than yours?"

He said, "No, you won't stay."

I said, "Make it a condition of the offer that I have to stay a specific period of time."

"JESUS!" he said, "You like to argue don't you, go home and I will think about it."

"Thanks" I said, "I appreciate it" and left.

Well, a few days later I got a letter from David expressing reservations about whether it was a good thing for my career, but if I wanted to I could have the position of Contracts Manager of Phonogram Records. He apologised for the salary, but he pointed out that you didn't have to be a lawyer to do the job. The salary was the same as I was earning as a qualified lawyer at a prestigious law firm ... I wrote back, 'When do I start?'

I was joining the music industry!

CHAPTER 3

BEING A MUSIC BUSINESS LAWYER

So I start work at Phonogram Records in June 1978. I am excited – I have to sign in every morning a bit like clocking in. The last time I had to do that was on a building site – but that's OK – my start time is 9.30am, but old habits die hard I get in at 8.00am.

The next person to arrive is pretty well 9.30am and I like the peace and quiet. I not only have my own office but I have an inner office for my 'charges' the artist contracts, I am literally the contracts manager.

My boss isn't David who interviewed me but a nice guy, Mike Brown, he is the in house lawyer –and he tells me he and his wife don't have a TV – unimaginable in 1978 but good for them.

Over a few days I get introduced to everyone. I am already known as the 'weirdo who gets in at 8am', but it's respect rather than disdain I feel. It's a nice bunch of guys and girls – most people go down the pub at lunchtime. At first I join them, but I don't love it – drinking at lunch time was never for me.

The managing director comes to see me – a very affable Scotsman who is liked by his employees. He greets me and has a good look at me, he tells me he wanted to check that I had two arms. I am puzzled, he said he had hoped in fact that I had only one arm – again I look puzzled, he is pleased with himself and he says I cannot tell you how fed up I am hearing from lawyers … on the one hand this and on the other ….

Cathy, David Baker's buxom secretary becomes a frequent visitor to my office but only after David has gone to lunch. David is also an early starter and turns out a prodigious amount of work in the morning, then goes off to his networking lunch and comes back in the afternoon to sign all the letters that Cathy has typed up in the meantime.

My job is not demanding. I find I can do it in two hours in the morning and two hours in the afternoon, but I am not bored – Cathy's visits are to update me on how she and her boyfriend spend their romantic weekends – energetic to say the least!

In the office to my left is the international manager, John Burn-ham – his energy is astonishing, he is always playing music, as he should – it's part of his job. He is also always playing pretend drums, even when talking to you about his weekend. He takes me under his wing – his glamorous secretary sits outside his office just to the left of my office and I can amuse myself listening to artist managers trying to impress her. One of the most blatant is Chris O'Donnell – one of Thin Lizzy's co-managers – a friend of mine to this day. It's a dilemma, he says to her, is it OK to park my Mercedes convertible outside and leave the roof down? I can picture her clearly, but sadly can't remember her name – actually it just came back to me, Jane – she looks like a girl that should be in the passenger seat of a Mercedes convertible but she has the measure of Chris.

Life is good – all my friends are impressed that I am working for a record company. There is no need for them to know how junior my role is, some think I was poached for my position – begged/poached, nearly the same thing!

But it is hard doing nothing, no-one worries what I do so long as I do my work. I have to send telexes around the world giving contract approvals for releases of compilation records – the telex operator is wonderfully named Theresa Greene, (trees are green)!

On a few occasions if someone has cancelled on David Baker he will take me to La Genova for lunch. This is a treat, but it's hard to work in the afternoon – in fact hard not to fall asleep after the alcohol consumption. Aperitif / starter / white wine / red wine / dessert / brandy – I 'pass' on the cigars.

David explains to me how stressful his job is – absolutely, I slur – he says his wife doesn't appreciate how stressful it is – terrible, I slur – yes he says and sometimes during dinner to release the stress he throws plates at the wall and my wife doesn't understand why I need to do this!

I am not slurring anymore, because I am open-mouthed! I say what does your wife work at? He replies, she works with autistic children – there is really no answer that could do justice to the picture that has just been painted to me – so I have another brandy.

So I got into a pattern, I would come in at 8.00am, work to 10.00am, walk around the office looking busy and saying hello to everyone and then leave the building. At first I would go shopping, but I have never been a great shopper so then I would start going to the Empire cinema, in London's Leicester Square for their 10.30am screening. Not many people saw Saturday Night Fever and Grease at 10.30 in the morning – but I did.

I was rarely missed and the novelty of working for a record company had not worn off – but I was, if I was honest, beginning to get bored.

Well be careful what you wish for. I had only been there three months when Mike Brown called me into his office with some big news – he was leaving. I had two questions, what job are you going to and who is taking over – both answers were a shock.

First, he was going to set up his own brewery called Brown's Ales! An unusual career move for a lawyer, and the good news was he had agreed on his successor with David, there would be perfect continuity … it would be me – HOLY SHIT. I knew Mike spent his time drafting contracts for artists and producers, but I had never done any drafting. It's a piece of cake he assured me – I wasn't convinced, but he promised to spend the next month teaching me to draft contracts.

So Mike left, and I was now a proper in-house lawyer. I was very nervous – but I certainly wasn't going to walk away.

Every law student's hero is the legendary Lord Denning, and as Mike left he gave me the wonderful news that in six weeks Phonogram had a court case in the Court of Appeal in front of Lord Denning. I was in charge but I had nothing to do. The barrister had already been instructed, all I had to do was go and sit in and listen.

It is one of my great thrills in life that I got to see Lord Denning at work in the flesh. Lord Denning's perception and intuition was on full display. After two days of complex legal argument and technicalities, it was time for Lord Denning to give judgement – not for him a week or two to prepare his judgement. He put down his pen and addressed the court in words that would be transcribed and reported in the law reports and studied by academics and law students in perpetuity.

He had a marvellous Cornish accent; "This case is about the recorded music industry. It is about a group of musicians who perform under the name *Cheap Mean and Nasty*" – and for decades I have been convinced that he then paused and went on to deliver the immortal line – "and as far as I am concerned that describes everyone involved in this case."

But now it appears that that so-called immortal line was a complete figment of my imagination as it is simply not there in this judgement in the law reports – memory is a strange thing, I was so sure he said it but he didn't and that was not his view of the characters involved.

I was no longer bored. I had kept my old job when I moved up a rung – I was working much more closely with 'the-man-in-white', David Baker. I learnt a lot from him – more regularly, if his lunch date got cancelled I was invited to join him. One lunch on the second brandy, he asked me how ambitious I was. I actually wasn't ambitious, I didn't have a plan – I had always tried to work hard and I found that made me lucky. As I say, I didn't have a plan, things just happened.

However when pressed, I said one day I would like to be managing director. I had no idea where that came from – and I was even interested myself that I hadn't said head of legal and business affairs worldwide. David smiled, and said "Right answer!"

Then one day Cathy came to see me and actually put lunch with David in my diary for 'tomorrow'. I had never had a planned lunch with David – what's that all about I said to Cathy –she tapped her nose as if to say 'none of your business', smiled mischievously and walked away flirting as she did so.

The following day I went up to David's office to head off to La Genova – it was always La Genova. Always the same table – same time.

I was obviously intrigued to know what this was about. These were the days before annual performance reviews so it wasn't going to be that, but it could be a general chat about how I was doing.

Anyhow, two and a half hours of eating and drinking in one of London's West End's finest restaurants was no bad thing and I was a big fan of David. So lunch with David was enjoyable and I always learnt about the industry from him – he was very cynical about it, and then on the first brandy he told me he had some news. Of course I was all ears – he said, "I am leaving." I nearly dropped my glass. I knew he did some work in his spare(!) time for John Cleese, and now he was going to work for him full time, WOW! WOW!

I was pleased for him as he was excited, but of course like anyone would be I was interested to know who my new boss was going to be.

"Well," he said, "it needs to be approved by Michael Kuhn, (group director of legal and business affairs), but current thinking is to give you the job!" I said shall we have another brandy. It was of course great news – thrilling, exciting, and daunting, but David emphasised it was subject to Michael Kuhn's approval.

I don't know why I haven't mentioned Michael before, he probably didn't need to approve my entry as a contracts manager, but he would have had to approve my move up to Mike Brown's role. Michael is one of the smartest and most personable people you could want to meet – a brilliant lawyer, but too creative to spend his life in the law. In the early days of my time at Phonogram, he wrote a play and I went to a performance – it had the wonderful cutting, arrogant, pompous line 'people actually live on the Holloway Road'.

I used to tease him about this, as I had pretty well been born on the Holloway Road and now irony of ironies Michael lives 30 yards from the Holloway Road, but in one of London's most beautiful and stylish spots.

Michael did give his approval, I learnt a lot from Michael and he was very supportive but I was soon to let him down, something I have always regretted. So in my new role I was very much at the front line of artist negotiations. Fortunately, there was one negotiation which preceded me.

Phonogram had an immensely talented A&R guy called Nigel Grainge. Nigel knew he wanted his own record label and he had decided it would be called Ensign Records. Phonogram wanted to retain the benefits from Nigel's talent, so they were prepared to fund Ensign but the terms of the deal needed to be worked out. Phonogram realised they were not going to have an easy ride when Nigel informed them that he would be represented by a USA attorney, Paul Marshall, who had a formidable reputation as a tough guy.

So the Phonogram team would be Ken Maliphant and David Baker. David would have been wary of Paul and would have watched silently knowing that Paul saw he and Ken as his prey. Ken was more of the bravado type.

So the morning of the negotiation arrives, and Ken and David are both nervous and apprehensive. Paul Marshall turns up 20 minutes late, that's another intentional 20 minutes for Ken and David to be nervous. Paul walks into the meeting with a bullying swagger and confidence and arrogance, but Ken has noticed something, and he understandably thinks this will be a great start to the meeting for him, and Paul will be on the back foot for the rest of the meeting. He can hardly suppress his delight as he says,

"Paul your flies are undone."

Paul doesn't miss a beat, he looks straight at Ken and says,

"Ken – THAT'S BECAUSE I HAVE COME TO F*CK YOU!"

We will never know whether this was planned by Paul or just a brilliant recovery, but if anyone has heard of a more dramatic opening for a negotiation then please tell me!

Well I was glad to miss out on that. I then started having my first introduction to USA music attorneys. I soon learnt that they were smart, experienced but aggressive. My first experience was with a lawyer we will call Peter. Peter asked to have a meeting with me to introduce himself. Of course, I agreed, he was affable at the beginning and then Peter told me he was representing one of Phonogram's biggest acts.

He told me he advised his clients that their contract was not worth the paper it was written on, and so they could 'walk'. However, he told me because he liked me and he was going to give me the opportunity to renegotiate their contract and be a hero ... 'Gee Peter, thanks'.

So a renegotiation dance began – I knew this was not going to be fun, and was not going to end well. I hired a top litigation team for the battle ahead.

Peter complained, "John, that's like an act of war – I was playing nice but now the gloves were off."

I said, "Peter, I didn't realise the gloves were on when you said the band was going to walk away from our valid contract!"

So Peter gave me a list of demands. It was the perfect list for me – as it was totally ridiculous. If we agreed it we would lose money on every sale, so we didn't need to agonise over our reply. We didn't want to go to court, but if we had to, so be it. Peter was not happy.

One day my phone rang;

"Hi John – it's Peter, my clients aren't happy and I am not happy."

I said, "Peter, you know this band had a wonderful relationship with this record company and now they don't – who knows if that can ever be put back together again, but my conscience is clear."

Then he put on his best menacing voice ...

"John, do you have family? ... do you have children?"

It was one of those moments when you pause and stare at the phone, which makes no sense, because the person the other end couldn't see me, and all I could see was - well, the phone!

I was thrown a bit, but I had one great advantage in this conversation. "Peter" I said, "You and your clients are making me work so hard on this case I don't even have ... a girlfriend." CLICK – the phone was put down.

A week later Peter asked to come and see me. I said I would rather he didn't, but we had to find some way out of this and he came in and was all sweetness.

He said, "John, it's our job to make this work for our clients."

I listened and he continued, "What's the biggest problem on my list?"

I resisted saying all of it – so I said, "The royalty."

He said, "John, the problem is, when I was hired I promised my clients I would get them a royalty of 40 per cent."

"Peter," I said, "it got you the client, but gave you a mountain to climb – as you know we have offered you half that."

"Exactly." he said.

I had been intimidated by Peter, but after his threat had fizzled out and I hadn't found a horse's head on the pillow of my flat in North London, there were bits of this which just seemed ridiculous, and I repeat, because his demands were so ridiculous I didn't lose sleep over whether I should be agreeing to his demands.

So, Peter became philosophical;

"John," he said, "for every problem there is a solution."

I listened and he said, "I have promised my clients 40 per cent, you are offering 20 per cent – how about you pay me 40 per cent" – I went to interrupt – he said, "No hear me out – but on 50 per cent of sales.

I looked at him – I nearly smiled, especially as I replayed in my mind his threat to my non-existent family, and I said to him;

"But wouldn't that be you being dishonest to your clients?"

I can't remember whether we went down his route, but from that moment the battle was over. He needed a solution more than me – within 10 days I was in the band's dressing room at the Apollo Hammersmith, London – we were all shaking hands and drinking champagne, signing new contracts. Peter and I clinked glasses;

"Friends?" he said. 'Yep' I thought – until the next time.

I seemed to have to deal with Marty Machat a lot. He was a physically small man with a big reputation as a USA attorney. He had done a deal for Frank Sinatra, and Marty told me that Frank had given him his elegant apartment overlooking London's Grosvenor Square, as either a fee or a thank you. I was sitting in the apartment as I was told this story. What sort of deal do you do to warrant a Grosvenor Square apartment as a gift! My visit to the apartment must have been in the early days when he was being nice to me – it didn't last. Marty saw my inexperience as an opportunity.

Marty had a reputation for taking on the big guys i.e. the big record companies and delivering for his artists. One of his big clients was the Charisma label – they had Genesis, Phil Collins, Peter Gabriel and more. My company Phonogram were part of Polygram Records, a global organisation – Charisma were a big part of Polygram's global turnover.

The Charisma contract had a year to run and both sides were keen to extend, but Charisma had the upper hand. I was asked by our head office if I would help out with the negotiation – I suppose I could have said no, but that didn't seem right. Marty and Charisma had all the cards – if we didn't agree their terms they could go to any other company. It wasn't my deal I was facilitating, I wasn't making the decisions – in theory I didn't have any responsibility.

Charisma were based in the UK, I was in the UK. Marty was in the UK for a limited time and I sort of ended up at the front of the negotiation. It was going quite well, nearly friendly. Then one day I got a call from Marty and Marty was in a different kind of negotiation mode.

"John I have a new point."

"Marty, we have been negotiating for two months, we are nearly at the finishing line, it's not the time for new points."

Of course, there were no rules to prevent him bringing up new points.

As I said, he was in the driving seat. He told me he wanted a 'key man clause' – this was both unreasonable and clever, but almost never given in a contract. The idea is that the label likes one individual at the company so much that they only want to sign if they know that executive is going to be around, and they reserve the right to leave if he, or she, isn't. No company should ever agree such a clause – it leaves them incredibly vulnerable to the demands of the named executive.

As an aside, later in life, a band I represented were signing to Virgin Records. At the last moment they asked me to get them a 'key man clause' – I said there is no chance of getting it – then they explained to me that during a long courtship by many record labels one A&R executive had been a complete arsehole – and they said they wanted to leave Virgin if they hired him. I laughed and said I would see what I could do.

I called Simon Draper, the legendary managing director of Virgin – one of the greatest record guys I encountered. I knew he was desperate to sign my clients – I told him they wanted a 'key man clause'. He was very irritated – but I explained this was a 'key man clause' with a twist - he laughed louder than me – he said 'fine' – if I hire that arsehole I deserve to lose the band!

Anyhow, Marty's proposal was a big problem. I didn't think he or his client even thought that highly of the person they wanted as a key man – in fact, they knew he was on shaky ground, but it might give them an option to exit from the deal early after we had paid them many millions of pounds.

I knew a flat 'no' wasn't going to go down well, so I said, 'OK how about I agree it but you can't exercise it for two years and you have to pay back all the unrecouped sums under the deal'.

It would actually have been a generous offer, except there were considerable non-recoupable monies under the deal. At first he liked the idea, and then twigged about the downside – so he went into 'Marty menacing mode' and said, 'John, I am only going to say this once, if you do not agree I will put the phone down and you will never hear from me or my clients on this deal again –will you agree a 'key man clause' for XXX?' I decided silence was better than a 'no' and waited for the inevitable 'CLICK'.

It was inevitable, but I still felt sick. What was I to do – I could call my bosses in a panic or what – what else? I decided on a strategy you won't have read about in those negotiating books that you buy at airports – it's called the 'sausage sandwich strategy'.

I cannot tell you how sick I felt in my stomach, I got up and I told my secretary that I was going for a walk. She looked at me as if I was mad – but I got up and into the lift down to reception and out into the fresh(?), well, open air of New Bond Street and walked round the corner to the greasy spoon cafe.

I ordered myself a toasted sausage sandwich and a cup of tea and I slumped in the chair. I didn't really know what to do next – I was numb – I knew I had done the right thing, but the really right thing to do would have been to pass Marty's request onto my bosses and let them say 'no'.

Well as my mum used to say, 'it's no good crying over spilt milk'. I tucked into my sausage sandwich – this was before it became widely accepted that a sausage sandwich might kill you, but anyhow I wasn't trying to boost my immune system – I badly needed comfort food.

I took my time, because once I went back to the office I would have to share 'developments' with others.
But I couldn't stay out of the office forever, so like a man having had his last meal and heading for the gallows, I headed back.

My secretary wasn't at her desk, but I went into my office, sat down and thought about who I would call first. My secretary came back and casually said whilst you were out Marty Machat called and he said can you ring him back!

I felt a conditional sense of relief – only conditional – who knew what the next development would be. I toyed with not ringing for an hour, and then after eight seconds called to my secretary, 'get Marty for me'.

I tried very hard to be calm with a casual,

"Hi Marty, you called?"

– but I knew I wouldn't sustain it, and he said,

"Hi John, we got cut off."

NO, NO, did he really just say that? NO, NO, - I was pleased to hear myself say, "We did Marty, and then I had something urgent to attend to."

He and I both knew I had nothing more urgent than this deal – then he came out with the blissful words …

"How soon can we sign this deal."

The lesson is … the 'sausage sandwich strategy' has mystical magical qualities – I bet they have never tried it at nuclear disarmament or peace conferences.

So life certainly wasn't boring. Hard work, long hours, and stressful, because all deals had to be closed quickly.

And then a wonderful thing happened – Michael Kuhn suggested to the chairman of the UK group company that I was made a director of Phonogram – not just a title but a proper board director. It was a wonderful thing to do – it was prestigious and felt like an honour.

Well how do you celebrate something like that? I had a burning desire to tell my mum – I would visit her regularly, and so on one of these visits I decided to tell her the good news.

"Mum," I said, "I got a promotion at work."

"That's good," she said.

"Yes," I said, "I have been made a director of the company."

"Amazing," she said, in a sincere and enthusiastic manner.

Then there was a pause …

"Would you like a cup of tea?"

"Yes please," I said.

So she went off to make a cup of tea which clearly gave her time to think. She came back in and gave me my tea, sat down and lit a cigarette … and carried on with her knitting. Smoking and knitting is quite a feat, but she was accomplished at it. I read her daily newspaper and then she delivered an immortal line;

"You don't think they are kicking you upstairs to get rid of you, do you?"

Well, there I was 26 years old but in my mother's mind my career in the music industry was nearing a swift end, with a master stroke on my boss's part – getting me out of the way by putting me on the board. Well they say, 'out of the mouths of babes …' well, what about mums?

Well, I suppose mums are supposed to make you keep your feet on the ground. Years later I visited my mum in hospital – she had just had her cataracts done. Again, I sat and had a cup of tea with her and I asked her how the operation had gone.

She said, "Oh, very well – I can see so much better."

"That's great" I said, and we sat for a while in silence, and then she said,

"Do you mind if I say something?"

"Of course not." I said.

She looked up at me and said,

"You know, I never knew you had such a big nose"

Thanks mum!

On the director viewpoint, I should really have seen that coming – my mother could see many things from a different perspective – a more worrying perspective than most. From my father's compensation money they had shrewdly bought another house to rent out and to supplement their income. For many years I was in charge of looking after the tenants and collecting the rents. I learnt often that it was best to give my mother as little info as possible – you never quite knew what she would do with it. On occasion my guard would slip – I would give her snippets of what I thought were good news – I would hand her the rents and she would say how are things around there?

Great, I would say, the new top floor tenants are making the flat very nice, they have even bought themselves a washing machine – they are nice people and I think they will stay a while.

"That's good – would you like a cup of tea?"

Cup of tea delivered, "Thanks, mum."

Pause …

"John, you don't think the washing machine will shake the house down do you?"

Weeks later, rent delivered – "How are things round there?" she says.

I reply, "Oh great, those nice Irish guys on the first floor have cleaned up the flat – they have done a great job – but the poor milkman! You should see how many milk bottles he has to take away – but great that they cleaned up the kitchen."

"That's nice – would you like a cup of tea?"

"Yes please, mum."

Tea delivered, pause …

"John you don't think they have been using the milk bottles to make bombs have they?" (They were Irish and the IRA were mounting a bombing campaign – but she was Irish for goodness sake.)

I decided on a simple 'no', rather than explaining that if they had, they would have done the milkman a favour because he wouldn't have had so many bottles to take away!

She was a truly wonderful woman – she brought up six kids pretty well, living hand to mouth, but as I have said we never felt poor.

When my father was back at work, he got paid on a Thursday, or when he became self-employed he went to the bank on a Thursday, because every Friday he would put three £5 pound notes under the TV aerial – that was my mum's housekeeping money to keep house and feed eight mouths. I have no idea what discussion led to that sum and I never saw it change.

A couple of years ago, I told Caroline there was only one thing I wanted for my birthday – three £5 pound notes from that era – framed. And I see it every day – it's not for any specific message, it's just a reminder, it was a symbolic constant in our house – under the TV aerial every Friday.

Except of course, when my father was in the hospital after his accident the money wasn't there then – imagine what that empty spot on the TV meant to my mum.

I often thought Irish mums and Jewish mums had lots in common – both worriers and great providers – they could offer their kids constructive advice, and even criticism, but god help anyone who said a bad thing about their brood.

My father was a provider, he earnt the money and that was his main role. Almost everything else fell on my mother's shoulders. I think that was common in many Irish families.

After his accident, my father was a man of very few words at home. In the pub he would come to life, a well-loved character with a great sense of humour. He had never lost his love of Ireland, never lost his strong Kerry accent. He never acknowledged the debt he owed to England for his life, his children's education and indeed the NHS – that stubbornness was one of his less endearing qualities, but he was a kind and good man.

He had two weeks holiday a year and they were always going to be spent 'at home', which you could have been forgiven for thinking was 15 Whitehall Park, London where he lived with his wife and children. But no, 'home' was OBVIOUSLY County Kerry which he had left decades before.

My mum and younger sister Anne would often join us on these holidays. My mum, and Anne, and I would go to Dublin a few days ahead and my father would arrive with the usual plan to drive us to Kerry. He had never passed his test – in those days in Ireland you could just apply for a driving licence. He would not have driven since the year

My mum's housekeeping money.

before. My uncle Paddy would hire a car, drive us to the edge of Dublin and point the car in the direction of Kerry. Not surprisingly, given his lack of experience, my father was a terrible driver. On the eight hour drive from Dublin to Kerry there was just one set of traffic lights, and unfortunately it was on a hill in Limerick town centre. My father could not do a hill start, so for the five hours of the journey that it took to get to Limerick my mum, and Anne, and I, and presumably my dad, would pray the traffic light would be on green when we reached it. The tension for five hours was palpable – if we got through on green the atmosphere would relax and we would stop for lunch – and I would get a new football and Anne would get a present of choice. If it was on red, the drivers behind would have to do the hill start for him with the constant tooting of horns.

My father was an 'armchair Republican', it wasn't a sophisticated stand, it didn't really need to be – in simple terms, as far as he was concerned, his country was occupied. However, it was undoubtedly complicated by the fact he had chosen to raise and educate his family in the home of the occupiers. Of course it was an economic necessity, emigration was not really a choice from rural Ireland – it was a fact of life.

No doubt, my father would have reasoned that if the British left Ireland the economy would sustain the population – however, there was no sound economic view to support that premise.

Anyhow, it was not a reasoned view, the Irish hated the English, it was ingrained with the males of my father's generation.

The following story is an illustration of his strength of feeling.

In 1974 I went to Guildford law school. It was hard work – my friends and I studied hard and only took Friday evenings and Saturdays off. On Fridays we would go to the pub in the local village, and for the first three Saturdays a group of us would meet in a pub called the Horse and Groom in Guildford.

Who knows how it got chosen, but that was our meeting place at 8.00pm on three consecutive Saturdays. Each weekend on the Friday the same crowd would have a quick drink at lunchtime in the pub opposite the law college.

On the fourth weekend, on the Friday I said goodbye to everyone and said, 'Horse and Groom tomorrow night 8pm'.

'Yes', everyone said – I headed off, but as I opened the door to leave someone said, 'Surrey University term starts this weekend – let's go up there instead' and great everyone agreed, and so we did.

That Saturday night at 8.30pm the Horse and Groom was blown to pieces by an IRA bomb. If it had been on any of the previous Saturdays, or if we hadn't gone to Surrey University instead, then our group would have been maimed or killed. We had a very lucky escape for which I thank God.

The following weekend I went home for Sunday lunch. My father came back from the pub - I didn't really need to go there, and I wasn't angry, or really looking for a fight, but I made the point to my father that I had had a near miss and that I could easily have been killed by his 'lot'.

He didn't miss a beat, he said "That's OK, you are English."

I thought my mum was going to hit him.

I actually tell the story for what it is – just a story, he didn't mean it. It was bravado and fuelled by a few pints at the pub, but there was a lifelong inconsistency between his supposed hatred of England and his life spent there. Of course I have often wondered, what he would have thought of his son receiving the Order of the BRITISH Empire from Her Majesty the Queen.

Would he have expected me to decline it, probably 'yes', and he would have said that in a moment again of bravado, but he wouldn't have meant it.

But the O.B.E. is a story for another chapter.

———————————————

And I am not sure how we got here when the chapter is called 'Being a Music Business Lawyer' – but so be it!

The train of thought came from my mum telling me that my promotion to director of Phonogram was a ruse by my bosses to get rid of me – but they should not have bothered ... I mucked it all up on my own!

CHAPTER 4

AMSTERDAM

So it's 1979, I am 25 years old, and I am working in the music industry – I am loving it and my friends think it's pretty 'cool'.

Then one day, Ken Maliphant, the managing director puts his head around the door and says, "What are you doing tomorrow?" I reach for my diary, thinking maybe I am being invited to lunch – my diary not surprisingly stares back at me completely empty … "Nothing special" I reply.

Ken says, "Great, come to Amsterdam with me." "OK" I say, "Fine – yep!" and I write Amsterdam across the whole of the next day in my diary, as if this was a usual development.

Ken explains, Thin Lizzy's American lawyer is flying into Amsterdam to meet with Chris and Chris, the managers of Thin Lizzy and they want to discuss a renegotiation of the Thin Lizzy contract –'okey dokey' I say as if I was a veteran of such meetings and negotiations.

Ken tells me we are on an 8.30am flight from Heathrow – great, I say see you at the airport – no problem.

Well you would not consider me well travelled personally, but this was certainly my first business trip – I just loved the idea.

That evening I casually dropped into conversation with my housemates that I needed to have an early night because I have to be up early the next morning. Of course they took the bait and asked 'why' and I casually said 'early flight to Amsterdam'!

So I had an early night and got up at 4.30am and was so excited that, in spite of the time in the morning, I put my vinyl copy of Dire Straits debut album on my basic record deck and played it as I got ready – I presume my flat mates were less than impressed.

I walked 'on air' to Archway tube station – briefcase in hand and started the one hour tube journey to Heathrow Terminal 1. And all was right with the world … UNTIL … UNTIL – I was one stop away from Heathrow when I went through my checklist; briefcase with relevant contracts to read on the plane – check – wallet – check – passport … NOOOO – I had forgotten my passport! My world collapsed – what the f*ck was I going to do – Oh NOOOO!

I would like to say I was calm and had a plan, but neither would be true. I headed up to British Airways check in – at the time, you didn't need to show your passport to check in so I checked in and got my boarding pass, and when it was safely in my clutches, I said to the British Airways check in lady, "I have a slight problem." "Oh yes sir, what is that?" "I don't have a passport" I said. She looked at me, and said "Sir, I would not describe that as a slight problem – I would describe it as a catastrophe." I said with a mixture of bravado and fear, "But surely this must happen all the time ... and there must be a contingency plan?" She said, "No, it does not happen all the time." Looking at me as if to say 'not everyone is as disorganised as you' !

I realised she was not sympathetic – but I thought I would bring her onto my team! "Susan," I said reading from her name badge, "what would you advise that I do?" She said, "Go home and get your passport?" But then a metaphorical light bulb came on above her head, and she said, "You can get a temporary passport from the post office." YES, YES! – I wanted to hug her, until she went on to say ... "But it doesn't open until 8.00am – and your flight is boarding at 7.55am."

SHIT! - thank you Susan – I reluctantly left her behind and headed off without a plan!

My flight was boarding – what should I do ? Well, logically, I should try and board, so I did.

I headed for the gate, and not surprisingly, as I approached emigration I heard the officer on the desk call out, "Passport" ... I said, "Well – actually no." "Sorry sir?" was the equally unsurprising response. I said, "I am afraid I don't have my passport with me."

He looked puzzled, and I have no idea where it came from, but I said, "You don't actually care if I leave the country – you and your officers are more concerned with people coming *into* the country without a passport." He looked at me as if I was mad – and then he said do you have any identification?" "Oh yes," I said nonchalantly, and produced my Royal Bank of Scotland cheque card.

Cheque cards were a common thing at the time, if you had one you could sign a cheque up to £30, and if the recipient marked down your cheque card number then the cheque was guaranteed by the bank – and in those days it didn't even have a photo on it.

The officer took my cheque card, looked at it, shrugged his shoulders and waved me through!

YESSSSS!

I now ran for the gate where Ken my managing director was waiting for me, and indeed it is fair to say, he was a little flustered. "You are cutting it fine" he said. "Not really" I said, as if I was a well-seasoned traveller, pointing to the 30 people in the queue ahead of us still waiting to board.

So we boarded the plane together and took our seats – I had no strategy, but astonishingly I was able to plough my way through a full English breakfast – 'waste not, want not'.

For the journey I was actually quite relaxed – for no good reason – but when the pilot announced he was beginning his descent, then more than a few butterflies found their way into my stomach.

At what stage should I share my little issue with Ken? At the last minute I decided … so the plane is on the ground, and we are standing up to retrieve our briefcases when I say to Ken, "There is a small issue."

"What's that?" he says. 'Well, I don't have my passport with me." It was a good job I hadn't told him whilst we were having breakfast, as it is clear that his coffee would have been spat out over the person in the seat in front of him.

Not unreasonably, he suggests it's not *really* a small issue – in fact, this happened to him once before, also funnily enough travelling to Amsterdam, when his travelling companion A J Morris had also left his passport behind.

I asked, "What happened?" He said, "They wouldn't let him travel." "Ah …" I said, "That's the difference – they have let me travel."

"Yes" Ken said, "but how?"

And then I heard myself say the following … "I explained the problem in Heathrow and that I was going to Amsterdam for a very important meeting, but would be returning the same day – they were very understanding and agreed to send an explanation by telex to Dutch immigration."

Ken didn't seem to focus on what an idiot I was for not bringing my passport – but seemed impressed I had things under control.

IF ONLY!

Clearly my wholly invented story was not going to buy me much time – and it wasn't going to get me very far!

I walked with Ken alongside me to immigration, where to my delight, and his horror, there was a long queue. I looked around the terminal and I saw an admin office, and found myself saying to Ken, 'You join the queue to go through, and I will be through in a minute"

Not surprisingly, again he looked completely bemused.

I went into the admin office where there was an immigration official sitting behind a desk with a typewriter in front of him and a queue of three people waiting to see him.

Again, I couldn't really believe what was coming out of my mouth – I said 'Excuse me,' to the three people waiting and went up to the official and announced …

"My name is John Kennedy, you will have had a telex through from Heathrow explaining my situation."

He looked at me as if I was mad – pointed to the three people and indicated that I should take my place in the queue as the fourth person.

I apologised profusely to him and the three in the queue, and said,

"I am sorry to be so pushy, but I am here for a very important meeting, and my managing director is waiting for me the other side of immigration – and I think you will have had a communication from Heathrow by telex explaining the situation."

The official was exasperated, but indicated I should sit down in the empty chair in front of him – the three in the queue sighed, but didn't stop me! The official asked me to explain the situation, which I did.

"Unfortunately, I don't have my passport with me, but I spoke to the immigration officials at Heathrow – I am only going to be in Amsterdam a matter of hours – and they said they would send through a telex explaining the situation."

He went over to the telex machine and of course there was nothing there. He shrugged his shoulders and I thought that's it … game up, but he put a form in his typewriter and barked at me; "NAME? – ADDRESS? – NATIONALITY? – DATE OF BIRTH? – IDENTIFICATION?

I produced my trusty Royal Bank of Scotland cheque card. He typed the number onto the form, and then pretty well ripped the form out of the typewriter, and asked me to sign it – which of course I did.

Then he indicated for me to follow him. I had no idea where we were going, but he headed towards the immigration queue where Ken was only half way up the line.

I suddenly realised that by a miracle of miracles he was taking me to the top of the queue so I pointed to Ken and said,

"He is with me – can he join us?"

The official shrugged his shoulders, so I motioned to Ken to join us, which he did and we went to the top of the queue, where the official indicated to his colleague on the desk that I could go through.

This was 'game, set and match' because I would now get to the meeting and I could worry about any subsequent issues such as getting out of Amsterdam and into the UK later!

But I tried one more roll of the dice ... and said to my man with the form; "How will I get through emigration this evening?" – and was stunned when he tore off the carbon copy of the form and handed it to me. YESSSSS!

Ken was looking at me with even more bemusement than before – but I was trying to give the impression that everything had simply gone according to plan – and indeed, to be fair, it had saved him from a long wait in the queue!

There was a car waiting for us and we headed off to the meeting place.

When we arrive, Chris and Chris, and their lawyer Greg are finishing a late breakfast – so we are not even late for the meeting.

In true 'rock and roll' style Greg had arrived that morning, overnight from Los Angeles – and from what I could gather, Chris and Chris had partaken of the delights of the red light district the night before!

We all then all adjourned to the meeting room. Two hours had been set aside for the meeting – so that we could get back to London in time for Ken to see one of our artists, Southside Johnny, who was performing at the Victoria Palace Theatre.

Two hours was plenty of time – this was just round one of what would be a series of sparring contests, where Chris and Chris and Greg would make outrageous suggestions for a renegotiation of the Thin Lizzy (already) signed record deal.

It was most enjoyable and I was thrilled to be at the table. I felt for Ken a bit because I wasn't bringing a wealth of experience – but you didn't need too much experience to recognise how outrageous their proposal was.

Anyhow, we parted on amicable terms, agreeing to pick it up again in January at MIDEM, the music industry festival in Cannes – another trip for me on the horizon – and hopefully with my passport firmly inside my suit jacket pocket.

Ken and I headed for the airport in our chauffeur driven Mercedes. What could have been a disastrous day for me had worked out just fine, though Ken did spoil the car journey by asking how I was going to get back in the UK.

I said, "I think it will be OK – and if it is – I will, if I may, join you at the Southside Johnny gig?"

"Sure" he said.

The truth was – my only hope was my RBS chequecard – but, if that wasn't sufficient to get me back in the country, I would have to try and get one of my flat mates to bring my passport out to Heathrow.

So, we had an uneventful flight back to London, with me tucking into a very nice evening meal.

We arrived and headed to immigration. We joined the queue, and I let Ken go in front, and said,

"You just head off, and if I can catch you I will – if not, enjoy the show tonight."

As the queue moved forward, I was looking hopefully at my RBS cheque card, and Ken got to the desk and showed his passport and went through. I optimistically said, "See you shortly."

But realistically, I knew I had gone as far as I could without a passport – and so I looked with no great hope at the immigration officer, and was absolutely stunned.

It was my roommate, also called John, from university – I had no idea he had become an immigration officer.

"Hi John" he said.

"Hi John" I said.

"John, I have a bit of a problem.

"What's that? he said.

"I don't have my passport with me."

And he said, "That's not a problem … I know who you are."

And he waved me through!

Ken had stood to watch what would happen, and was standing the other side of the desk just shaking his head.

"What was that all about" he said.

I replied, as if it was always part of the plan …

"Oh, that's my room-mate from university!"

Ken just looked bemused and baffled. He couldn't make up his mind whether I deserved his respect, or I was just 'jammy' – of course, the latter is the right assessment.

I enjoyed the Southside Johnny gig, and a few beers – and of course, Ken asked me to tell our mutual colleagues about our day trip to Amsterdam!

CHAPTER 5

A MIS-STEP

Phonogram was certainly not a cool record label, but for me it was my label and it was fun. Then all of a sudden there was a changing of the guard.

EMI was a very successful label – they had the Beatles. They were THE label in the UK. However, there was some fallout at EMI, and as a result four very important executives came from there to uncool Phonogram. It was a shock to us – and to them.

The most senior was the very suave Ramon Lopez, then there was Brian Shepherd who became Phonogram managing director, Chris Briggs a talented and experienced A&R man, and Roger Ames.

They were to transform the Phonogram company.

About the same time, Michael Kuhn had bought the Decca record company who had many great assets, including the Rolling Stones catalogue and a hidden gem, a very, very young A&R guy named Tracy Bennett.

All of these people would in due course become a big part of my life, especially Roger Ames.

They all really still wanted to be at EMI – but they had made their bed and now they had to lie in it. They formed a clique within our company and none of the existing Phonogram team were part of that clique, including me.

Resentment flourished, as part of their deals to leave EMI they had all been promised and given BMWs with great sophisticated music systems, whereas if you were lucky enough to have a Phonogram company car it would have been a basic Ford or Vauxhall with just a radio.

I didn't bear any resentment – I just sat open-mouthed watching what was going on. All four of them were different to anything I had encountered before, each in varying degrees.

Ramon was the boss and the other three were his disciples and soldiers. Ramon was astonishingly charming and impressive. He was always polite to me and even respectful.

One day he came into my office and sat down to chat. He said he had heard that I had applied to the London Business School to do a MBA. I said I had, and been accepted, but hadn't made up my mind whether to do it. He was effusive 'it was such a great idea – it would send my career into the stratosphere' – there was no doubt that if he was me he would do it.

As he left I was on 'cloud 9' – he had given me his time and the benefit of his wisdom. Then, after he had been gone a while, it dawned on me he was trying to get rid of me. They had their own lawyer over at EMI who they wanted to bring in.

When I tell the story over a few drinks, I say that made up my mind that I wasn't going to do the London Business School course – I wasn't going to make life easy for them in getting rid of me. But in fact, I was probably wondering about how easy it would be to get back into the music industry if I left. Certainly at no stage during his conversation did Ramon say, 'there will always be a job for you here' – nor did he say 'we will fund you on the course'. Ramon trying to get me to do the course wasn't really so different from the scenario my mum had pondered – getting rid of me by kindness!

So I turned down my place at the business school and got stuck in with the new team.

Ramon never complained, maybe I even went up in his estimation, and he continued to impress me.

One evening I was sitting in my office with two attractive female colleagues - I think my attraction to them was that I was one of the few people who had a fridge in their office, in fact a fridge full of alcohol.

Just as I was about to open a bottle of wine Ramon appeared at my door to discuss some weighty matter – he saw I had company and apologised. I said, "Of course, no problem, how could I help?"

But he insisted it could wait and admired the company I was keeping – being effusively and convincingly charming about the two young ladies keeping me company.

He then looked at me in horror ... "MR KENNEDY, what are you doing?" What I was doing was opening a cheap bottle of plonk that I was going to pour into three paper cups.

"NO, NO, MR KENNEDY, that is not how a gentleman treats two beautiful young ladies." They of course were loving this. He said, "I will be back."

Five minutes later, he returned with three glasses and a bottle of cold Dom Perignon – opened it, poured it, and insisted he could not join us. Now that is what you called style – and fun.

So, Brian was the MD, and a great motivator, Chris was enigmatic and even a bit mysterious, and then there was Roger. He more than any of them had been reluctant to leave EMI. I used to say, even five years later, if you cut

Roger in half you would find those three letters E-M-I engraved in his body. Now I have never been endowed with the mantle 'cool', but Roger was 'cool'. I recognised that – I didn't recognise that he was also very good looking and was considered so by almost every female. It was not unusual to get into a lift and literally hear two females saying to each other 'he is SO good looking.'

He was wary of me and so I reciprocated. I am, and was then, pretty sure it was him who had sent Ramon to usher me out the door. Roger insists, as he often has over the years, that I am paranoid – he means it as an insult – I take it as a compliment in my line of work.

Everyone was impressed by this new team. Roger earned a further notch of respect from me when I realised, as he headed off on holiday, that his girlfriend was a travel agent – so he got free holidays.

One Phonogram employee, Dave Bates, had tried valiantly to make Phonogram competitive, but he had been a lone soldier – we did have the incredibly successful Dire Straits but they were almost like an outlier. He now had some comrades to help make Phonogram a force to be reckoned with in the competitive world of new signings.

Literally overnight Phonogram had become a 'happening' place – I was learning so much and meeting really interesting people. I wasn't yet even in my late 20s, but there were people who were much younger than me making an impact.

Tracy Bennett at Decca was a natural talent, but Roger took him under his wing and nurtured him, and at the same time learnt from him. Whenever Tracy came into my office he was like a tornado of energy that overwhelmed some but energised me.

At its best the music industry in the 1980s was like what the technology industry was to become later – 'oldies' could learn a lot from the uncluttered, confident, innovative thinking of the youngsters. As I say I wasn't even 29 at this stage but I am including myself in the group of oldies.

Until now Phonogram was not likely to win a competitive field to sign a 'hot', trendy, new artist. What 'wins' Phonogram had came from the likes of Dave Bates – brilliantly spotting, at a very early stage, some new talent that no one else had heard of, or indeed were interested in.

But this EMI team were professionals and experienced winners – when they wanted an artist, they were going to get them. The rest of us were not yet 'winners'.

I remember turning up at a Spandau Ballet gig at The Angel in Islington, London on a Sunday night. I felt I had pulled out all the stops to look like a cool record executive. I knew my T-shirt looked the business, carefully selected from my wardrobe –nice colour, nice design.

The following day Roger explained to me, helpfully but not gently, that if you were part of a team trying to sign the hottest, unsigned band around it was not a good strategy to wear a T-shirt bearing the name of the last band that you had told them and the industry that you were going to make them global superstars ... only for you to sign them, not sell a single record and then drop them!

Style ego in tatters ... but point taken!!

Not the best calling card for persuading a potential new signing that we were the right partner to launch their career into the stratosphere.

To be fair, my T-shirt was not the death knell for our courtship, nor the reason we didn't sign them. We put in what we thought was a very competitive offer and yet more than 40 years later I can't think of a more cutting put down – by way of a reply, their excellent manager Steve Dagger said "Clearly, we are taking you more seriously than you are taking us!" They signed to Chrysalis and sold millions of records.

And then, talking of learning from youngsters – there was Stevo! He was, in these early heady days, a trailblazer, an entrepreneur, and unique, all at 18 years of age. He stood on no ceremony, he didn't make appointments to come into the building, or into anyone's office, he just barged in, and in doing so he brought Soft Cell into our lives. Stevo was certainly not the most educated individual, but he gave real meaning to that phrase that you could be educated in the 'university of life' – and he was smart. There were many great hits, but 'Tainted Love / Where Did Our Love Go?' just crashed into all our lives.

At the time, we didn't get chart predictions, we just got news of the new chart, when on a Sunday evening the BBC played the Top 40 as a countdown starting from 40. Until you heard your record announced as a new entry you didn't know it was in the charts.

'Tainted Love' and Stevo, and Soft Cell had resonated round our offices for many, many weeks – but who could be sure how successful the record would be. It was the focal point of the soundtrack for the new Phonogram – it was to be a summer release. I was actually on holiday in France (in my new company car – I cannot tell you how much I wanted a company car) and I reached Calais on my way home on a Sunday evening in time to get the chart show on my radio.

I knew the ambition was to try and tuck the record inside the Top 40.

Reaching just 38 would be a great result. I sat waiting to board the ferry with my then girlfriend ... 40 / 39 / 38 / 37 / 36 / 35 – no sign of it – and I had given up hope, fearing it was the wrong side of the top 40.

And then to my astonishment, there it was at 32! My girlfriend told me I hadn't been that excited at any other time on my holiday - I don't think it was a telling off. But honestly, it was one of the most exciting and important moments in my career in the record industry – not just then but looking back nearly 40 years later. I really had been part of the team that signed Soft Cell and there was the fruits of my labour in the chart countdown.

That was only the start –Phonogram were to become the coolest and most successful label of the next decade. Soft Cell had hit after hit, Dave Bates signed Tears for Fears for £2000 after listening to a tape that came through the post, Roger found Junior Giscombe, the whole team worked on trying to get ABC – literally the coolest band around and with the legendary Trevor Horn producing. Dave Bates had already signed Def Leppard – and he and Chris working together made them one of the biggest selling bands in the world.

It was like a waterfall, Phonogram was a success, profitable for the first time in a long time, fun and admired from afar.

Roger had signed and worked with Dexys Midnight Runners at EMI and he had a special relationship with Kevin Rowland, the wonderful lead singer. Roger almost irritated me when he kept saying he wanted to work with Dexys. I think I said something like 'and I would like to work with Michael Jackson but he is signed to CBS and Dexys are signed to EMI'.

But Kevin also wanted to work with Roger and again to my immense irritation I was asked to look at the Dexys /EMI contract. I was busy! I didn't think I had time for such a futile exercise, but I took a read and as I did so I got increasingly excited – in that I was pretty sure Dexys were out of contract. EMI had forgotten to exercise an option to extend the contract. Roger was thrilled, Kevin was thrilled, and so was I!

So how did I enjoy all of this other success which I was a part of? I took a major mis-step – I decided to leave. Even now I feel sick thinking of what I did and how stupid it was.

I am sure if I had discussed it with my mum, when I subsequently endured the misery of having left, she would have told me these things always work out for the best. In the course of time she was right, but it didn't feel like it during a long and painful 1982.

What possessed me to leave – well, I was self-taught in the craft of business affair. I had been given the chance to learn on the job, and I had grabbed the opportunity with both hands, but I didn't really know if I was doing things properly.

I was poached by CBS – they were the professionals of business affairs – they were even in the habit of sending their executives to business school for three months – and I saw it as an opportunity to polish my expertise and craft. I didn't even push the negotiation that much financially, I just thought it was something I needed to do.

God almost saved me. In the interview with Obie, the chairman of CBS, he said, "Why would you want to leave those nice people at Phonogram?" Obviously hoping I would give him some cogent reason ... but to his horror I said, "You know I can't think of one good reason." and got up to go. He made me stay and threw in a small signing on bonus, and probably thought I was a brilliant negotiator, but my heart was not in this move.

However, I did give in my resignation and resisted all efforts to change my mind. I felt sick from the moment I did it and for months I would have the same dream. I was playing in a football match and I would keep scoring own goals. I particularly felt I had let down Michael Kuhn who had given me many chances and opportunities – I felt I had betrayed his faith and trust in me. There was a good reason I had that feeling, because I had!

So, I joined CBS in January 1982. I learnt a lot, as indeed I had hoped to, but it was a very, very unhappy year for me – but the positive is I can't remember another unhappy period in my life. I could say, 'what doesn't kill you makes you stronger' but that would be too dramatic.

I missed Phonogram desperately, but I was the director of another record company – they had Adam and the Ants, Michael Jackson, Abba, Bonnie Tyler, and numerous others. I was earning a good living, there were parties, lots of wonderful girls, and I wasn't yet 30.

To show I was not in penance, I remember at the sales conference in Torquay I managed to run up the biggest expense account for a sales conference. A record I kept long after I left and funnily enough at the same sales conference in a game of football I did score an own goal from 20 yards – and, if you know anything about football, you would know that should be an impossibility!

CBS was a great company and very successful, but I wasn't really part of that success, much of it came from America. I don't think I sulked – I was encouraged to take people out to lunch every day to the best restaurants – I was actually told at one time I was not spending enough on expenses.

I might have found my way through it but I found myself with two bosses.

The great A&R maestro Muff Winwood, (brother of Stevie Winwood), gave me some advice – he told me I might find I got on better with my bosses if I didn't disagree with them ... even if they were wrong. It wasn't that Muff was more subservient than me – he was just a better politician.

I noticed one day as I drove into work that I was pleased when the lights were red – not a good sign.

I was working on one particular deal and had arrived at work at 8.00am to take a final run at the paperwork for it. At 8.15am the chairman Obie came in and told me he wanted me to look like I was trying to get the deal – but make sure I didn't get it !

At 8.25am the managing director Paul Russell came in and told me he had never wanted a deal more.

The previous day Paul had treated me like dirt in front of a top manager and when I had picked him up on it, looked at him as if to say 'WTF'. He had come up with the marvellous phrase 'why do I need to bark when I pay you as my dog'.

Anyhow, as Paul told me he wanted the deal more than any other deal I asked him to come with me. He didn't take direction easily, but I took him into Obie's office and told them both of my 8.15am and 8.25am conversations.

I think it's fair to say that was a resignation move, but most of this was about me not them – they were incredibly successful executives, with even greater success ahead of them, we just didn't chime.

––––––––––––––

So, for ages, I had been desperate to be in the record industry. By luck and hard work I had got myself not one, but two, senior jobs in the music industry and now I had resigned ... potentially not just from a job – but maybe from the industry itself.

I had no job ... no plan ... what was I thinking of!

I think that totals two mis-steps!

CHAPTER 6

J P KENNEDY AND CO
DON'T LET PERFECTION BE THE ENEMY OF PROGRESS

As a title for a chapter this will not make any reader think this chapter is going to be a page turner!

I was so thrilled when I joined the music industry working for Phonogram – just so thrilled.

And then I sort of mucked it up by not just leaving them – but leaving at the wrong time, but all the clichés apply, nothing ventured, nothing gained, what doesn't kill you makes you stronger, etc. Yes they all apply – but there were so many times, in fact most days, that if I could have turned the clock back I would have.

I was loving Phonogram, I had made great friends, they were treating me well, I had been made a director at 26 years old – everything was perfect. Then I got an offer from CBS Records, the market leader, to join them. It wasn't really a lot more money, but as I said, I had basically been self-taught at Phonogram and I thought the new role would broaden and deepen my experience – and they also sent their senior executives to business school for three months.

My reasons were mature but they took me into a torrid spell in my professional life. There really is no doubt that it worked out for the best in the end, but there were times when 'in the end' felt more like 'Neverland' than around the corner. From the moment I accepted the new role, I felt sick in the stomach, I felt disloyal. I would have a recurring nightmare where I was playing a football match, but kept scoring against my own team – own goals. You did not have to be Freud to analyse that.

I joined CBS in January and there were so many nice people but it felt very corporate. An early development was I had two bosses, both of whom disliked and competed with each other. One was particularly unusual – he had spent time in Australia and seemed to think he needed to play up to a particular alpha male stereotype.

The directors including me were based on the 6th floor and the ladies loo was on the 6th floor, with the gents on the 5th floor. This executive insisted on using the ladies loo, rather than go down one flight of stairs – shouting 'cover up girls' as he stormed through the door.

He suggested it was 'only just a bit of fun' and this was the early 1980s – but years later I was told how horrific the girls found it and just imagine doing that now. He was a very smart talented individual but I suppose I wouldn't add sensitive to that list. He was managing director, and Maurice Oberstein the chairman, was a legend called 'Obie'. Gay but no obvious partner, Obie was a larger than life character with a Rolls Royce, a chauffeuse called Shirley, and a dog called Charley.

He and Charley were inseparable. There were occasions when Obie was being played a piece of new music and Obie would ask Charley what he thought of it … and Charley would crap on the carpet.

Obie was immensely successful, and talented, and rich from his success. He had a deserved reputation for being ruthless but when my father was taken ill and I needed to be absent for a couple of days to bring my father home from a trip to Ireland, Obie's message was simple, "John, family ALWAYS comes first." All the more impressive as he literally had no family.

I realised I wasn't enjoying work when I was hoping the traffic lights would be red on my drive into work, but then one day I brought things to a head. I resigned and with nowhere to go!

Actually, both my bosses were understanding and supportive, and actually sent me to New York for a week to see if I fancied working there.

It's inconceivable that in my twenties with no family, no responsibilities, and no job, that I didn't want to work there – but I just didn't. If anything, it was even more corporate and I felt I would be working in a legal and business affairs silo.

I had a long notice period to work but funnily enough we all relaxed a bit more and just got on with things.

I really did not have a plan and I do remember thinking a bit how, financially, I was making life uncomfortable for myself, giving up on a decent salary and bonus which comfortably exceeded my outgoings. I can't remember if I had any savings, but I did have a house which was converted into two flats, so one of them gave me rental income.

And then life / God played the next card. My dear friend from Phonogram, Roger Ames asked me to go for a drink with him. Roger was, and is, the smartest and coolest person in the music industry – even now 40 years later my family remark what an odd combination we make. If I say 'what do you mean', they will say 'well Roger is so cool, and trendy, and well …'

On the second beer Roger told me that Polygram, the parent company for Phonogram, wanted him to restart London Records. Wow! – that was big news – congratulations Roger. He then asked me what my plans were and I said I didn't have any but something would come along.

He said, 'he and Michael Kuhn thought I should start my own law firm and the new incarnation of London Records would be my first client'! They would even give me office space. In almost every sense this was an unbelievable opportunity, but I didn't know how one set up a law firm. I suspected it was not straightforward. I was flattered, grateful – but daunted, and went away to think about it.

Planning is important but sometimes if you are cautious, as indeed I am, if you think about things then you will find more hurdles than reasons to believe what's possible. Don't let perfection get in the way of progress.

At some stage I must have said 'yes'. Yes … with butterflies in my stomach and in May 1983 I set up J P Kennedy and Co. At first operating from my flat in Highbury, North London and with one of the best things that ever happened to me … my secretary Lesley.

I actually remember sitting there thinking what do we do now, as at first we had no work because London Records had not yet relaunched, and then … the very, very silent phone rang so loudly it made me jump!

It gave me a shock and my first non-London Records' client (irony of ironies) the call was from Clive Bank – the person with whom I was trying to do the deal that the CBS managing director wanted, but the chairman didn't. He had an artist who needed legal representation – Clive has been a dear friend ever since and has introduced many clients to me.

So, J P Kennedy and Co, and Band Aid (but not just yet), and my wife Caroline and our children were to be my life – but J P Kennedy and Co was to be … ONLY for 13 years.

I soon moved into the office that London Records had promised me. It was a win / win situation, I saved on an office overhead, and they never needed to find me when they needed me – I wasn't on the end of a phone, I was there!

London Records was THE happening label of the time and there were two other record companies in the building. It happened many times that one of the other record companies would offer an artist a record deal and the artist would pop in to see me and ask me to represent them on the record contract.

It was hard work, but satisfying and enjoyable, and clients became friends as much as clients. Word of mouth was good and I got asked by many artists who did not have record deals to represent them. In theory that was not a good financial model, as of course they had no money – I had a simple business model – I got paid if and when a band got a record deal.

I never turned anyone away – my mantra was 'who knew who was going to have success and who wouldn't'. I was just 30 so I wasn't like their dad, but more like their older brother. I had to manage their expectations and make sure they weren't ripped off.

I was not particularly sophisticated myself, but I did say that sometimes when my clients were being wined and dined by record companies (with me by their side) that as they looked bemused at the array of cutlery in front of them (though so often it was a Japanese restaurant and chopsticks) I would whisper to them 'start on the outside and work in'. And then 12 months later we would be having a meal and they would be telling me what the best restaurants are in New York, Los Angeles, Sydney, Tokyo, Rome and Berlin.

It has often been said that boxing was a route out of poverty for a working class boy – but I was witnessing how record and songwriting deals could transform people's lives.

My clients came from all over the British Isles – yes some from London, but more from Glasgow, Edinburgh, Belfast, Dublin, Newcastle and Liverpool – in the 1980s Scotland particularly punched above its weight.

Sometimes, the artists were under 18, so I had to give parents the reassurance that signing the deal was the right thing to do.

Of course there was a temptation to think that getting a record deal meant you had made it – but of course that was only the first step to stardom, and for most, even with a record deal, stardom was elusive. I hope I helped keep clients' feet on the floor. The hope was that even those who didn't make it still earned enough from advances to buy a terraced house back home to help ease them out of the business when it was clear they were not going to be superstars .

As I write this, it is less than 12 hours since Sinéad O'Connor died. I cannot tell you how sad that makes me. When Sinéad was 18 years old she was offered a record deal by the brilliant Nigel Grainge.

Nigel had a middle-aged office manager called Doreen who was working for him. I adored Doreen and was friends with her until she died.

Hard to believe it but Sinéad was naive back then, actually NOT hard to believe, the public Sinéad was not the private Sinéad!

So Sinéad was told by Nigel that he was going to offer her a record deal, and so she needed a lawyer. Of course Sinéad didn't know any lawyers – a fact she expressed to Doreen who was already keeping a very watchful eye on this absolutely beautiful young woman. Sinéad told me that Doreen looked around the office to see who was watching and listening, and then wrote something on a scrap of paper, and in a cloak and dagger manner, slipped the piece of paper to Sinéad and made her promise to not tell anyone where she got the information from. Doreen then ushered Sinéad out of the office saying 'call him'. Sinéad told me she was a bit bemused, and left the office, opened the piece of paper, and on it was my name and telephone number.

Sinéad called me, and subsequently with her amazing smile, said she couldn't keep a straight face when she heard that Nigel said to someone 'how the f*ck did she find Kennedy' – Doreen kept her head down.

Sinéad was at our wedding and we were at her very small wedding where she wore her mother's wedding dress. The Sinéad that came into my office was always a very shy person, but very clear about what advice she needed, which she would debate with me, and we would mutually agree a plan.

When 'Nothing Compares 2 U' was about to be released she was temporarily manager-less and had a new record company, so I took her in to meet her new record label.

At this stage I had no understanding of the demons she was dealing with – just no idea – I only ever got the smiling Sinéad.

I only had one very gentle falling out with Sinéad. I begged her not to smoke because I feared it would damage her voice, but she totally ignored me. One-on-one she had a very deep voice that simply belied her look!

I have worked with, listened, and watched many artists, but no other artist has got close to shocking me with the power and passion that came out of such a tiny body! As has been said by so many, she simply did not seem to be aware of her astonishing natural beauty. And then there was that smile!

The evening she died I messaged my kids to say that maybe I didn't realise it at the time, but perhaps she was one of the most important people I ever met – and I have been lucky enough to meet some very important people!

In the end she became the subject of much ridicule – but she was an artistic genius, and as an activist in many ways years ahead of her time. As the world learned of her death one of the most poignant messages of grief was, 'I hope she knows how much she was loved'. Yes, I hope so, but I suspect she didn't, and in the manner that happens to many famous people it seemed that the world only recognised the talent of Sinéad as a musician and an activist on the evening that they learnt of her death.

I was brought up in a deeply Catholic Irish family, and I still am a Catholic, and I was shocked when she tore up the photo of the pope on TV – but the point she was making was correct, and she was years ahead of her time.

At that time, the Irish population had a blind devotion to the Catholic Church, and of course considered what Sinéad did as beyond sacrilegious – but by the time she died, that blind love affair with the church was over, as abuse after abuse came to light. I doubt if many woke up and said Sinéad was right (but actually, maybe they did), and by a different, and let's say less radical and less controversial route, the vast majority of the Irish population had ended up in the same place as Sinéad – dismayed by the Catholic Church's failure to address their many mistakes.

There was a dramatic fall in church attendances in Ireland – she was a pioneer in the subject of the wrongs committed by the church. I actually think that, by the time she died, most of the country would have given her a state funeral.

The shame (probably the wrong word, as I don't think she had regrets about speaking out) is that her personal life became more at the forefront than her music – but her music is a truly unrivalled body of work. Years ago on a panel, I was pressed to say what my favourite album was – I refused to choose one, but chose two; *'The Lion and the Cobra'* by Sinéad, (and *'This is the Sea'* by The Water Boys).

And a couple of days after the shock of Sinéad dying, I received a 'heads up' message – a will had been found naming me as one of the two executors of Sinéad's estate – but a later will may turn up! In fact a later one did turn up, but I was privileged to be 'invited' to the small, private funeral service.

It is a tradition in Ireland for mourners to pay their respects to the deceased in an open coffin. The first time I experienced this it was a shock, but standing alone in the room by Sinéad's coffin it did feel a better way of paying respects and saying goodbye.

The funeral was an astonishing reminder of her life and where she had ended up in people's esteem. The service was conducted by a Druid with strong spiritual messages, and a group of eight Muslims reflected her conversion to their religion with a wonderful joint blessing through gentle chanting.

I was not surprised to see Bono, Edge and Adam from U2 there, as I knew of their musical connection and friendship with Sinéad, nor was I surprised to see Bob Geldof there as they had shared the same bus stop since she was 11 years old – but I was stunned to see the President of Ireland and the Taoiseach in attendance – oh my goodness, the transition from reviled to revered was now patently visible.

Then after the service the cortège drove along the Bray promenade where thousands had lined the streets to show how much she meant to them. Some were playing '*Nothing Compares 2 U*' but most were throwing flowers and kisses! In the days before the funeral, as I have said, many commentators had posed the question, 'did she know how much she was loved?'

I suspect she did in terms of one-on-one engagements with the public, but the national and media outpouring of love, thanks and respect, with pictures on the front pages of newspapers globally, showed we were all saying goodbye to an extraordinary musical talent, who was an important activist way, way ahead of her time.

May she rest in peace, with a beautiful body of music left behind for us all to remember her by.

And then six days after the funeral service I was told that the 'new' will was not a will after all – so I was still joint executor of Sinéad's estate – but then it all took another twist and I wasn't.

I would never have been friends with Sinéad if I had not started J P Kennedy and Co my law practice.

J P Kennedy and Co lasted from May 1983 to June 1996, during that time I represented some fantastic clients, some of the names will not be as familiar as they were then, but I have listed them in the next chapter.

I loved my work – meeting innocent, young musicians with the world at their feet, many of whom would become household names. I have often been asked, how I put up with the prima donna behaviour of musicians, but I struggle to recall any examples of such behaviour.

I was on their side – I was their big brother, their legal adviser, their consigliere sometimes, not just in law but also life. Yes they paid me, but no one got a bill that they could not afford to pay and if anyone had said they didn't want to pay, then that was fine – no big deal. In the 13 years of J P Kennedy and Co I only had three unpaid bills. Many clients became dear friends – I would attend their weddings and birthday parties.

And who knows, J P Kennedy and Co may have still existed today, but for one conversation just after Easter in 1996. A bit earlier, I had given an interview for Music Week where I answered a question about my future plans with this; 'job is for life, wife for life and something else for life'.

The journalist finished the write-up of the interview with that quote – hardly painting the picture of a radical personality, but then that was who I was, and I wasn't trying to impress anyone. I also didn't think my clients needed me to be a 'larger than life' personality, just that I was there for them when needed .

As well as artists, songwriters and record labels, I represented many record executives including the supremely talented Roger Ames who I mentioned earlier as the cool guy who came to Phonogram. I had just represented Roger in a negotiation that made him head of Polygram Records worldwide, reporting to Alain Levy the CEO of the Polygram music and films conglomerate. It had been a tough, spikey negotiation involving trips on Concorde to New York, but all ended well.

Within a week of the negotiation Alain asked me to have a drink with him to thank me for my tenacity and professionalism in the negotiation, that was a surprise but a pleasant one.

We met on a Friday evening and on the second beer he delivered a bombshell. He said he wanted me to take over from Roger as his successor, as chairman and CEO of the UK music and film company. I had not seen this coming for even a millionth of a second. He said, 'you are working far too hard and this will get you a better work/lifestyle balance' – this was a novel approach, someone hiring a CEO to work less hard.

Because I was working hard I was making a good living – in fact more than the new role would normally pay and I pointed that out, Alain said, "Don't let money be the reason not to do this – if you want to do it we will make the package work for you."

I was reeling! This was an offer to run the biggest and most successful record company in the UK ... and a film company. I would go from having six employees in an office in Paddington to 800 employees across eight different sites.

It also immediately threw up a huge issue – at any one time, I was negotiating about 10 deals with Polygram, so even the offer gave me a conflict of interest.

I sort of surprised myself by not just saying 'thank you, I am flattered, but no thanks'. I said the first two limbs, but instead of the third, I said "Can I think about your amazing offer." "Of course," Alain said, "I am available at any time to discuss it." and gave me his home telephone number. So I went home in a daze, and delivered the news to Caroline, opened a bottle of wine and slept on it. On Saturday I asked Caroline what she thought, and she sensibly said, "It has to be your decision, I am happy with a yes or a no."

As I was agonizing, Alain called and said, "Let's have a drink Sunday evening to discuss how your thinking is going." I readily agreed.

As I thought about it, I reached the conclusion that if in years to come I was lying on my death bed contemplating life, I might regret passing up the chance to run a music and film company, but I probably would not regret having tried even if it didn't work out.

So I went to see Alain on Sunday evening and said, "We have a lot to discuss." He said "That's fine with me." I said to him, "If I was to do this and give up my business, then I need to make it work for 15 years for the decision to have been a good one."

I saw him go pale, and just as he was about to say 'I can't give you a 15 year contract', I said, "I know you can't guarantee me 15 years, but I would want a 5 year contract." He said, "No problem."

He also said I could keep an interest in my business in case I ever needed to return to it. I said I appreciate that offer, but I was adamant about the fact that, in my mind, there would be an irreconcilable conflict between those two positions – I would have to make a clean break from J P Kennedy and Co.

I then repeated my concern about being in a position of professional conflict by just having these discussions and said we would need to move very quickly.

"Fine with me," he said, "come to my office at 9.00am tomorrow to discuss terms – see if we can reach an agreement."

I said, "Thank you, that is a good idea."

So after a sleepless night, I turned up at Alain's office in Berkley Square and over a coffee we discussed commercial terms and reached an agreement in 45 minutes. That was impressive and I said my worry is how long will it take to document it. To my astonishment, Alain said, "I used to be a lawyer" and he got out an A4 pad and started writing down what we had just agreed and then gave it to me to read. I read it and said, "Yes that's correct", and to my further astonishment he said, "OK, let's sign."

I realised that if I wanted to do the job, and if I wanted to avoid the professional conflicts that I was concerned with then that was the right thing to do, and so less than two hours after entering Alain's office we signed and shook hands.

I headed back to my office in a cab digesting the enormity of what I had just done. So I returned to my office in Paddington, which I had converted from an Indian restaurant!

I went up to my office and asked Lesley my personal assistant from day one of J P Kennedy and Co to join me. I said you had better sit down … I told her what I had done and said of course I wanted her to join me at Polygram – and thankfully she agreed. If she hadn't agreed, I would have suffered an enormous loss.

I then called up Richard and Mark the two young lawyers who worked for me, again I asked them to sit down … and said I have some big news for you, but news that represents a great opportunity for you.

I had already decided that I didn't want to try and sell my business. My clients were like friends and family – not a commodity to sell. So I was going to basically give my very successful, very valuable business to Richard and Mark for free. There was only one condition, I said the name would have to be changed.

I then sat and drafted a letter to every client telling them the news and telling them of my mixture of natural excitement combined with sadness that I was walking away from our relationship. I explained my decision not to sell my business, and in the last paragraph told them they were under no obligation to stay with Mark or Richard – but strongly recommended one or other of them on the basis of who was the better fit for that particular client.

And so … after 13 years … J P KENNEDY AND CO was no more!

Richard and Mark decided to bring back a previous partner of mine and Babbington, Bray and Krais was formed, but that is now Bray and Krais.

Ninety five per cent of my clients stayed and Richard and Mark took the firm from strength to strength – not only keeping clients but adding household names like the Rolling Stones and Ed Sheeran to name but two to their client list.

The music industry, lawyer landscape is a very competitive arena, but I think there are few that would argue against the notion that Mark and Richard are numbers one and two in that arena – or probably more appropriately both joint number one, with former team member Kieran Jay working to oust them from that spot.

———————————

And now I had a new career – chairman and CEO of Polygram, the UK music and film conglomerate.

CHAPTER 7

1983 - 1996

ADVISING CLIENTS AT THE LEGAL COALFACE

Before I start telling about my new career as a CEO of a record and film company, let me mull over the events of 13 years of J P Kennedy and Co.

During these years I was a qualified solicitor, but as one person once said to me 'not a proper lawyer, a music business lawyer'. I did not know how to set up a law firm – but I did, necessity is the mother of invention.

My goodness, I worked hard. At almost the same time as I started my law firm, at that time 'Saint Bob' had not come into my office, ... but there was Saint Caroline.

I suppose she knew what she was getting into from the beginning. I would leave home just after 7.00am, work 8.00am to 7.00pm in my office, then drive home, eat and watch a bit of TV from 7.30pm to 8.30pm, and then work 8.30pm to 11.00pm – but ONLY if I was not out seeing a band.

Caroline would often come with me to see the bands and many clients enjoyed her company more than mine – very pretty and the same age.

I joke that once I put a wedding ring on her finger she stopped coming to gigs. She quite fairly points out that a wedding ring was followed pretty swiftly by a bump!

If there was no gig to go to, then Friday night was no work, as was Saturday night, but only after 6 hours in the office – I only did three hours on a Sunday.

I used to say I was only working those hours until my new business was established, and then I was going to ease up – but that was before Bob asked 'JUST FOR ONE HOUR'.

Having said all that you may not be surprised by this story. During COVID we all had a bit more time and my daughter Ellie took that opportunity to go through an old box of her belongings. I heard her crying out "I have found it ...I have found it."

I asked, "What have you found?"

"I knew it existed" she said. "WHAT?" I said.

And she showed me her school book from about 1994 when she was four years old. Clearly she had gone into school on a Monday and been asked to write about her weekend ... 'we had a lovely weekend, it was a sunny day so

Mummy, Conor and me went to the park, and 'THAT JOHN' came too!"
Ellie's teacher asked to speak to Caroline about 'THAT JOHN'!

It was a fabulous 13 years, I never knew who was going to walk through the door – most of the time it was new artists, many of whom would go on to become household names, some were enjoying medium success, and some were established artists.

In one week Mike Scott from the Water Boys and Shane McGowan became clients, that was a stellar week! And then a year later, I got a beautiful letter from Mike saying, *'I bumped into Shane over the weekend and we both agreed how lucky we were to have you watching out for us'.*

A treasured note !

I list below many of the clients – knowing full well that I will have made some terrible omissions:

ALISON MOYET
ALAN MCGEE
ALL ABOUT EVE
BLACK LACE
BLUR
BONNIE TYLER
BOYZONE
BROS
CAST
CATHERINE ZETA JONES
DELAMITRI
CHRISSIE HYNDE
CREATION RECORDS
CUTTING CREW
DEACON BLUE
DEAD OR ALIVE
DEPECHE MODE
DEXYS MIDNIGHT RUNNERS
DUSTY SPRINGFIELD
EDWYN COLLINS
EMF
ENYA
FRIENDS AGAIN
GO WEST
GUN

HUE AND CRY
JESUS AND MARY CHAIN
JIMMY SOMMERVILLE
JOHNNY HATES JAZZ
KEVIN ROWLAND
KIM WILDE
LLOYD COLE AND THE COMMOTIONS
LONDON RECORDS
LOVE AND MONEY
MARC ALMOND
MIDGE URE
MIKE JOYCE
ORBITAL
PAUL YOUNG
PHIL LYNOTT
PREFAB SPROUT
ROBSON & JEROME
SCRITTI POLITTI
SHANE MCGOWAN
SIMPLE MINDS
SINÉAD O'CONNOR
SKUNK ANANSIE
SOUL II SOUL
STATUS QUO
STEWART LEVINE
SWING OUT SISTER
TAKE THAT
TEXAS
TEN YEARS AFTER
THE BLOW MONKEYS
THE BLUE NILE
THE CHEMICAL BROTHERS
THE CRANBERRIES
THE DAINTEES
THE KANE GANG
THE JESUS AND MARY CHAIN
THE MISSION
THE PAINTED WORD

THE PRETENDERS
THE SHAMEN
THE STONE ROSES
THE THE
THE VERVE
THE WATER BOYS
THIN LIZZY
T'PAU
ULTRAVOX
VAN MORRISON
VISAGE
WET WET WET
XTC

I really could tell one or more great stories about every one of them – but actually it would be a whole book!

I dedicate full chapters to Mike Joyce and The Stone Roses later in this book – however, here are a few vignettes.

Go West were two young men Peter Cox and Richard Drummie. They were so excited when they came into my office, telling me that Chrysalis Records wanted to sign them. I always got a buzz out of the clients' 'buzz'.

We completed the record deal, celebrated with some champagne with the record company, and then typically I would not see them again for months. The February after the deal was signed I bumped into them in the gents at the BRITS, (the prestigious TV music awards show) – we decided not to shake hands. They could not believe they were at the 'Brits' – their record company had invited them, they were on cloud 9.

I saw them again at the 'Brits' the following February, but this time not in the gents. They were on stage collecting the Best Newcomer Award. How great and how fast is that! And the next time I saw them was also on stage where they were playing to a sold out Hammersmith Odeon when they amazingly took time in the middle of the show to thank me for all the advice and support I had given.

It was 99 per cent fun, but one day I got a call from another lawyer, he was a friend.

He said, "John, I am sorry to be making this call."

"Don't worry Russell," I said, "how can I help you?"

He said, "I am afraid I am calling you for client Z's files, she wants me to represent her."

I was disappointed, I liked the client and I very, very rarely lost clients. I was a bit bemused. I asked, "Russell, what reason did she give?"

He replied, "I don't want to say."

I pressed him and he said,

"She said your bills are too high!"

I said, "Russell, you will have the file this afternoon – but let me tell you – I have represented that artist for two years, done a fair bit of work but never charged a single penny because I didn't think she had the funds to pay at the moment."

Artist X was a client and a household name – he was a nice man and a great creative talent, at times a genius. He was fed up with his record label. In the end, he tortured them so much that they agreed to release him from his contract.

So one day I came out of a meeting to a phone message from his manager, 'Phonogram have agreed to let X go, can you please get paperwork sorted out before they change their mind.'

Interesting I thought, and went into another meeting.

One hour later I came out of the meeting to a more urgent message from the same manager 'John, X is sure that the record company are going to change their mind so please call them to confirm the verbal agreement and get it confirmed in writing as soon as possible.' So that is what I did. The manager and X were very happy.

Six years and 364 days later the girls in the office give me a call.

There is someone in reception who wants to see me – I go down and there is a stranger who serves me a writ.

Artist X v J P Kennedy and Co – a writ for negligence for getting him released from his contract. The 364 days is significant because if it was 366 days it would have been time barred.

This was an incredible low point.

However, by good fortune I still had the messages from all that time ago, but no one likes being sued and I felt sick to my stomach, a situation which remained for some time. I can only mention this as the writ took it into the public domain, but in fact at the last moment I have changed the artist's name to artist X.

It made me sick and very sad. I instructed lawyers to defend the case and we filed our defence and everyone was confident I would win, but the sick and sad feeling would not go away.

Then one day someone called on behalf of X. They said, 'X has come

to see us and asked if we will ask you if you will let him drop the case?'
I smiled and thought of the sadness and sickness and knew it wouldn't just
disappear. I said 'I would' and they said 'but what about your legal fees?'
I said, 'I will let them go because I never really felt it was X – but that he
was being badly advised by one particular individual'.

So the case was over. A few months later, the phone rang, it was X,
and he asked to see me, I didn't really want to, but he said 'please it is
important to me'. I reluctantly agreed and had a cup of tea with him.
The sadness and the sickness returned, before and during the meeting,
but X had come offering a sincere apology. What could I do?

I accepted his apology and he then went a step further and asked me to
forgive him. I hesitated but said 'I did' – I could see this was part of a healing
process for him.

Even if I say so myself I did many great deals for clients. I was good at
playing off one record company against another and creating a bidding war
to sign my artist client.

There was one client for whom I got a deal of £2 million an album and
remember this was 30 years ago! The advance reflected not what the client
was currently selling but what we all hoped the artist was going to sell in years
to come. The client was thrilled, well at least initially.

After 6 months the artist came to see me, he explained he felt the deal
and the sales expectation was a burden for him. I listened sympathetically,
I just wanted to be clear 'you do realise that if you sell no records you still
get the advances and never repay them as a debt'. He did and I was satisfied
he knew what he was doing, and I knew why he was doing it .

I called the chairman of his record company.

I said, "You have been in the business even longer than me, but I think
this will be one of the strangest conversations you have ever had."

"Well John, you have just set yourself a tall order."
And he listed the large number of legendary and difficult artists he had worked
with over the years. I said, "I am still betting on what I said being right!"

I continued, "You know you have to pay my client £2 million an album."

"Yes John, I remember that very well." he replied.

"Well, I have come to renegotiate."

He was about to scream at me that he would not give me a penny more
– when I said, "Please hear me out."

I silenced him. I said, "My client wants to reduce their advance from
£2 million per album to £1 million per album."

Silence the other end of the phone ... and then,

"I think I can accommodate that John."

And just as I went to put the phone down, he said,

"And it still only makes the top five of the strangest requests I have had, not number one."

"Wow!" I said, "We need to have a beer, so I can hear the other four!" I reported back to the client, they were relieved and I completely understood their thought process. I decided not to charge the client for this negotiation as 'Fee £1000 for making sure you did not get £2 million (£1 million x 2 albums)' seemed out of kilter with my normal line of work – though actually the aim on every deal is to have a happy client, and that is what I had !

Over the years I developed a reputation as an artists' champion. It was true I negotiated strongly on behalf of my artists, but always being careful not to overestimate their negotiating position.

I did represent record companies, in fact, I liked record companies. Artists needed record companies – so it was true I fought hard to get the best deals for my clients and they were usually artists, but actually I would say I fought to get the best deal for my clients even if they were record companies or publishers.

One record executive told one of my clients that they viewed me like Freddie Krueger from Nightmare on Elm Street - I never saw the film but I took it they meant it was like a horror movie having me on the other side.

Midge Ure called me one morning, he said he had been out for dinner the night before with BMG, his record company. The purpose of the dinner was to discuss the release of his new album, but he said the German record executive spent the whole evening discussing what a nightmare I was to deal with. I asked him for the name of the executive. He gave me the name, I said Midge would you be surprised to know that I have never met or spoken to that gentleman. Yes ... Midge was surprised!

All of this meant no record company ever recommended me to artists – but my word of mouth was good and I was busy. In fact some record companies would say to artists they would not deal with the artist if they hired me – it was foolish, it was like a marketing budget and those artists would beat a path to my door! I never ever spent one pound on advertising.

Because of this 'artists' champion' reputation, no one was surprised when I represented the Stone Roses in their restraint of trade case, but they were stunned when I was the expert witness for Sony Records when

George Michael sued them. I knew George a bit, and I thought he was one of the greatest artists ever born, but I was not convinced of the wisdom of his court case.

The music industry is an ecosystem. I made money from it, my artist clients and songwriter clients needed these companies to invest in their careers, not just in the UK, but globally.

It could take hundreds of thousands of pounds, if not millions, to develop an artist's career. If the artist could walk away when they were successful then no one would invest any more.

The Stone Roses contracts were terrible. Actually, the first George Michael contract was terrible and may have been worth litigating over, but it had been renegotiated at least once with many, many millions of pounds being paid in advances and royalties. If George could walk away, then I believed the investment/risk/reward ecosystem would be damaged. One very successful artist manager said to me, 'what are you doing, if George walks free then all our artists walk free!'

My choice to support Sony's position was not a popular decision.

So I went into the witness box at the Royal Courts of Justice against George Michael. A witness box is a lonely place to be – you certainly do not want to be there if you need to tell a lie!

The judge and barristers have decades of experience – they know if you are lying, it is as if your nose gets longer, like Pinocchio, if you tell a lie. But, I had no lies to tell. I was cross-examined for the best part of a day and by all accounts acquitted myself well – I scored some really good points.

However, I did not win the case for Sony – though they did win – and nor did the expensive and brilliant barristers..

The case went on for weeks and weeks. The case for George was that his contract was an unreasonable restraint of trade – basically, he was arguing it stopped him from earning his living.

George gave evidence in a manner which was polite and showed how smart he was. I don't know if by this stage the judge was fed up, bored, or astute, or all three. But he suddenly turned to George and said,

'Mr Michael', or was it 'Mr Panayiotou?' Either way, he asked George how much he was worth. George was taken aback, "I am sorry?" he said.

The judge politely said, "You heard me."

George's barristers were protesting about the crassness of the question, and George said to the judge, "I would rather not say!"

The judge persisted, "OK, I will respect your privacy, you write your net worth on a piece of paper, and only I and the two lead barristers will see it."

I believe from the moment the judge turned over the piece of paper George had lost. I don't know what the sum was that was on the piece of paper, but it was certainly many, many, tens of millions of pounds.

I believe the judge took the view that when George signed to Sony he was worth zero – and now he was one of the wealthiest people in the country. Of course, this was largely down to George's immense talent, but it was a stretch to argue that a pact that had made him so wealthy was stopping him earning a living – especially when he had been advised by the top lawyer in the music industry that he should sign it. I think common sense prevailed in the judge's judgment.

I confess, I have struggled to limit the stories over this 13 year period – it was rarely boring, certainly unpredictable, and often very entertaining.

One Saturday night I came home from a nice dinner and a bottle of wine with Caroline. As I mentioned above, I worked hard, so Saturday night was supposed to be an oasis of rest and relaxation. As we paid the babysitter she said 'oh a guy called Paul Boswell had called and said can you call him when you get in'.

He had left his number, but I was tempted to leave it until the morning, but he had said it was urgent and according to the babysitter it was something to do with a 'beast'.

I called Paul and he said,

"Thanks for calling, I have a new client for you … a Beastie Boy!"

Well, Beastie Boys were global legends and certainly at the cutting edge. Paul filled me in. On the Friday night the band had appeared in Liverpool and after 10 minutes a riot had broken out.

The band had subsequently headed to London, but now the police had arrested Adam Horovitz and charged him with assault causing grievous bodily harm. He was locked in a police cell in central London. I reminded Paul I was not a criminal lawyer, but he said,

"I know, but please do what you can to help."

Even with my limited knowledge of criminal law, I knew with a charge like that, Adam was not going to be released without a bail hearing – and that was not going to happen before Monday morning. I told Paul I would be at the police station at 8.00am and I was.

The police were enjoying having such a celebrity under their 'care'. I asked to see Adam who of course was not enjoying this experience.

Whilst I was with Adam the police sergeant told me that Merseyside police had arrived to take him to Liverpool. I asked if I could travel with him – and the answer was a resounding 'No!'

So, I took a train to Liverpool and then got to see Adam that evening when I gave him the assurance that the following morning he would be released. That gave him some comfort, but no one enjoys two nights in a police cell. Of course there were no mobile phones, so having checked into a hotel I called Caroline to give her the surprising news that I was no longer in central London but was in Liverpool.

I was up early Monday morning to hire a barrister to get Adam released. By the time we got to the court, the press were out in full force, but the hearing was a success – Adam was freed on bail but would have to return in due course to face a full trial. Adam thanked me but of course headed off swiftly. Within 24 hours I was contacted to have my bill paid – but was advised that my services would not be required for the full trial. That was in any event a sensible decision – and I certainly did not feel bad when I learnt that my replacement was the president of the Law Society.

Chrissie Hynde was not only a great recording artist and songwriter, she was an animal rights activist, especially on the subject that 'meat is bad'. Every meeting with Chrissie was interesting, but soon after one meeting I had heard on the news that Chrissie had been particularly vocal about her disdain for McDonald's.

In fact, she was alleged to have told people to boycott McDonald's restaurants and her message was alleged to be so strident that the police were considering charges of 'incitement to criminal damage'.

Again one Saturday evening, again of course long before mobile phones, I was having a rest and recuperation evening with a bottle of wine with Caroline in a restaurant in Highgate. I was beyond surprised when a waiter said that there was a call for me and the phone was in the kitchen. To this day I have no idea how the caller knew I was at this restaurant. I picked up the phone and said, "Hello?"

"Hi John, it's Chrissie"

and when I paused for a second, she said, "Chrissie Hynde."

"Hi Chrissie" I said in a bemused tone.

She said, "John, you are not going to believe this, but someone has firebombed a McDonald's in Milton Keynes, and the press is saying it's my fault!"

I have to admit I was shocked, but I reminded Chrissie that the number

JUST FOR ONE HOUR

one rule was ... 'do not panic, lie low, don't answer the phone and certainly don't talk to the press'.

Saturday evenings were proving to be less restful than I had hoped!

All of my clients were creative people. That usually made them interesting and unpredictable, and no matter how much experience I had, I realised that if I listened to my clients then I could often learn from them.

Alan McGee is a legend in the music industry. He started out as a client, became a friend and client coming to my home for dinner, and is now just a fascinating and entertaining friend who I seem to bump into all over the place. I first met Alan in 1984, soon after I moved into my basement offices in London Records.

Alan had 'discovered' two young brothers, Jim and William Reid who were in a band with the wonderful name, The Jesus and Mary Chain.

Alan was not looking for a deal for them, he was going to form his own record company and put out their records. I asked him if he had a contract with them, and he said,

"John, I don't need a contract – we are like brothers."

I said, "Alan, see those files on the floor – those are actual brothers suing each other."

Anyhow, this was the start of the legendary Creation Records. At the time the music papers were incredibly influential, and I started seeing the band on the front pages as even more than the next big thing. I saw that they were going to be playing North London Polytechnic the following Thursday. When I next spoke to Alan, I said,

"I am going to come down on Thursday."
I thought he would be pleased by my show of support.

"NO, NO" he insisted in his broad Glaswegian accent, "DON'T do that!" I said, "Why not?"

He replied, "It won't be safe, there is going to be a riot and bottles flying around."

I said, "How do you know?" and he said ...

"Because we will start the riot!" "What!?" I said.
He explained, the band only have enough songs for 15 minutes, but 'we have accepted a booking for 50 minutes – so after 12 minutes we will start a riot and leave the stage'. I chuckled, this was serious rock and roll! So I turned up in spite of Alan's advice, made sure I stayed at the back of the venue with my back against the wall so I couldn't get hit from behind.

If this was anarchy and punk – it was very efficient anarchy, the concert started on time, as did the riot. Again, I chuckled.

The press coverage was extraordinary and the reputation of The Jesus and Mary Chain was legendary after one gig!

Eat your heart out Malcom McLaren.

I worked with Alan as his label grew and I loved having him as a client. We got on very well, but he did tell me there was a time in the summer of 1985 when he was frustrated that I wasn't as available as usual – and then one Saturday in July he turned on his TV to see a global jukebox on two continents and realised why I was distracted – he forgave me.

Alan built a well respected and successful label with his partner Dick Green. Every band wanted to sign to Creation. Alan was brilliant at spotting talent, but once an artist was signed if he had a fault he indulged them in the creative process, especially in the studio. The label was an enormous creative and credible success, but then one day Alan and Dick came to see me to confess that their finances did not reflect the public, industry and press perception – but not to worry, Sony Records wanted to do a deal with them.

Alan and Dick and I discussed what was needed to pay off the accumulated debts, fund the company and give Alan and Dick some money. I set off to see Sony one Thursday afternoon with something resembling a business plan to negotiate a deal.

We made good progress on the headline commercial terms and we agreed to work Friday and the weekend to close the deal. We worked until midnight on Friday and until 9.00pm on Saturday, but still had a bit of a way to go, and so we resumed on Sunday. We were confident we could sign by the end of Sunday, so we brought in Alan's father who was a small shareholder.

The numerous documents got closer and closer to the finishing line.

Then the Sony executive who was leading the negotiations for Sony asked me if he and I could have a word in private.

"Sure." I said, a little bemused.

He took me into an office and said, "John we have a Problem." ... WTF?

He said, "Sony head office want to see last month's accounts before we close the deal."

I said, "But that's not right – we have agreed a deal, and now we are just writing it down."

"John," he said, "There is nothing I can do – that is head office's condition to approve the deal."

I went to find Alan and Dick, and told them of the problem ... then watched Dick go paler and paler! I said, "OK, what will they see if they see the accounts they have requested?" And Dick said, "A huge loss."

"OK – but will the figure we have agreed for funding still cover the debts and the next few years funding?"

"Yes." Dick replied – with more confidence than I expected.

So I went back to the Sony executive and said,

"Your new condition probably means that the deal is not going to happen ... but I have one suggestion. We don't have the accounts you want, but we want to close tonight – so we could close tonight on the basis that the deal is not finalised until you get the accounts."

This seemed to satisfy Sony. I was a bit surprised, as I wasn't saying 'you get the accounts, you review them, and then you decide if you want to close the deal'. I was just saying 'we deliver the accounts, you see them and the deal automatically completes'. I was never sure if this was close to sharp practice on my part, or whether Sony UK were fed up with their head office's interference and just wanted to close the deal.

Anyhow, we signed the deal Sunday evening on the basis I suggested. There was no champagne because technically the deal was not finalised. The following morning the accounts were delivered – and once they were delivered the deal was closed. Sony could not pull out because the accounts were horrendous – which they were!

As I say, I don't know whether or not Sony knew what they were doing but I was not representing them. And if my suggestion had been bordering on sharp practice it was the best thing that could have happened to Sony. If they had the right to pull out when they saw the accounts they probably would have done so ... and then they would have missed out on one of the biggest bands Sony UK ever had the good fortune to have on their roster ... OASIS!

Alan loved music – he was seeing bands all the time. He travelled the world spotting talent, making records, and promoting his acts – and he discovered Oasis when he went to see another band who turned up late.

As he worked and travelled Alan partied. He left much of the day-to-day running of the business to Dick, and my law partner started liaising with Dick on Creation matters.

Alan and I were not in regular contact, but I suddenly started hearing that Alan was not in regular contact with anyone – he had headed back to Glasgow which really surprised me. He was ill. I was concerned but I was told his instructions were that no one including me were allowed to contact him.

Then Dick asked to see me. He said Creation again had huge financial problems, they could not pay staff or artists. He said Sony were fully aware of the situation, they were prepared to cover the debts but they wanted Dick and Alan's remaining shares in Creation. Dick had agreed that was the only solution and he wanted me to come to Sony to close the deal.

I went to Sony with a heavy heart. At the meeting I was told of the dire financial state of the company, but was again informed Sony would come to the rescue and pay all the bills if they got Dick and Alan's shares for free! It was left that I would call Alan in Glasgow and recommend this course of action. Though there was no guarantee that Alan would take my call.

I got a taxi back to my office with a heavy heart – if I had had a mobile phone I would have immediately started dealing with all the issues that had arisen whilst I was in meetings with Dick and Sony.

In the absence of a mobile phone I had time to think. What I thought most is that one day Alan will get better and even if he agrees to this course of action then he will be bitterly disappointed. Of course I also wondered if he was mentally in a position to make such a decision. So I called Dick and said I am not prepared to make that recommendation to Alan. Dick was horrified he said 'we will go bust' and I said 'I am not sure you will'. I will call Sony next.

I called Sony and said, "I am afraid I cannot recommend your plan of action." They told me I was mad and that "that would be the end of Creation Records".

I said, "That would be like you cutting of your nose to spite your face, as you own 50 per cent of the company."

They said, almost sarcastically, "OK then, what do you suggest."

I said, "I suggest you continue to fund the company and pay staff and artists, all of that will be a loan from you to the company, and that may well mean, that eventually, you do get Alan's shares for free.

Then two things happened ... Alan got better ... and Oasis got bigger and bigger – and Alan and Dick kept their shares, until they were ready to sell them, which was basically the last deal I did before I said 'adieu' to J P Kennedy and Co.

I did not say goodbye with a heavy heart – I was excited but nervous about the new venture and I knew I was leaving all those wonderful clients in safe hands!

CHAPTER 8

THE STONE ROSES

Before I move on to my new career – three stories from the J P Kennedy and Co. era to tell.

The first is about that iconic band the Stone Roses.

This was an all-encompassing, exhilarating, frightening, satisfying, but ultimately I suppose frustrating episode in my life.

As I write this book I am reminded that, as I have already said, there was no way of knowing what the next phone call would bring. Music Week did an interview with me where they were fascinated that it was a rule of the office that the phone should be answered after three rings. I have no idea why I issued this edict but the team of wonderful secretaries / PAs that I worked with got it.

This was largely our clients ringing, the people who paid our wages, and no one wants to be on the phone with the phone ringing out – it's simply not customer service. At the time, phone and letter were our only means of communication – both pretty inefficient, but all we had.

In recent years I have particularly fallen out of love with the phone. What are the chances, when you phone, that I will be free and that the most important thing I could / should be doing is speaking to you?

I adore email. I do understand that it's not for everyone, but it was and is a boon for me. My whole life I am busy, unless I am sitting with a pint of Guinness, preferably in Ireland, overlooking the sea or the high street of the local village - I like being busy.

Email enables me to be my own air traffic controller. I can look at my inbox and immediately prioritise which ones need to be dealt with first. Even more importantly, I know at a glance how long it will take to reply – usually not very long. Astonishingly efficient, granted not very sociable but efficient. 'Hi' can usually replace 'How are you?' And I suspect 90 per cent of the time people ask 'How are you?' and they really don't want to know.

We used to joke in the office that there were two clients/friends and they were in on the joke, that you should not under any circumstances ask them how they were. If you did, astonishing tales of woe would be unloaded.

I can't believe this as I write it but the arrangement with one client, a very dear friend, was that the wonderful Lesley would, when he called, ask him how he was – and then pass him onto me for the business part of the call.

One day I heard the phone ring and I heard Lesley say, "Hi Dave, how are you?" Lesley has commented to my wife that I have astonishing hearing. Anyhow, the call came through to Lesley at say 2.15pm. I was working on a document and keeping an ear out for the immortal words, "OK Dave - I am just putting you through."

Well, it got to 2.20, 2.25, 2.30, and now the caller is putting Lesley behind with her work – and I can hear he is telling her what a nightmare his wife was – and this was a fact very well known to Lesley, every other girl in the office, and indeed all of Dave's friends, and of course Dave.

Even though I could only hear what Lesley was saying, not what Dave was saying, I gathered his wife's recent behaviour had been even more nightmarish than usual. After 20 minutes, I called out to Lesley, 'please send my Caroline a huge bouquet of flowers and an even bigger box of chocolates'. Dave could hear me shouting and asked Lesley what I had said, Lesley now laughing used this as an excuse and said 'ask him yourself I am putting you through'.

So Dave asked me what I said and I told him, and he said why did you say that and I said to thank the Lord and Caroline that I am not married to your wife! Dave laughed, and he laughed, and he laughed, and he has a great laugh. I said, "Now what did you call about?" He replied, "... You know I can't remember." After more than 40 years, Dave is still a very dear friend.

Anyhow – after that diversion! So whilst the girls were working in the office the phone was answered after three rings, but before they arrived and after they had gone I used to have to juggle answering the phone – as well as actually being on the calls.

One evening at 6.30pm I answered a call.

"Is that John?"

"Yes this is John." I replied.

"Hi John, this is Gareth Evans."

I responded with an enthusiastic, "Hi Gareth" and trying to think who Gareth was ... "Yes, I manage The Stone Roses" came the reply.

My heart missed a beat. The Stone Roses were the coolest and most exciting band around by a very, long way. He said could we meet – I said sure, when would you like to come in, reaching for my diary. The call then took a sort of clandestine turn, and he explained he didn't want to come in. I had to meet him in a coffee shop on the Cromwell Road, West London.

No problem – we arranged to meet at 11.00am a couple of days later.

I went as arranged to the agreed spot and waited and ordered a coffee. Gareth turned up at 11.10am, looked at my coffee and said, "What are you doing?" I was worried that I was going to sound patronising, but I said, "I am drinking a coffee."

"Now," he said, "this was the meeting point – not the place for a meeting." I shrugged, paid for my coffee and followed Gareth to his car which for some reason I think was a Rolls Royce or similar.

We then drove to a similar coffee house where we sat in the conservatory. I realised this subterfuge was in case we were being followed. I wasn't sure why we would be followed, and if we were, they certainly could have done so in the slow moving traffic of Cromwell Road – but I had already blotted my copy book by ordering a coffee in a coffee shop, so I was now treading carefully.

I liked Gareth, which made it sad that we eventually fell out, for reasons outside my control, but of course Gareth didn't see it like that i.e. not my fault. Anyhow, he was engaging in this first meeting and as I hoped he was giving me the chance to represent The Stone Roses – I loved the idea. The band had had some commercial success, and even greater critical acclaim, and their Spike Island concert was in the planning – to use a phrase, 'they were happening'.

The plan was to renegotiate their contract. They were signed to Silvertone Records who were owned by Zomba, which in turn was owned by Clive Calder and Ralph Simon, both of whom I knew well. It was agreed that Gareth would get me the recording contract.

As I was about to leave, Gareth said, "Shall I get you the songwriting agreement?

"Sure," I said, "who is that with?"

"Also Zomba" he said.

"Interesting" I replied.

As I went to leave, he said, "You should know the band have no money … they can't afford to pay you."

I said, "Don't worry, it will work out."

The reality was very few of my clients had money to pay me when they first walked through the door. It was my job to get them deals where they could pay me and where my fees were a sufficiently small percentage of the income from the deal to cause my clients little or no pain.

So Gareth got me copies of the record contract and the publishing contract, and I set aside an hour to review them, and took a cup of tea to the meeting room. I could not believe what I was reading. Over the years, I had read and knew a lot about the English law concept of restraint of trade – it was an important concept whether I was advising record companies or artists.

Well these documents were like spoof contracts for a law student exam so that the student could point out the flaws. They were extraordinarily bad – I made notes, and as I went through these contracts I was both fascinated and relieved. I was relieved not because I thought 'great we can break these contracts' but because Clive Calder for whom I had immense respect was a notoriously tough cookie. At the time most record companies would reward a bands success with a renegotiation, where both sides would give things to each other.

However I knew Clive did not really subscribe to that school of thought, but when I read the agreements I thought well now he has no choice, and in his own interests he needs to replace these contracts.

Well, I was completely wrong. The last thing I wanted was litigation, I did not have a litigation team and I didn't think it was good for the band, and to put it even more simply, I preferred to make deals rather than break deals.

I reported back to Gareth along the 'make not break a deal' lines and asked for permission to start the renegotiation and got the all clear to do so.

I contacted Clive Calder's business affairs guy, Mark Furman, an experienced and affable guy, and asked for a without prejudice conversation which he readily agreed to. I told him what I thought of the contracts – but said I was calling to make a deal.

He put up a brick wall at a relatively early stage. Of course because Clive had told him to – but said if I wanted I could make a proposal. My heart sunk, I could smell what direction this was going in. So I prepared a proposal for a comprehensive renegotiation of both contracts. Frankly on this occasion, this was as much in Zomba / Silvertone's interest as the bands. I ran it by Gareth, and with his permission I sent it to Zomba. Until now my sole intention was to renegotiate, not least because Andrew Lauder at Silvertone was the guy who had given the band their break .

It did not take long before I received a resounding rejection for my proposal. Almost in desperation I asked if they wanted to make a proposal and then I received a desultory in fact insulting proposal. My heart sunk, I called Gareth and said I need a meeting with you and the band!

By the time I got on a plane to Manchester for a meeting at the airport Hilton my spirits were lifted. I could give my clients two choices – stay or go –

but with the road to departure a long and rocky one.

It was a good meeting with the band, they were friendly, intelligent and streetwise. I went through with them how bad their existing contracts were and told them that Zomba wouldn't really budge. They immediately responded in a way most people would react, but especially creative people, they didn't like being taken advantage of – they didn't mind that they had been 'rolled over' on the original deals, but all that they asked was that they now be treated fairly.

The message was clear, if Zomba won't offer a fair contract then, if they could, they should 'walk'.

I warned them it wasn't an easy route but they said if you are up for the fight then we are too. It was entertaining – they wanted to make a deal, but if we couldn't then like a band of brothers we would take on Goliath!

It was agreed I would go away for a week and think of the next steps. I did not underestimate what we were about to embark on!

So I knew the interest for the Roses from record companies would be immense, but only of course if I got them free of contract. I would have to do the heavy lifting and then it would be a crowded party once the band were free and the band's financial resources were limited, very limited.

So step one was to go and see my dear friend David Davis, the ace litigator. I took him through why I thought the recording contract and the publishing contract were unenforceable. We agreed we had to write a formal letter to Silvertone / Zomba saying we believed the contracts were voidable because they were in restraint of trade and we were now voiding them.

We knew that meant that Zomba would seek an injunction to stop the band going off to another record label and David and I agreed that to save costs though it was probably sensible anyhow the band would submit to an injunction, ask for a speedy trial, and agree not to release any material until that trial had taken place.

The clever thing about that was the band could write and record whilst all this was going on but not release. I had already discussed this with the band and that worked for them with everything else they had to deal with including that well known obstacle, the second album.

I already had a busy workload and this venture was of course going to be extremely time consuming and it is not an exaggeration to say that the eyes of the industry were on me. If The Stone Roses could 'walk' from their contracts then who else could.

In reality this was not as groundbreaking as some people thought, we were not creating new law, we were relying on the well-established principle of restraint of trade which was more enshrined in English law than many other legal systems.

Not that long ago the Frankie Goes To Hollywood record and publishing agreements had been declared by a judge to be in restraint of trade. I now had a Jekyll and Hyde existence. On the one hand I was the devil incarnate – I was trying to get a band out of a record deal and a publishing deal, and according to some, if I succeeded I was going to destroy the industry which built its financial model on long term contracts.

On the other hand – 'Oh my goodness, what if he succeeds ... we MUST sign the Roses!'

So behind my back I was talked of as if I was about to destroy the industry – but at the same time I was being wined and dined by the industry just in case I got lucky and got the band free!

Everyone wanted to sign them – EVERYONE.

My strong advice to Gareth and the band was that they should not make themselves widely available for the inevitable 'Japanese dinners' where everyone told them they were the best record company in the industry. That process would start out fun, soon become boring, and ultimately draining – anyhow, they should be writing songs.

So I said I will field the interest. I will prepare a wish list of commercial terms we wanted, send it to any credible interested party, and see who falls by the wayside, and who is in for the long run.

After a while it came down to two main contenders, Polygram led by the eccentric but brilliant Obie and Geffen Records led by Ed Rosenblatt with the legendary David Geffen in the background.

One of the biggest problems was that Polygram was strongest outside the USA and Geffen was strongest in the USA. The simple answer was to do a deal with Polygram for the world ex USA and Canada and with Geffen for the USA and Canada. Unfortunately, I could not get both companies to agree that. They were largely in the right area on commercial terms but neither wanted to split the deal even though it would also have split the risk.

Of course this deal had one big quirk from normal deals. Whoever the band agreed to 'sign' with were assuming we would win the court case, and the big deal was that I wanted them to fund the court case, and whether we won or we lost that sum was a non-recoupable sum.

From memory I think the sum I had decided I needed for the court case was £300,000 – not chicken feed as Obie pointed out to me.

We had narrowed the field down to two contenders and so the courtship began. To be honest I can't remember the detail but it was easy for Polygram because they were based in the UK. Obie was relentless as a formidable dealmaker but he especially knew how to close deals. Geffen were ready to fly the band to Los Angeles but the band were having none of it – with great Mancunian aplomb they said if they want us they come here! You had to love that!

So from memory I think Geffen sent their top A&R team to seduce the band – anyhow it worked, the decision was made that it should be Geffen for the world.

First job was for me to deliver the news to Polygram and Obie. He did not reply 'thank you John for taking the trouble to let me know' – in fact he got more swear words into one sentence than I thought was possible. He was not a good loser – that's what made him so good. I checked my birth certificate and my anatomy to make sure that not all the things he said about me were true.

So now to Geffen my words would be that 'it's now yours to lose'. That's because, especially then but actually even now, companies have a habit of promising the world and the moment you say 'yes we will sign', they start backtracking.

Time was tight – we had got an earlier trial date than we expected. We were about to go into court and we did not have the money for the court case. It was agreed that Geffen would come to London to close the deal. They would come over a weekend, they would base themselves at the Halcyon hotel in Holland Park, the band would also be there, and we would start on the 100 plus pages of paperwork with a view to agreeing it on the Sunday evening and the band signing it then.

The negotiation was friendly, at most times, but Geffen's business affairs guy did what he considered his job – he wanted to really see if we needed what we had asked for and indeed they had already agreed – yes we did!

They wanted huge loopholes on the arrangements regarding funding the court case. I had no wiggle room on that, and I needed the money now – not of course if / when the band won!

Then I had a bit of luck. I never found out how, and sadly Obie is no longer with us, but Obie found out that we were all staked out at the Halcyon Hotel. I really have no idea how he found out, I hadn't even told my wife, why would I, not that it was a secret, why would she care what hotel we were meeting in?

Whilst I was locked in a room, actually a very nice suite, negotiating with the Geffen team the band were having a great time. Geffen were picking up the tab for all room service and they were watching films. Obie decided to hang out with them and came up with an inspired offer to persuade the band to sign to him - I will come back to that.

There was one very important point I had to address in the Geffen negotiation. Geffen were having a problem accepting it but to my mind there was no choice. The band had, as part of the injunction, not only agreed not to release any records, but also not to sign a new record deal. That was tricky – actually of course the band needed the money for the court case and no record company were going to fund that and just hope the band would sign to them if they won. They needed a commitment from the band, but then there was that injunction.

So having negotiated from 10.00am Saturday to 9.00pm that night I called an end to the day, and went home to wrestle with that thorny problem. We were to reconvene at 9.00am Sunday.

I came into the meeting the following day with a spring in my step.

I said we would have three documents:

A - The main record deal, undated and unsigned.

B - A letter whereby Geffen funded the court costs to a maximum sum, win, lose or draw.

C - The band would sign a letter agreeing that if they won the court case, so that the injunction was discharged and no appeals possible, then they would sign document A.

Geffen didn't love it but I said there weren't any other options and Obie was 'in town'.

Anyhow, it was agreed and the negotiation continued with food being delivered at meal times.

As we were putting in our lunch order I chuckled as I looked at the menu. Eddie Rosenblatt, one of the nicest guys you could expect to meet, especially in the music industry, said, "What are you laughing at?

I relied, "I just saw steak tartare on the menu.

He said, "That's good, have that."

I recounted a story back in 1979 when I was holed up in a hotel like this – that time representing the record company and trying to sign Dr Hook who were huge at the time. Same thing, we negotiated all over the weekend, but managing on sandwiches – I was a very unsophisticated 26 year old. At 6pm on the Sunday evening we were done and the contract was agreed, and we all decided to have a beer and supper before we went our separate ways. I was starving and I loved steak and chips (see what I meant by unsophisticated). It came to my turn to order and I said steak tartare – I think everyone was impressed.

I said to the waiter, "Does that come with chips?"

I saw him raise an eyebrow and he said, "No sir."

"Then add a large plate of fries and some mayonnaise please."

 "Certainly, sir."

I could not wait for the food to come – it had been a good day and I was on my second beer when room service arrived and the waiter with a wry smile whisked off the cover to reveal my raw steak!

Anyhow, back to The Stone Roses' negotiation. By 8.00pm on Sunday we were done – and the Geffen team were booking flights for the morning. I reminded them I had to go through everything with my clients but I did not anticipate any problems.

So I went to the room where the band were all gathered, knocked at the door and went in, and said, "I think we are done."

Only to be greeted by "SHOOSH" …

"What the f*ck?" …

"SHOOSH!"

They were watching the film '12 Angry Men' and now I was on the receiving end of their Mancunian spirit. They wanted to see the end of the film before discussing the documents that I thought they were about to sign. I was about to blow a gasket – I would like to get home to my family.

But first I asked, 'How long left?'

… "20 minutes."

I don't know where I found the patience but I figured I was going to get better focus from them if I let them finish the film.

I said, "Fine I will go for a walk."

And as I left Rennie said, "And there is something we need to discuss!"

So I got some fresh air and returned 25 minutes later.

"Right" I said, "I think we are there – I am going to go through these very important documents and at the end you will, if happy with them, sign two and not sign one."

Rennie said, "We need to talk to you."

"Fine," I said, "I am all ears"

"Obie came to see us."

"Yes" I said, "I saw him" and added … "too late!"

"Not necessarily ..." someone said.

"What do you mean?" I said.

"Well ... he offered to add £100,000 to the Geffen deal and fly us all to New York on Concorde – and we all said what a great idea – we can sign the deal when we are halfway across the Atlantic!"

I was stunned ... I sank into my chair ...

"Are you serious?" I asked, "We have spent ages discussing which company would be best for your career – YOU decided that you would sell more records with Geffen and now for a bit more money, and a joy ride, you are going to switch allegiances!"

I was clearly furious and then one joker threw in ...

"But JOHN, you get to come too.!"

I screamed, "I HAVE BEEN ON CONCORDE!!! ... and if you sell records then you will go on Concorde many times over!"

They were clearly not shocked by my anger – and in fact seemed to be enjoying it. Then someone, I think it was Mani, put me out of my misery.

"John," he said, "this is how it works ... we tell Obie and Polygram that we are going to sign to them ... we get on Concorde, we get halfway across the Atlantic and when they produce the contracts and say sign here ... we say 'no' ... what can they do ... we then get Geffen to meet us in New York where we do sign their contracts ... and they then put us on Concorde back to London – what a story that will make – John, we will be front page of all the music papers and maybe even the Financial Times!"

Well, I had to marvel at their ingenuity and I did smile, but I said, "NO ... over my dead body!"

I could hear 'SPOILSPORT' ringing through my ears, but I said 'NO' in a manner that made it clear that was not going to happen – it was too disrespectful to Obie.

I made them sit down and we went through the paperwork, but there was another twist to come!

So I went through everything and we all agreed it was a great deal. I explained because of the court case they would not really make money from the first album, but it would only be the second album and big sales that would produce the cash flow.

It was now 11.00pm – I knew we were in court in the morning and I wanted to get home and get some sleep. I wasn't actually the advocate in court but I was bearing the responsibility for this whole venture and now it wasn't just under the scrutiny of the music industry but the wider media were interested.

So I suggested let's go to the Geffen suite, open a bottle of champagne and sign … BUT NOT ALL THE DOCUMENTS.

"NO," the band said, "we need a Concorde plan from Geffen."

I did lose it a bit – I said, "We don't have time for this!" … but they weren't budging.

I don't know who came up with the idea – I think it was as if it were a negotiated settlement between me and them. We went to the other extreme to Concorde – the contract would be signed on the top floor of … a red London double-decker bus!!!

I wasn't so tired that I couldn't see a flaw in this (as this was before regular night buses) – we had missed the last bus available that night for contract signing!

"No problem," they said, "we can sign tomorrow."

I looked at them, but you know I got it. This band had a legendary reputation to live up to – their fans would have loved the Concorde story if it had played out, and would think the red bus was a bit of a laugh. It wasn't, as it might look now, about being spoilt brats – it was about being unconventional. It may even seem childish, but I really did 'get it' – the music papers were very influential at the time and this story would be all over the front pages.

"OK," I said, "a couple of issues, I have to go to court in the morning and bizarrely even though you are the claimants you don't have to be there, and the Geffen team will be on flights to Los Angeles."

"No," they said, "We want you and the Geffen team to be there."

"OK," I said, "I have no idea if I can make this happen, but 2.00pm tomorrow on the first bus that stops at the bus stop opposite the hotel."

And then I took a weary walk up the steps to the Geffen suite. They were surprised to see me come in alone.

"We have a small problem …" I said, but before I could finish they said,

"John, you have made us break every rule of deal making – ENOUGH."

"No," I said, "actually this won't cost you anything … well, maybe a few bus fares." They looked at me as if I was mad – and so I explained the plan.

Eddie, a really nice man, was absolutely furious – he made noises like 'I have a business to run'. I said to Eddie you have come this far, and when he was still not budging, I told him the ALMOST Concorde plan – and it broke the ice – and after a few expletives from Eddie we agreed to meet at 1.55pm the next day at the bus stop across the road from the hotel.

Little did I know what I would have gone through by the time we met at that bus stop!

So it had been a busy weekend – but Monday was a court day. This was a time well before email, and mobile phones were not part of my world – I was not an early adopter ! So it was only when I met up with the litigation team Monday morning at 8.00am that I was able to bring them up to date with the weekend's developments.

I thought I was coming in as a conquering hero. The most relevant thing for the litigation team was that I had secured the funding for the court case – we had been running on financial fumes until then … we had been running on ZERO.

I sat and had a cup of tea with David Davis and told him what had happened – if he was concerned he didn't show it – but nor did he appear elated.

We went off to meet our barristers as usual – we had a wonderful formidable female QC Barbara Dohmann. David said to her can I have a word and took her to one side – it was clear I was not to be a party to the 'word'.

After about 10 minutes David came over and said to me can I have a word. He always had a wicked sense of humour and I thought his next line was one of his best until I realised he wasn't joking.

"Have you brought your toothbrush?" he said.

I looked quizzical and he said, "As you know, our two barristers have two of the brightest legal minds in the UK and they are both of the view that the documents that you let the band sign put the band in breach of the injunction – and as such they are in contempt of court and they could go to jail … but Barbara thinks that because this was done on your advice … you should offer to go to jail in their place."

I laughed out loud and then stopped mid-laugh – not an easy thing to do – because I could see this was not one of David's little jokes. My heart sank but I remember not for long – now this was a time to cower or fight – and I chose the latter.

"BOLLOCKS" I said.

"Yes" David said, "I understand."

"No," I said, "I don't mean I have made a bollocks of this – I mean those two brilliant legal minds have got it wrong."

"Really?" David said, "you have got it right and they – two of the best and most experienced legal minds in the country – have got it wrong?"

I continued, "Yes."

And he replied "So do you want to tell them?"

"I do." I said.

So I went over and, not surprisingly given her view, I got a very frosty reception from Barbara. She reminded me I may have been responsible for hiring her – but I was not her client – the band was. I took her through my thinking ... they would be in breach of the injunction if they signed a record deal but they had signed a piece of paper committing them to a record deal ONLY if they won the case and the injunction was discharged. So they could never be in breach of the injunction as they were only signed to the record deal if the injunction was discharged.

Barbara was brutal, "John I know you think you have been clever, but I am afraid your linguistic somersaults have not worked."

I was both angry and frustrated because I thought our own legal team was now going to create a problem where there was none. The clock was ticking against us it was eight minutes until the hearing resumed.

Barbara said, "I am sorry but I am an officer of the court and I have a duty to the court and to my colleagues on the other side. I am going to give them a copy of the documents. They will read them and they will make an application for contempt of court." I had little time for a longer debate.

I said, "OK Barbara I have no choice, I only have one request and I accept you don't owe me this, you owe your clients this – I want you to present the documents to the other side in a matter of fact way with no hint of drama."

"John do you take me for a fool?" she hissed.

"Of course not." I apologized – but I was very anxious that they did not score an own goal.

Was it arrogance that I knew I was right – and yet two of the greatest legal minds in the country were wrong. Yes it was arrogance, but if you are going into a battle like this it is not a time to be faint-hearted.

So I stood at the back of the court and watched as Barbara gave the documents to the QC on the other side. I watched as there was much gesticulating and pointing at watches.

She came back and said, "They have asked for a half hour adjournment to read the documents and I have agreed."

It was a long half hour – with David Davis trying to keep my spirits up with gallows humour about my spell in prison being a good opportunity to lose weight.

The other side indicated they were ready to resume, and just before the judge came in, Barbara said,

"John I will do my best but you have put me and your clients in a difficult position." It was much worse than being told off, she was putting considerable distance between me and her.

The QC on the other side rose to his feet and we braced ourselves for a dramatic application regarding contempt of court.

"My lord," he addressed the judge, "over the weekend the plaintiffs have signed a number of documents which I submit to you now."

"Yes, yes" said the judge, "and do you want me to read these now?"

"No my lord, they are just for completeness for your file ... I would now like to call my next witness."

And with those words the application for contempt of court disappeared into thin air. It was clear the other side had interpreted the documents in the way I intended them to operate.

I hadn't been shaken in my belief that I was in the right, but to say the least, it is not fun to have two great minds cast doubt on it. I hope my huge sigh of relief was not audible and I was pleased to see David Davis smile and when he leaned over to me I was expecting to hear 'well done' – but no, no concession from him ...

"JAMMY!" he said and shook his head.

What could I say ... and I joked back ...

"Is that spelt with a G ... as in G E N I U S."

Barbara turned round and said "SHOOSH." I had heard that phrase before in the last 24 hours !

Well, now from the sublime to the ridiculous. Apart from having many other clients, no mobile phone and pre-Blackberry, I had to get myself a bus ticket for the No.38 bus and headed back to Holland Park.

Time had not healed with the Geffen team, especially Eddie Rosenblatt. The band were in good spirits – I told them about the toothbrush story and they loved it – quipping, "John, we would have come to visit!"

So a happy band and a photographer who someone had whistled up got on to the top of the bus with a grumpy Geffen team. The band had champagne (no glasses), of course ordered on room service on Geffen's tab.

It actually was fun and the documents were signed. Of course, if the contempt of court bit had gone wrong I could have pulled the plug on the signing – but we would have had no money for the court case, and we all had a swig of champagne and went our separate ways.

The truth of the matter was the court case wasn't going well. We didn't have one of the country's top judges – we had an inexperienced judge from Manchester, ironically, who was clearly of the view that if you signed a contract you made a deal and you were stuck with it.

He didn't like being told by a woman, i.e. Barbara, that he was wrong; she could be prickly, and she was brilliant.

I will never forget the first two minutes of the case. Her rather grand and pompous opposing QC rose to his feet, and addressed the judge saying,

"My Lord, the case before you today is a copyright case."

There was a kerfuffle and I could see the noise was Barbara collecting up her papers and books as if she was leaving. The judge was astonished,

"Ms Dohmann, what on earth are you doing?"

"I am terribly sorry my Lord, but I just listened to my learned friend's opening sentence and I am worried I am in the wrong court ... the case I am here for is not a copyright case at all but a contract case."

The learned judge and her learned friend were not amused – David and I smiled – Barbara was going to take no prisoners! It was going to be an interesting few weeks!

So yes the first part of the case was not going well. The judge thought a 'contract is a contract' and to be fair that is largely the case under English law. In general a contract will be enforced even though it's unreasonable, or even harsh, and unconscionable. However, restraint of trade is an exception to this approach, because I suppose it's considered a fundamental right to be able to earn a living. Again, I suppose, reflecting in its most extreme modern form that slavery is wrong.

When 'The Artist Formerly Known As Prince' was trying to get out of his record deal he had the word 'slavery' emblazoned on his forehead. These Stone Roses contracts were some of the worst I had seen – but this judge seemed to be taking the view 'how bad can it be to be paid for making records and writing songs' – and maybe some coal miners would have been sympathetic to that view.

Anyhow, we were losing the fight – but then the case took an interesting turn. Before a case reaches court, both parties have to go through a process called 'discovery', where they have to show to the other side all documents, memos, letters, emails, etc. that they have in their possession.

One day the QC for Zomba was reading from a document which referred to a couple of documents that we had not seen. Barbara jumped onto this impressively – she complained to the court that clearly Zomba had not disclosed all relevant documents, and seemed to lay responsibility for that on the shoulders of her learned friend who she pointed out as an officer of the court had a duty to ensure his clients complied with their discovery obligations.

Very professionally, Zomba's QC took this to heart and agreed to ensure that a review took place to see how reliable their discovery process had been.

Barbara however saw an opening – a review can be stalled and take time and she insisted that the judge adjourn the day's proceedings IMMEDIATELY so that her learned friend, and his assistant, and Zomba's solicitors, could go to Zomba's offices and see what undisclosed documents there were, even if they had to work all night. The judge agreed and Zomba's QC was on the back foot so did not put up any resistance.

The fact that some documents hadn't been disclosed could easily have been a minor incident – but Barbara had made it a major dramatic issue, her instinct was right and this was a major turning point.

Whilst the Zomba lawyers are burning the midnight oil let me take a diversion. Discovery had caused some problems for our side. It had revealed a document that I didn't know existed. A management agreement between Gareth and the band. Very unfortunately this document was also onerous and unreasonable.

Well before this, it was clear the relationship between Gareth and the band was poor to non- existent – and the news of how unreasonable the management agreement was, was the straw that broke the camel's back. However, the back was already fractured and was going to break with or without a straw.

There were two developments – one evolving and one immediate. The immediate one was that it was decided now that Gareth had to have a separate barrister and solicitor, and everybody including Gareth expected me to arrange it, and find the money for it. To be fair, who else would have done, but the cost put an additional strain on our limited fighting fund and certainly pushed back the day when I was ever going to see a penny for my efforts.

The second development, and it was already in train, was that Gareth blamed me for the schism in his relationship with the band. I actually had zero responsibility for it. The truth of the matter was the band had come to loathe him for a multitude of reasons – and I had enough on my plate without wanting them to be managerless! Anyhow, suffice to say I was the villain as far as Gareth was concerned and a couple of years later I woke up one

Sunday morning to read an article about The Stone Roses in the Sunday Times in which Gareth made the unveiled threat to the effect that he would get his revenge on John Kennedy one day – and that wasn't a threat that I dismissed lightly.

Anyhow, the following day the Zomba lawyers returned with bundles of additional documents and the case resumed, whilst in parallel our team went through the papers.

Barbara like most great QCs could have been an actress. The papers contained an internal memo which she could not wait to read to the court. Of course, nearly 30 years later, I can't remember the exact words but it was an internal memo which was sent whilst I was trying to renegotiate with them. It basically said, *'offer them this, i.e. xyz, they will probably take it because they don't know how bad these contracts are'.*

Barbara read each word as if it was a sword slicing through their defence. "THEY - DON'T - KNOW - HOW - BAD - THESE - CONTRACTS - ARE ! Barbara made each word sound like a sentence!

It wasn't a golden bullet to win the case, that only happens in TV shows and films – but it did make the judge realise he needed to take Barbara's arguments more seriously. He did that, but there was absolutely no indication as the trial carried on as to who was winning and who was losing.

And then the trial comes to an end, the judge thanks everyone and goes away. He will give his judgement but you literally have no idea when. To me that is beyond bizarre but it's the system. It was pretty hard to explain to the band that I literally have no idea whether we have won, or we have lost, and I have no idea when we will find out.

Neither Barbara nor David had a view, they simply didn't know – and we knew we would appeal if we lost but that was it. And I wasn't sure where the money for an appeal would come from.

The music industry is at the best of times a gossip machine and I had no idea who the judge would share his thoughts with. The then managing director of Zomba told my good friend Roger Ames that they had been told they had won and that my career would be ruined. I had no idea if either was true. But losing was certainly not going to enhance my reputation.

Whilst all this was going on my father died. It was of course very sad but it was a long time ago and as I write this it reminds me that, whilst waiting for The Stone Roses decision, the 10 years London Records negotiation was full on. I would work until say 11.00pm on that, go home for a few hours sleep, and go and sit by his bed for a couple of hours – he was in a coma so this was as much for me as him. And yes my wife was, and is a saint.

So my father passed away peacefully, never waking from his coma and we planned his funeral at our family church in North London. People in the music industry were both kind and sympathetic and one day I got a call from Ossie Kilkenny. Ossie was U2's business manager at the time, a larger than life character and a good friend. The Irish are good at dealing with death, and Ossie offered me his sympathy and we joked about a terrible story I had told him about my father.

The conversation was nearing an end and Ossie said,

"When are you taking your father back to Ireland?"

I paused and said, "We aren't."

Ossie nearly went berserk. He knew from previous conversations that even though my father had brought up and educated his six children in England, and even though England had been good to him, my father was Irish through and through. I finished the call with Ossie's admonishment ringing in my ears and called my brothers and sisters – why are we not taking Dad back to Ireland? No one had an answer, but thanks to Ossie, the penny dropped – we were on the verge of making a terrible mistake.

Bear with me – this is relevant to the Stone Roses!

If you can guess how then you are a genius.

So plans were changed – there would be a funeral service at the church where my parents and all of us were married, and then his body would be taken to Ireland. Of course the whole family went to Ireland – well, we had a three day wake though unusually for Ireland at first without the body.

My father's body had been driven across on the ferry and then on to Kerry. Ireland is a small place and the driver of the hearse stopped for a pint when he was an hour away from the funeral parlour.

Now, all Irish publicans are the source of all knowledge, and this one said to the driver, "Did you hear Michael Kennedy from Inch Strand passed away."

It took a lot to surprise a publican but he wasn't expecting the reply,

"Jesus, haven't we got the very man in the hearse outside."

My father had now been dead for a number of days, and he had been ill for a long while, and so hopefully we can be forgiven for making the weekend a celebration of his life, rather than a sad occasion. Let's say the Guinness flowed, and my young daughter learnt to sleep on a pub bench with much bedlam around her. Interestingly, she has trouble sleeping now and listens to dolphin music to help her nod off. I think next time I am in Ireland I will record Foley's bar at 11.00pm on a Saturday for her – it certainly worked all those years ago .

So we all returned to Stansted airport having done my father justice – if it was a celebration he wanted, yes that is what he would have wanted. Caroline, Ellie and I got home at a quarter past midnight and our live-in nanny had gone to sleep. As I was about to head up myself I saw a torn envelope on the stairs with something written in pencil on it – I nearly ignored it but didn't. It was a written scrawl with a blunt pencil but I could see it was supposed to relay a phone message;

'Roses / judgement tomorrow 10.00am' – I FROZE.

Of course I hardly slept that night.

I knew if we lost, the industry would gloat, but it was what it was – there was nothing I could do about it now. So in 18 hours I had gone from drinking in Foley's bar in Ireland, listening to tales from the locals about my father, to the Royal Courts of Justice in the Strand, London. The media was out in force including even TV cameras.

David Davis and our barristers knew the result but were not allowed to tell me – instead they offered commiserations for my father's passing.

So the judge came in and started giving his judgement. For the first half it sounded like we had lost ... and then there was a 'HOWEVER...' and the judge went our way and agreed the contracts were unenforceable. I felt relief rather than euphoria and remember no mobile phones, no emails. We went for a celebration lunch with the legal team. The consequences of losing were immense – and having won I think I was just numb. The band were thrilled, as were Geffen – now the band needed to come back strong.

THEY DIDN'T ... that's the right two words ....THEY DIDN'T!

About a couple of years later I was asked if the litigation destroyed the band – it didn't. They just loved taking on the establishment and winning – they were very appreciative, but they started an internal combustion which has been catalogued elsewhere, and I don't need to repeat it.

I invited myself down to Rockfield Studios to hear how the new album was progressing. I was excited as we arrived, my toddler son got to play on the drums, but you could feel the atmosphere – it was toxic. I could smell lethargy, arguments, probably drugs, and certainly the absence of any credible, creative process.

The album did actually get finished, but got a lukewarm reception

Geffen away with it

Roses freed to pick up £20m deal

BOB DYLAN'S 50TH BIRTHDAY

NME spesh!

THE STONE ROSES have won the case brought against them by record label Silvertone/Zomba, and have signed a long-term deal with US label Geffen said to be worth a cool £20 million.

The legal battle, which has been raging in The Strand's High Court since March 4, climaxed on Monday. Presiding Judge Humphries declared their recording and publishing contracts with Silvertone/Zomba "entirely one-sided and unfair".

The band were not in court, but delighted manager and fellow defendant Gareth Evans told *NME*: "Gazza misses out, but The Roses clean up". According to sources inside The Roses' camp, the triumph was unexpected.

The Roses and Evans were awarded £100,000 costs, and the judge also permitted inquiry into damages suffered by the group while under temporary injunction banning them from recording for any other party. No inquiry will take place until Silvertone/Zomba have decided whether to appeal against the decision.

Silvertone/Zomba pleaded that the band were in breach of contract in seeking another deal (with Geffen), and wanted a court ruling obligating the band to record for them. The Roses claimed successfully that their oppressive contracts with the company were not enforceable by English law.

The Roses return to the studio this week to record the follow-up to their platinum '89 eponymous debut album. A spokesperson for the band told *NME*: "A single will be released as soon as humanly possible". According to insiders, Ian Brown and co have already demo-ed enough material for a double album release.

Meanwhile a massive open-air comeback gig is reportedly being considered for sometime this year. The band have been rehearsing in a West Wales studio during the last month, but insiders have expressed doubts whether a show could be staged before the summer is out. However, representatives for the band have reportedly viewed several prospective locations in the South of England in the last few weeks. Plans are also afoot to stage two major US gigs.

BOB DYLAN, maybe the most influential figure in the history of rock, is 50 this Friday (May 24). To celebrate, *NME* offers the following morsels:
● Pg 9: a **Material World** from 1965
● Pg 21: 50 things you didn't know about Bob Dylan
● Pg 22/23: Four lives (including **Bob Willis** and **Keith Floyd**) that have been touched by Dylan
● Pg 24: Bob and The Dylans (the groups!)
● Pg 25: What they say about him
● Pg 35: win new Dylan books
● Pg 58: Complete Dylan discography – and the eight LPs you should own
● Pg 61: Dylan cover versions chart
● Pg 62: Lowry on Dylan
● Pg 63: The Dylan Story!

25 May 1991 New Musical Express—Page 3

The Stones Roses 1991 legal case – as reported in the NME.

'To John - Love and Respect!'
from Ian Brown of The Stone Roses.

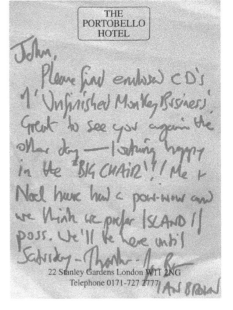

A note from Ian Brown on starting his solo
career after The Stone Roses disbanded.

and lukewarm sales – the songs weren't terrible, some were even really good, but it was as if the public could sense this was no longer a band of brothers.

After the release of the second album John and Ian both asked for separate meetings. Pat Savage, their accountant and my friend, was to join me at both meetings.

I was about to embark on a dramatic career change but that's for another chapter – the meetings were sad, disheartening affairs.

It was clear the band was over – and the suggestion was that they were only staying together because they owed me £82,607!

I said to both of them, 'if that's the reason you are staying together then forget it, I won't chase you for it, do what is going to make you happy'.

After the meetings were over I was very sad to see what had become of these friends. Pat looked at me and said with his great humour 'if you hadn't already decided on your career change that would certainly have made up your mind'.

I ended up being chairman of Ian and John's record company – John with his band The Sea Horses and Ian asked to come in and see me as he had made a solo album. He played it for me – there and then after 45 minutes, I agreed a solo deal with him.

It took a long time, but the multi-million pound reunion came, many, many years later – and the week of the first concert a book about The Stone Roses was published.

It mentioned the £82,607 – and when I went into the dressing room just before they went onstage for their big Heaton Park homecoming, and after we had all hugged each other, someone said,

"John, we still owe you £82,607!"

"Oh … forget it." I said.

"Thanks John!" they said, "You have always been good to us!"

———————————

What a rollercoaster it had been – but I wouldn't have missed it for the world.

CHAPTER 9

MIKE JOYCE

It was an incredibly busy time, work was flowing, Band Aid commitments never went away. My family were either understanding or just put up with it.

Monday to Thursday were leave home 7.20am, a cheese roll for breakfast in a cafe round the corner (what was I thinking of ?) work 8.00am to 7.00pm, drive home, dinner 7.30 to 8.30pm, work 8.30 to 11.00pm – and Fridays no evening work!

Weekends were much more relaxed probably only eight hours on Saturdays and five hours on Sunday.

It was hard work but enjoyable, stressful – but less stressful if I put in the hours because less time was spent on being chased by people. Those hours working enabled me to keep ahead of the curve on deals rather than on the back foot.

In spite of the workload I really did appreciate at the time how exciting and interesting it was.

Things would just come out of the blue. I remember one Saturday in the office opening the post and their being a nice handwritten letter asking if I would represent this guy Dave Dorrell on a single he had with other musicians under the name M|A|R|R|S.

I never turned people down and I like to think we tried to treat everyone the same out of common decency, but also because one of the great things about the music industry is today's nobody can be tomorrow's huge star.

I arranged to see Dave the following week, he had a single but no record deal. He played me the record – he loved the fact I wanted to hear the record – apparently not all professional representatives did. And the music was part of the buzz of all of this – it was exciting hearing music at the beginning of its life in the industry.

The single was a track called 'Pump Up the Volume' and it went on to be a huge global hit and Dave Dorell became a big player in the industry, but was just an overall great guy. I am sure we made fees out of the relationship with Dave, but the prize was being involved at the beginning of such an important record, and watching and hopefully helping Dave 'grow' to the very heights of the music industry and take on presidents of labels for his artists – he became a formidable force.

When I sat down this morning I wasn't intending to write about Dave Dorrell ... my post-it note said 'Mike Joyce'.

Mike was a great example of the beautiful uncertainty of life. One day I came out of a meeting to a phone message, Mike Joyce from the Smiths would like an appointment. I asked Lesley to call him and arrange for him to come in. I was excited, maybe he was sent as an emissary to ask me to represent the Smiths, in fact it was more interesting than that. Mike came in, sat down and said,

"I don't know if there is anything we can do about this but ..."

I was all ears, I can only write about this because it is in the public domain as you will hear later.

I knew that Mike Joyce was the drummer in the Smiths, who had now disbanded, and he went on to explain that when they all started out he thought the four members were equal in respect of their recording activities – but after a while the splits of income became unequal.

One split for Morrissey and Johnny Marr, and a lesser income split for Mike and Andy Rourke; 40/40/10/10.

I became a bit like a doctor asking for symptoms,

"Did you sign anything to agree this split?"

"No." he replied.

But he seemed to have accepted accountings on the 40/40/10/10 basis for some time – which was a potential problem.

Now as a music business lawyer you don't actually practice much law – you negotiate deals and you draft contracts but you operate in a quite limited area of law. In fact, I remember being at a client's wedding in Scotland when a guest on the other side of the table called across,

"John what do you do for a living?"

I said, "I am a music business lawyer."

"Ah," the reply came back, "then not a proper lawyer."

The whole table all laughed and I certainly didn't take offence, it was almost like a badge of honour, a bit cooler than being a proper lawyer. Though, as my wife and children would be quick to point out, the words 'John' and 'cool' should not appear in the same sentence.

Actually I prided myself that I had a good legal mind, and over the last few years I had been wrestling with the fact that a number of my clients were becoming more successful, they were proper businesses. The problem was at the beginning of their careers they simply didn't have the money to spend on legal fees for a partnership agreement. Then later on when they did have the money I learnt very quickly that trying to prompt such a discussion was more likely to break up the band than instil harmony and remove uncertainty.

I had drafted many partnership agreements for bands but I am pretty sure in the 12 years that I practiced as a music business lawyer none were signed.

So Mike was sitting in front of me and I did something I don't think I did at any other time in front of a client. I went over to my tiny law library, about 5 books, and took out a book and read it in front of my client. I was reading the Partnership Act 1890.

After about five minutes of silence, letting it all sink in, I told Mike, you know I think there is something you can do about it – but I have three pieces of advice for you go away and think about :

    1 - Are you ready to declare war on Morrissey and to a lesser extent
       Johnny? (I had a feeling Johnny would be less dogmatic about it.)
    2 - Do you have the stomach for a few years of the litigation?
    3 - Does Andy Rourke want / need all this?

I don't remember at this stage raising with Mike the cost of the litigation, because in the early stages of developing this idea I wasn't worried whether I would get paid.

So after some days thinking time, Mike came back with Andy and told me that they had both discussed it, and they both felt so aggrieved about it they wanted to right the wrong if they could.

In one respect my heart sank because I knew this was a tough road ahead but I couldn't walk away now.

I didn't have a litigation team so I used to work with my mentor and friend David Davis, but to save money I went to see Nigel Davis a barrister that I knew from other matters. I was surprised to find Nigel fairly sceptical about my line of argument for this litigation.

He was a very bright man who always treated me with respect, but he wasn't used to seeing me without the artillery and support of David Davis behind me, or indeed very often in front of me. I think his opening words, (a bit like the guest at the wedding) were 'John, and what do you know about the Partnership Act 1890?' At one time during our discussion I was tempted to say 'Nigel by the sound of things a lot more than you.' I realised he was playing Devil's advocate with me, but at one stage I was ready to wilt under his surprisingly strong 'push back'.

Anyhow, we left it that he would go away and think about it .

I can't remember whether the next stage was a call or another meeting, but he came back to me as every barrister does, quite rightly, and said we need lots more information.

He was very concerned that because Andy and Mike had received accounting statements over a number of years accepting the different splits, then that was evidence that they had agreed or at least acquiesced in the arrangement.

I became quite passionate about that and sort of said 'if that was the case then the law is an ass' and that in fact I believed, unlike Nigel it seemed, that judges were better than that. Nigel subsequently became a well-respected judge!

I said to Nigel it was our job to demonstrate that it was not normal for musicians to study the accounts in the detail that they might if they were me or him. And particularly, I argued that the onus should not be on them – but that it was incumbent on Morrissey and Johnny not just to achieve a change from the Partnership Act 1890 by changing the accounting method, or by imposition, or even by implied threats.

I said this is not Animal Farm where some members are more equal than others. If the 25 per cent each presumption of the Partnership Act was to be rebutted, then common sense dictated that an agreement, even if it was as simple as a letter, needed to be drawn up, given to Andy and Mike, and they should be told to get independent professional advice!

I think Nigel was surprised by my strength of feeling and hopefully a bit convinced.

As a general rule I hate taking clients into litigation. It is never a pleasant experience and there will be many sleepless nights. Even now I have a draconian note that I will send to friends, family, and clients if they are contemplating litigation.

When I sent it to one famous client, he called me up,

"What the f*ck, it frightened and depressed me."

"YEP!" I replied, "that was the intention."

My reluctance as a litigator was shown to be a good instinct. I was sitting at my desk one morning when at 8.03am the phone rang. I was the only one in the office so I answered the phone to a cheery voice that I recognised. But my cheery tone disappeared as I was told that last night Andy Rourke had signed a letter accepting that the 40/40/10/10 splits were acceptable to him.

I tried to make light of the situation but I was anxious to get off the call, when I put the phone down I just stared ahead of me thinking we are totally and absolutely f*cked.

It was now effectively three against one, not that I thought Andy had gone over to the other side – more that he was not in a great place and he had bowed to the immense pressure he was put under.

I can't remember whether Mike had heard by the time I called him, but I don't think he had, I said we needed to have a chat so we arranged for him to come in. I explained, as he already knew, that this made what was already a difficult battle, one in which the odds were now really against us.

He asked me what I thought and I said, in spite of what anyone else said, I actually thought this did not change the law and a good judge would get that. In fact, I argued because I believed they had now asked Andy to sign something, then that supported the idea that something needed to be signed to move away from the Partnership Act presumption of an equal 25 per cent each.

I think I had been sent a copy of what Andy had signed, and I didn't think it was fatal as far as Mike's position was concerned. I suggested to Mike he should not be aggressive with Andy because I believe Andy would come to regret what he had done. And if his evidence remained the same, but he said he needed to avoid the stress of litigation, and was pressed upon one evening to sign. Then maybe a judge would disapprove of what had happened and decide it was irrelevant to Mike's rights under the Partnership Act 1890.

I wasn't just trying to be positive – I really believed this to be the position. And, in fact, Andy remained supportive of Mike's case, including giving evidence in the trial. .

The next unexpected development was that I was, as you can/will/have read elsewhere in this tome, invited to take over as chairman of Polygram. I tell of the agony of that decision elsewhere, but I was very concerned I was bailing out on Mike on a difficult road that I had I sort of led him down.

I wrote him a long letter and asked to see him, he was gracious and understanding. Most importantly, I was leaving him in the hands of David Davis and Andrew Sharland – two great litigators.

Of course, I told Mike I was on the end of a phone and he should feel free to call for advice, but in any event to keep in touch. I meant it, but we both knew I was about to have a lot on my plate running a company with a turnover of £500 million and 900 employees.

Well sadly, but not surprisingly, we did not keep in touch. I knew he was in great hands and he knew where to find me, I hadn't exactly disappeared from view. By the time the judgement arrived the case had been going more than six years, with Mike having legal aid to fight the good fight.

I got my update on the case in the most bizarre way imaginable. I had arranged to have dinner with two friends of mine, Ian Mill and Pat Savage. I don't know how it had come about but we used to see a fair bit of each other, but simply hadn't over the last couple of years. I was looking forward to it but I had never had dinner with both of them before at the same time. Ian was, and is, the top music QC in the music industry, and is also 'top' in many other fields of practice. Pat is a very successful, popular and talented accountant.

I remember I arrived to our dinner first, but it wasn't long before I saw Ian and Pat come over to the table. Ian was clearly furious about something, if you are in litigation you want Ian fighting your corner, and one of the reasons is that he is not a good loser.

At first it wasn't clear what was going on, but I managed to establish that Ian and Pat had been in court that day for a judgement on a case that they were involved in. I could tell from Ian's adjectives about the judge's intellect that things had not gone particularly well.

I kept trying to ask what was the case about but I was getting nowhere, and then from some clues, I deciphered that the case was Mike Joyce v Morrissey, and that Ian and Pat had been on Morrissey's (and Johnny Marr's) side – and the judge had found resoundingly in favour of Mike. Oh dear, this was not going to be an easy evening.

"Ian," I said, "I will pay, and you choose the wine."

Ian, a wine connoisseur and entrepreneur, said, "I will."

And I watched his eyes go to the bottom of the list!

We changed the subject and enjoyed the wine.

The next day, Mike Joyce very kindly called me to thank me for my help, he was a relieved and happy man.

The judgement in the case and in the appeal are in the law reports and it is fair to say that Morrissey did not impress the judge, and it is fair to say Morrissey was not impressed with the judge, or indeed many of the other participants in the case.

Things started gently – the judge leant towards Morrissey in the witness box and said,

"What shall I call you?"

"Morrissey" came the reply along with a curt,

"and what shall I call you? ... Judge?"

"No ... 'My Lord' would be more appropriate."

(Not well received by M.)

"Well, MISTER ... (not well received by M) ... Morrissey!

I get the impression, apart from the legal considerations in this case, that you don't like Mr Joyce very much?"

Cue, inhalation of breath from M's legal team, and then apparently, allegedly, the reply came. In fact, LET ME EMPHASISE, I now believe this is a mythical tale that spread like wildfire.

"Well, MY LORD, if I was driving a car and I saw Joyce crossing the road up ahead then I would put my foot on the accelerator and run him over."

His legal team desperately trying to catch his attention, but M is in full flow ...

"AND MY LORD, I would then turn the car around and go back for him again."

"Thank you," said Mr Justice Weeks, "that is most helpful."

Now of course even if that exchange had happened, which it didn't, it would not have changed the law, but as the appeal court was clear to point out – Morrissey 'clearly forfeited the judge's sympathy'.

Indeed the judge took the extraordinary step of describing Morrissey as 'devious, truculent and unreliable where his own interests were at stake'.

I have rarely heard such strong language.

It is amusing to read in the court of appeal judgement – (only Morrissey appealed, Johnny Marr didn't) – the appeal court judges doing linguistic somersaults to say that when the judge used the words 'devious truculent and unreliable' that of course was mere judicial language, not a character assassination ... yeah right!

I have not been able to verify the above exchange between the judge and Morrissey, even though someone told it to me at the time as if it was gospel. So, I present it as an 'apocryphal myth', but in his autobiography Morrissey leaves the reader in no doubt as to what he thinks of Mike Joyce.

The main reason I am certain that the exchange above is an apocryphal myth is that no matter how angry Morrissey was and maybe still is I am sure he is not a violent man and would not dream of wanting Mike Joyce to suffer physical injury .

More than 20 years later I was asked to advise a famous musician about his legal and general relations with his colleagues. Unusually the client had done some research himself, and after a few minutes chatting, he said, "I want to ask you about a case I heard about, The Smiths – have you heard about it?"

AH, I SAID, NOW THAT IS A STORY!

———————————

In his autobiography, Morrissey writes 50 pages about the case. It is an incredibly gripping albeit bitter read. He is stunned that he lost the case and he reports that Mike Joyce's win was worth many millions of pounds to Mike. Morrissey loathes Judge Weeks for his decision-making and his treatment. He just cannot understand how, or why, he lost. His writing is as good as you would expect from one of the truly great songwriters and he finds it impossible, almost understandably, to comprehend how he was undone by a hundred year old piece of law. The 1890 Partnership Act.

It's a good job that act was there in my extensive legal library of five books – well good for Mike anyhow!

CHAPTER 10

BAND AID

So Chapter 7 told in a few thousand words the story of 13 years of my professional life, but it omitted an astonishing story – not words to write lightly, and I hope you will understand why I think that even if you don't end up agreeing with that description of 'astonishing'.

I never own up to this but I was not at the recording of the Band Aid single. I was sat that day in my, then girlfriend, now wife's rented shared terraced house with an outdoor loo.

It was 1984. I had been working in the music industry for six years and I loved it. I had met Caroline nine months earlier. When I first asked her out earlier that year, she had tried to cool my ardour with the cliché 'she was washing her hair'.

I said, "That's a shame as I have tickets for Billy Joel, and the after show party." Quick as a flash, the response came back,

"I can wash my hair another night."

And Billy Joel kept the next 39 years on track!

On the day 'Do They Know It's Christmas' was recorded, 25th November 1984, we had our Sunday tea watching the evening news where there was footage of the stars turning up to record what became known as the Band Aid single. I am of course biased, but that song is a great song that has stood the test of time.

Anyhow, I don't know why I am bigging up the song, because at this stage in the story I am an onlooker, just one of millions watching the story with interest. The (no central heating) house was freezing, and so we were watching TV, eating our 'tea' with our coats on, and I took note of the story and the news moved on.

At the time I was a freelance music business lawyer – you know that from an earlier chapter, J P Kennedy and Co. My office was one room and that had literally only room for my desk, and a record player and speakers. My wonderful secretary Lesley was a number of rooms away. We were based in the newly formed London Records and it was a win-win relationship. I got a central London office rent-free and they got a cheap in-house lawyer. I was based where there was a lot of through traffic of artists who I could represent, if London Records weren't trying to sign them and if the artist wanted me.

You might think the last paragraph is a bit of a ramble but it has a purpose. In most offices a secretary sits outside her boss's office and protects against unwanted visitors! I had no protection, only a door, never locked, sometimes open, and sometimes closed. On this Monday morning, the day after the recording of the Band Aid single, it was closed and this was supposed to signal I was busy. Indeed I wasn't pretending – I was busy.

All of a sudden, it is as if my office has been hit by a tornado. If a door can slam open – it did. In this case sound travelled faster than light as I heard the sonic boom, 'KENNEDY!" before I could see who it was coming from.

To my absolute astonishment, there in front of me was the man from the news last night, Bob Geldof. He was not a client, not at that stage even a friend. Of course I knew of him and we would have known each other a little when I was in-house lawyer for the Boomtown Rats' record company Phonogram. I would have recognised Bob in the street, but I doubt that he would have recognised me.

Anyhow, he had found me and apparently for some reason to my immense surprise he had been looking for me. I then heard a sentence that would haunt, and reward me, from then until this very day – and also I suspect until I part from this world.

"Kennedy, I need you to do one hour's work and you can't charge for it ... JUST FOR ONE HOUR."

"Sure," I replied and reached for my diary and suggested Thursday 2pm.

"F*CK THURSDAY!" he replied, "COME WITH ME NOW."

This was my first experience of the modus operandi of Bob Geldof, a style of operation which literally the whole world was about to experience. If I had said to myself that it was something that presidents, and dictators, and Maggie Thatcher, and Mother Theresa would come to experience, then I would have asked myself, 'what drugs was I on'!

It was November, so I submissively got my coat and it almost seemed rude to ask him where we were going, but I did anyhow.

He said, "We are going to see Phonogram and I want you to negotiate the best deal possible for my charity record."

Phonogram were expecting Bob, and not me, but they welcomed me. We immediately jumped into discussions of how quickly they could get the record out. In fact, incredibly, they managed that in just four days.

And then Bob wanted to discuss what would be a good financial deal. I want to emphasise that I was pushing at an open door, everyone at Phonogram was into this project, heart and soul and pocket.

He asked me what would be a good deal for a top artist – I said 'xyz' and he said 'we would want that' and Phonogram nodded.

I said, 'but phonogram would still be making a profit and these nice guys wouldn't want to take food from the mouths of the hungry in Africa'.

'Right', Bob said, 'they wouldn't' – so we agreed a no profits deal for Phonogram in the UK.

Then I said the record might sell overseas – it might, everyone agreed, (in fact it sold one and a half million copies in America alone). I knew what Phonogram got paid for their sales overseas and I said we should get all that. And everyone agreed, BUT I said that would mean those nice companies overseas would be making profits and that wasn't right. Again, everyone agreed that wasn't right, so we agreed an unprecedented royalty for overseas sales, which I calculated should ensure all net profit came to us. Whoever 'us' was?

As I say, I was pushing at an open door. I was negotiating with Tony Powell, the acting managing director and John Watson, the head of business affairs. As long as I made a good point, they simply agreed – they weren't pushing back. They had bought in one thousand per cent.

The Phonogram team left and I asked Bob if I could have a word.

"Bob, I can see I am now going to have to paper this contract, but who is the money to be paid to?"

"Good question." he replied.

"Thanks," I said and I waited for an answer, but clearly one wasn't immediately forthcoming.

"We will give the money to a charity," he said, "we will decide who later."

"Bob," I said, "I don't want to be cynical, but you know what the UK press is like – this will start with euphoria, and before long it will be 'where did the money go?' And, that's fair enough.

"What do you suggest?" he said.

I was really winging it now, I asked,

"How much do you think it will make - a quarter of a million pounds?" Bob said he had previously been advised it was going to raise £72,000 (a remarkably specific figure). And he said that was a lot of money at the time.

I said, "I think we will need a proper charity, and I think it will do a lot better than that!"

"Good," he said, "You deal with all that, you can be our legal adviser."
It wasn't a request but a direction. I didn't get the chance to say, but as agreed I am only here 'JUST FOR ONE HOUR', instead I found myself saying,

"Bob, actually I know nothing about charity law, but I will see what I can do. I'm not sure, but I think we will need trustees."

"Fine" he said.

"Who?" I asked.

"Well, he replied, "me and you."

At that moment the phone rang, it was Chris Morrison, Midge Ure's manager. He was ringing with some questions about the release of the record and he was with Midge who, of course, had written the single with Bob and produced it.

Bob answered the questions Chris had asked, and said to Chris;

"Tell Midge he is going to be a trustee and Chris you can be a trustee as well."

No assent was required, nor actually any knowledge of what a trustee was or what they did.

Wow, it had been quite a morning. I had no concept of what I had signed up for, nor did anyone else, including Bob, but I had a nagging feeling that 'JUST FOR ONE HOUR' wasn't entirely accurate.

I tried to reclaim the rest of my day catching up on the work I had promised clients I would do, but in the back of my mind I was thinking what the 'feck' do I know about charity law. Of course we had no money to hire lawyers and actually I didn't know any charity lawyers.

During that week I got the Phonogram agreement and that was familiar territory to me even if the provisions were unprecedentedly favourable to us. Phonogram wanted to know who was the contracting party for our side – I said I will tell you Monday.

That Saturday morning I went to Highbury Barn library and sat reading a book on charity law. As I did so, I learnt a lot and came across the trust deed used for the families of victims of the Aberfan tragedy. That disaster had made a huge impact on me as a boy as I watched it unfold on TV one Friday in the 1960s.

There didn't seem many other precedents, so I photocopied it, and started adapting it for our purpose. I suppose it wasn't a work of genius to decide we would be called The Band Aid Charitable Trust, but that's the name I chose. The actual earlier choice of the brilliant name Band Aid for the single was something I had no hand in.

The next few weeks I had a ringside seat to an absolute phenomenon – people's kindness and generosity. Even now, I can easily well up at the extraordinarily wonderful side of people that Band Aid brought out.

There was lots going on behind the scenes. Bob just grew and blossomed in a role for which there was no training and no precedent. He was determined that the song should be on the next Top of the Pops. He got through to Michael Grade, the BBC controller, and demanded (which was a modus operandi for which apparently he needed no training) that the song be on Top of the Pops on Thursday. Michael made the mistake of saying I am sympathetic but it's against the rules, no songs go on unless they have been released. Well for some people that would be a brick wall. You won't be surprised that Bob told Michael, I am not looking for your sympathy, the hungry of Ethiopia need and deserve that, I want your action. Michael said OK call back tomorrow.

To his credit Michael did not take the simple approach of not taking Bob's call and he agreed to give Bob five minutes before the Thursday night's Top of the Pops. What a coup, our own slot which Bob then turned into PR dynamite by persuading the legend that was/is David Bowie to introduce the video. It was just astonishing. Sadly, I often use a phrase 'no good deed goes unpunished' – well, Michael was rewarded for his initiative by being conscripted as a trustee! Like all of us he is still working on the project 39 years later.

I really don't know what comparisons you can make, but the British media and the British public bought into the cause in an amazing way. The UK music shops were initially not keen to give up their profits, as the run up to Christmas was the time of year they really made their profits to cover losses from earlier in the year. Brian McLaughlin at HMV was prepared to take the lead amongst the dedicated music shops, but he said it's not fair us doing it if the supermarkets don't.

I have built a career on a reputation of being a good negotiator, but I now watched and learned the hoodwink method. The big supermarkets thought charity should begin at home, and by that they meant the profits from the single should stay in their pockets. They wouldn't budge, so Bob then backed off from berating the biggest supermarket and they couldn't work out why.

So Bob told them, "It's not my problem, it's yours."

"What do you mean?" they said.

Bob replied, "Well all your competitors have agreed to give us their profits on the single, so all the superstars on the record will be telling the public to buy the record from your competitors. And whilst they are there to buy the record, they will do their Christmas shopping there!" Much sought after Christmas footfall. They looked at Bob and said,

"Bob, that's blackmail." Bob just gave them a quizzical look;

"What do you mean blackmail, I am just telling you the facts." And with that, they caved. Of course, none of the other supermarkets had agreed to give up their profits, but once they heard the market leaders were going to then they 'altruistically' agreed.

For some, as in this example, hoodwinking and brinkmanship were required, but for the vast majority of people they not only went with the flow they fuelled the direction of travel. There literally were butchers taking meat out of their windows to put 7 and 12 inch pieces of vinyl in their place. 'People in Pinner' really cared about what was happening to the poor of Ethiopia.

It's very important to understand this was an era, in fact a year where it was considered 'greed is good' and Maggie Thatcher had said 'there is no such thing as society'. This Irishman was actually pulling at a thread which showed how people were not as selfish as the zeitgeist at the time suggested.

Subsequently, Bob developed a more dubious technique to sit alongside the hoodwink strategy. Sometimes, people would sigh when they realised that the phone they had just answered had Bob Geldof at the other end and would agree to whatever Bob wanted to get him off the phone – content in the notion, they would deny they had said yes – after all, it was only their word against Bob's.

But when the inevitable call came from the manager trying to deny their artist had agreed to Bob's request, then Bob would say,

"But I taped it, because my memory is not so good with everything that was going on."

The manager would freeze with horror, and realise that a reluctant 'yes' by his artist, which he was now trying to turn into a 'no', now had to be an enthusiastic … 'YES, NOTHING WE WANT TO DO MORE.'

We all know now of the persona that is Bob, or even Saint Bob, but this persona was evolving in front of my eyes at very close quarters by the minute – it was astonishing to watch.

Someone questioned, "How did this come to be – Bob doing it?" I know for a fact, from them personally, that U2 were stunned their old mate from Dublin was now this philanthropic activist and campaigner.

Indeed, when someone said, "How come Bob?", another responded by saying "Well God needed someone to help the poor of Africa, and He was busy himself, but he knocked on a door and when a scruffy Irish musician answered, he said, well, you will just have to do!"

Even Bob didn't know it at the time but there could not have been a better person for the job.

Along the way the UK music industry's leading light Maurice Oberstein, 'Obie', was cajoled into being a trustee. Before he accepted, Obie called to ask me if I thought it was a good idea.

"You know," I said, "I never had the chance to wonder about whether it was a good idea. I don't know if, for you personally, it's a good idea – but you should do it and your presence will bring us wisdom experience and gravitas." He signed up.

Somewhere along the way one more trustee, Lord Harlech, was seconded but I never knew how or why, and sadly I never met him, he died in a car crash before our first trustee meeting.

In the meantime, I was desperately trying to get our operation registered as a charity as we were probably operating outside the law. At the time it seemed as if there was only one person at the charity commission. He was overworked but extremely helpful, he said he thought we could get the charity registered in six months.

I asked can I come and see you.

At the meeting, I sat opposite him and said,

"If we can't get this registered almost immediately, one or other newspaper will, regardless of the facts, decide this is a scam."

So he helped and pulled out all the stops to try and speed up the registration process. We agreed our charity objective was 'the relief of hunger and poverty in Ethiopia and the neighbourhood thereof.'

I hated every day that we didn't have our formal registration as a charity – it was a media achilles heel, but we were doing everything by the book and there was a good paper trail.

Now, I just went upstairs to take a look at my copy – we signed the trust deed on the 26th April 1985, the very second the charity commission would approve it, but basically five months after the record was released. Fortunately the press never knew, and most importantly, no harm was done.

This was all very time consuming and at the same time I had a business to run. It was the beginning of a long term balancing act – I was embarking on an extraordinarily rewarding adventure, but I had to earn a living.

From day one, no trustee got a penny, no coffees, no taxis, were reimbursed. Even when we visited projects that we had funded in Africa we paid for our own flights and hotels. It may seem cheesy but we had in mind over the years the astonishing generosity of the public, for me for whatever reason, I focused on the mythical 'Beth of Basildon'. In my mind, over the years, she donated directly or indirectly to our charity not out of spare cash but out of money she didn't have to spare. Making the donation even more poignant.

So even in 2020, 35 years later I recommended to my fellow trustees that we refuse one grant application because 'that isn't how Beth wanted her money spent'. It would have been a betrayal of the greatest magnitude if we wasted her money – so no trustee fees, no sandwiches, coffees, or taxis reimbursed, no paid for offices and certainly no jollies.

Our only expenses over the years were accounting and audit fees – we would not cut corners here. We wanted the public not to just trust us, but to know that we were being watched and monitored – we were being properly audited.

After a number of years, the charity commission insisted that we take out annual trustees insurance – so we did. That was our only other expense apart from accounting fees, and even those expenses weren't paid out of Beth, or her peers donations, but out of our commercial trading income which 39 years later earns us more than a million pounds a year!

In 2005 at Live 8 I walked past a top manager and someone I considered a friend. They didn't see me but I heard them as they looked around at the spectacle that was taking place, and one of them said,

"Just think how much Geldof, Goldsmith, and Kennedy must be making from this."

I just walked on past them, I had to as I had just had a call – in the USA, Beyoncé wasn't going to go on stage unless we changed a clause in her contract! To be fair, it wasn't her being a prima donna – it was, as is often the case, her management and the tiniest tweak removed the problem. I looked over at my 'friend' and the top manager, and thought I can look 'Beth of Basildon' in the eye – that's more important to me than what you think and it really was.

So back to 1984, and it soon became apparent that the record was going to raise a lot more than £250,000. It wasn't just selling in the UK, it was selling everywhere. It became the biggest selling single ever in the UK, selling more than three million copies in what was really a matter of days. All our estimates were wrong – the record made £8 million and nearly 40 years later it still makes £300,000 a year!

Some people went in to record shops and bought 50 copies of the single and then gave back 49 so that the shop could sell them again. Fortnum & Mason sold thousands of copies in their restaurant.

The video was completed in 48 hours and helped create terrific demand. We were pressing more than 300,000 copies a day, every vinyl factory in the UK and Europe worked at full capacity and it still wasn't enough – even our T-shirts were continually running out of stock.

I will warn you now, that if you think at any time Kennedy 'bigs up' Geldof a lot, well I do. It was fascinating to watch what he was growing into. Admittedly, we have had and continue to have our fights and disagreements, sometimes quite tough falling outs as you can imagine over the years – but my respect and admiration has never faltered and I don't apologise for that.

Back to December 1983. Bob is, as you will all know, very eloquent and from nowhere the sound bite came that 'The price of a life this Christmas is the price of a piece of plastic with a hole in the middle.' Marketing genius!

And a few weeks later he coined the phrase 'a global jukebox' to encapsulate his vision for a concert.

The single was sold for £1.40. How could you not be moved by that 'price of a life' phrase – moved emotionally, and moved to put your hand in your pocket, wallet, purse or handbag!

We hadn't yet started our formal trustee meetings but we were having informal gatherings. This was an emergency, it was not at this stage about long-term strategies, and if the song was about words then we now needed actions.

With the success of the record came the huge responsibility to spend the money wisely. Bob had a clear vision of what was immediately needed – of course it wasn't rocket science ... it was food and medicine.

Friends and clients over the years have described me as having a paranoid and cynicism streak, and if they meant it as an insult I took it as a compliment given the line of work I was in.

I said to Bob it was not enough to buy the supplies and wave them off at Southampton, there were already stories of government aid being stuck on the docks. I told Bob whether you like it or not you have to go with or meet the shipment and see and report that it got into the camps.

Maybe he had got to that viewpoint himself though I am not sure as he had told journalists, in no uncertain terms, that he would not be going. (The media wanted a front cover of Bob with dying children.)

There was no doubt in my mind that Bob going was essential, and it was agreed that Midge would go with the second shipment, and I would go with the third. In his autobiography, Bob acknowledged that I had made it clear he had no choice but to go!

But of course at the time, and in retrospect, it was nonsense to think he could avoid going. I was adamant he should go because I wanted him to demonstrate to the public, and the media, that Band Aid did not just intend to spend the money raised and hope for the best – but that it was wisely spent – we would supervise and follow through. As it turned out the trip performed two other functions, one emotional and one practical.

I had nearly forgotten this 39 years later, and it seems amazing that I could forget, but the press had started calling Bob 'Saint Bob' and on the trip, by chance, Bob met another saint, Mother Theresa and the photographers got a picture of the two saints together.

If you haven't already read it, you should put it on your to-do list to read Bob's autobiography, 'Is that it?'

It's a great and at times astonishingly moving read, and I will quote from a tiny part of it now. If Bob had been devastated by the Michael Buerk report of the famine when he went to Ethiopia he was suddenly transported to the reality of it.

At one of the many feeding camps he visited, Bob wrote;

'... a circle of people in the process of being fed. They were like the grotesque creatures of some distorted imagination ... they stared through an impenetrable window at the meaningless succession of events ... they did not want to eat any more ... eating hurt the stomach. They sat on the ground with the milky, high-energy porridge dribbling from the corners of the mouths while their seeping eyes were sick with flies. The eyes were looking at me. I began to cry. I was angry. Crying was useless and a waste of energy ... It reminded me of the films I had seen of Auschwitz!*

Bob converted that anger into renewed energy and after absorbing the horrors of the reality he focused on getting advice from the right and trusted people as to how the Band Aid money should be spent.

He found and we lent on Brother Gus O'Keefe, an Irish monk who ran the Christian Relief and Development Association who were coordinating relief activities. The monk and the atheist made for a compelling partnership.

And from now I had a front seat watching Bob evolve from the pop star to the most powerful activist. His intellect was in no doubt but now he was learning new skills on the job – a job he had never planned to do. Few could match that intellect, but none – none could match the passion.

Nobody would be surprised to hear it said that Bob doesn't suffer fools easily, but exhaustion from what he saw and physical fatigue made him tired and impatient, and he learnt that that was a good thing. He had no time for niceties, or false diplomacy, and he learnt for the first time on that first trip to Ethiopia that he could say things other people could not say.

Aid workers sometimes had to walk on eggshells, politicians had constituents to worry about, but Bob learnt that not only did he have money he could spend without strings, but as he said,

'I represented nobody but myself and the millions who wanted to help. A constituency of compassion.'

To my mind 'Beth' was there amongst the millions.

Bob didn't know it at this time but that was a constituency he was going to mobilise to even greater effect at Gleneagles, 20 years down the line. In fact, if you told him he would still be an activist 20 years later you would have depressed him – all he wanted to be was a musician.

Of course, he had always had a great sense of humour, but if anything, he became sharper and certainly blunter. He was embarrassed by people treating him as a saint – when one religious soul said to him,

"If Christ was on earth he would be with you."

Bob replied instantly,

"If Christ was on earth I would ask him why he wasn't in Africa."

But to many a 'saint' he was, and if Christianity was losing followers then Bob was gaining them, whether he wanted to or not .

At the time, were we young?

Well, sort of, I was 31 years old and I was trying to build a business. I often say, if we had known what we were getting involved in we would have been too scared to do it – but we started in the shallow end, and were lured into the deep end without ever making a conscious decision to get more involved.

In early 1985 I was spending at least 12 hours a week attending and preparing for the grant spending meetings. And maybe as much again on the rest of the stuff, so I embarked on the seven days a week x 15 hours a day which would dictate my life for a considerable while, but at least I was plural between my business and Band Aid.

Bob completed an already scheduled Boomtown Rats tour, but then was simply full time on Band Aid. Remember … no mobile phones, no emails, communication wasn't quite by distant drum, but nearly.

He had ignited something quite extraordinary at a time when greed was considered good. Bob had ignited compassion and people didn't have to be courted or goaded into doing things, but both those were skills Bob had in abundance, many, many people were self-starters.

As I have said, the maxim of Band Aid was that the public's money would not be spent on overheads – there were no employees, no consultants. For an office we had a warehouse – actually, a disused bus garage that was acquired free of charge. Furniture was donated and two ladies Judy Anderson and Valerie Blondeau were either executive assistants or chiefs of staff. A husband and wife team of Kevin and Penny Jenden became the de facto management of the operation, but there was certainly no time for the niceties of job descriptions or titles. Penny set up and ran the committee of aid experts that would make recommendations to the trustees on grant applications. Penny and I seemed to have a tense relationship from the start, that didn't mean I didn't respect her it just meant I didn't always agree with her, and she certainly didn't always agree with me. Kevin was like a ceo – especially for logistics. I would get much of my news on Tuesdays and Thursdays.

At an early stage there were 'Truckers for Band Aid' procuring free vehicles for use in Africa and 'Builders for Band Aid' acquired building materials to be shipped out.

I would hear about these developments, but not be involved in them – there was no vetting, no criminal checks. Can you imagine running an organisation like that today – just trusting people.

But yes, the Band Aid Trust trusted that people were good. We applied a light touch, except on the public's money – every payment required two signatories, that was not delegated, and for 39 years nearly every payment has been signed by myself and Harvey, with another trustee stepping in if either of us were on holiday.

In 39 years we largely avoided litigation. At the beginning, a madman suggested Bob had stolen his idea and was going to sue us, we said 'bring it on' and he didn't.

We nearly sued someone for selling our merchandise, but they stopped, … and then, there was Band Aid v Kenneth Martin.

Ken Martin was a shipping broker, and he suggested to Bob that we could save money by chartering our own ships. Bob liked the idea – we would charter the ships and we would give other aid agencies space for free.

I said to Bob, "WTF!?" (though this abbreviation was perhaps not in use at the time, but yes something like WTF) ...

"What do we know about shipping?"

Not for the first, or last, time Bob would say, "KENNEDY FFS!" (again the abbreviation not perhaps in use at the time) ...

"Don't be so negative."

I suggested 'cautious' rather than 'negative' – Bob suggested 'paranoid' rather than 'cautious'.

"KENNEDY, just meet with Ken Martin."

So I did meet with Ken, and this is not with the benefit of hindsight, but I didn't get a great feeling from the meeting. It would be fair to say that frankly I was scared of us as trustees getting into chartering ships. It's a complex and dangerous business, and in fact most of the court cases in the highest court in the UK are about things that have gone wrong in the world of shipping.

However, I knew my brief was not to come back to Bob and say, 'Nah, let's not do this.' My mission was to make it happen and minimise our risks. In fact it was good that we did it. However, I thought Ken's altruism did not ring true, but I did think he knew what he was doing. Ken was not only to run our shipping operation but also to be in charge of purchasing procurement for us.

So we had ships called 'Band Aid' sailing the high seas. Even now I can't believe it – how did this happen, but it did and it was a success. However, we feared Ken was not as honest as the day was long.

It's to our credit, in spite of our light touch, we discovered that Ken wasn't just in the 'doing good business' it seemed like he was in the 'doing good for Ken business'. We suspected he was using ships that we paid for, to carry cargo that he was charging others for, and he was not simply asking us to indemnify him for costs he incurred, he was overcharging us. We were not people who tried to sweep such matters under the carpet – we sued.

Ken denied the allegations, but continually failed to comply with court orders, and a court ordered him to pay the trust £2.5 million, which was a conservative estimate of what we were due. We never received the money – Ken went bankrupt, but the proceedings sent a strong message that a light touch did not give people the right to fill their pockets at the Trust's expense.

Far from feeling vindicated in my suspicion of Ken I was glad that we had launched the Band Aid ships. The net benefit in savings and logistics outweighed this betrayal of our trust, but even now I just can't believe that our courage, or our folly, took us into the world of shipping – what were we thinking of? However, we had 33 successful voyages and assisted many aid agencies with such trips.

Let me take a minute to talk about Midge Ure. I think Midge was at times frustrated about having the secondary role in the trust – living in the shadow of Bob, but there wasn't of course a stage at which that was decided, it just evolved. I am afraid it was sort of destined I suppose, since 'God knocked on the wrong door'.

It wasn't in Midge's make up to do the things Bob did – I am not sure it was in anyone else's make up. Midge also had a demanding music career and Bob makes no secret of the fact that, at the time, the pause button had been pressed on his own career.

Midge is a wonderful, talented man who I adore and admire, he has been a trustee throughout, he performed at Live Aid and Live 8 and has contributed to the trust more than anyone other than Bob. And before the first record was sold, he had made the most astonishing and unmatchable contribution – he had created 4 minutes 38 seconds of magic – the song.

Bono told Bob and Midge that they had written a hymn. I am sure I will be laughed at for saying this was 'a Lennon and McCartney moment' but I suspect that song has made, indirectly, more money than any Lennon and McCartney song. It was the acorn from which the oak tree grew. It begat Live Aid, 'We Are the World' (Band Aid à la Pete Waterman), Band Aid 20, Band Aid 30, Live 8 and most important of all influenced the G8 at Gleneagles.

It's also a little known fact, that Comic relief was created as a result of Band Aid, and as we know that has raised a billion pounds.

There was another crucial thing Midge did – he gave Bob confidence.

In November 1984, Bob's confidence was at an all-time low.

Difficult to think of a version of Bob with no confidence, but as he said himself the reason that he was home that day at 6pm to watch the news was because he was not busy with his career as a musician, and he had lost confidence as a songwriter.

The fact that Midge thought that he and Bob could write a song in 24 hours was a huge boost for Bob. The fact Midge encouraged and was complimentary about Bob's role in their collaboration lifted Bob, I learnt this listening to Bob at a 'pitch' meeting regarding a documentary.

I will come back to what monies that song raises, what debt relief was achieved and what trade was facilitated – suffice to say it was a lot!

None of that would/could have happened without Midge's talent as a songwriter and producer! And also thank you producer Trevor Horn for your help too!

So Christmas itself came and went, and the money came in, and the Band Aid Trust took on an a compelling life of its own. We agreed we would have trustee meetings every Tuesday and Thursday, these were primarily to decide on how to spend the money. Alongside us a group of aid experts had been created (that's professionalism for you) to sift through the large number of grant applications we were receiving, but soon tension arose between that group and the trustees. I don't think it was an exaggeration to say that that committee was at the start patronising to us. They expected us to just rubber stamp their decisions, but these trustees were not a group who rubber stamped.

Obie often sat next to me at these meetings and if I had a streak of cynicism he was almost the embodiment of it. As we were sitting as one of the most high-profile charitable trusts of the time, or maybe even any time, he would whisper in my ear in his American accent 'there ain't no such thing as Santa Claus' – he was cynical about all the altruism he was surrounded by.

The workload was overwhelming. At the beginning, we met on Tuesdays AND Thursdays, the meetings each lasted five hours – and there was a huge amount of paperwork to read up front. We also had lots of fun. When we had the energy we would go out for dinner after the trustees meetings, and there were some receptions we attended.

What was touching to watch was the great relationship between Bob and his partner Paula. The trustee meetings were often intense but one evening someone came into the meeting (no mobile phones) and said Paula was trying to get hold of Bob.

Bob was chairing the meeting but he went to take the call, and he came back and told us Paula had locked herself out of their house. I thought he would put the keys in a taxi and then carry on with the meeting – but no, that was the meeting over for Bob, he was off to let Paula in. We carried on without him – just!

I told my girlfriend, now wife, Caroline the story and she suggested I wouldn't have done that for her – I took the fifth amendment.

Caroline was watching this madness from afar, but of course she came to dinners, receptions etc. As we walked out of one fun evening she crushingly put me in my place. She said,

"You think Paula fancies you, don't you?"

"What are you talking about? I replied.

She said, "I can tell you do."

My firm denial was not cutting the mustard – she was very fond of Paula who had been kind to her. (Caroline was 23 at the time, we were all young but she even more so.)

"It's a wonder to behold," Caroline continued,

"I just watch as Paula works her magic, she works the room, not because she needs to, or wants anything from anyone, but she doesn't drink and it's how she parties – and every single man in the room leaves thinking Paula fancies them – you are not the only fool." she kindly said!

So there was great fun and excitement, but many of us took comfort that we were doing a good and efficient job at spending more money than we ever expected to raise. Bob had told me he thought it might raise £72,000, then he upgraded it to £250 000, but in fact it had raised £8 million and the money continued to flow in.

Then one Thursday Bob came in and said we were going to have a concert. I was not the only one who thought 'oh my god, my life will never get back to normal'.

Obie leaned across, and didn't even try to whisper – when he got angry his voice became high pitched – he screamed at me in a high breaking pitch,

"Kennedy, you have to stop HIM he has gone mad."

I thought … 'JUST FOR ONE HOUR'.

I laughed, and said,

"Obie, you are the one who is mad if you think any of us can stop him."

The next day Obie called me and asked how he could resign – I laughed again,

"Obie are you sitting down?

"What the f*ck Kennedy?"

"Obie," I said, "when I drafted the trust deed, (it was the first and almost certainly the last trust deed I drafted), I put in a clause 'APPOINTMENT OF TRUSTEES' – but I forgot to put in a clause dealing with RETIREMENT OF TRUSTEES." The words "F*CK YOU KENNEDY" resounded in my ears as the phone was slammed down.

Sadly Obie is no longer with us – perhaps he realised that the only way to no longer be a Band Aid trustee was to depart the mortal coil.

Anyhow, back to that trustee meeting – the concert was not a point on the agenda for discussion ... it was a fait accompli.

I actually think Bob did say 'are we all agreed'?

Then allowed a split second for a response and said,

"Great well done – well I have had a chat with Harvey Goldsmith ..." Half an hour later Harvey was in the meeting and was now our final trustee. Harvey was not the only promoter involved, but he was the lead by a long way, as a great larger than life character and he gets things done.

There would be huge arguments over the next decades between Bob and Harvey, and to a lesser degree between myself and Harvey, but it would be completely trite to say that without Harvey there was no Live Aid and without Harvey our accomplishments would have been diminished.

Many years later I was asked to do one of those tribute videos – Harvey was being honoured as man of the year. Our relationship was such that I felt it was OK to gently say – 'I heard Harvey was trying to get in shape ... and I didn't realise the shape was round!'

Why were the rest of the trustees not as excited as Bob about the idea for a concert? It was not that we didn't have the enthusiasm, we just had no idea where the time was going to come from for all this, but we just had to find the time.

Did my business suffer during this time – yes.

Did my earnings suffer – yes.

However, I had an experience money could not buy.

You may remember Bob had said, 'I want you to do an hours work for free' – well, I only regret one thing, I wish I had kept a Band Aid time sheet, just for the hell of it. And a number of trees would have had to be felled for that paper record, and the fees would literally have been millions, yes many millions of pounds, but as I said, 'some experiences money could never buy'.

The reason for the concert was that Bob had realised from his visit to Ethiopia that our £8 million was a drop in the ocean.

But even worse, he had seen at first hand that some or much of the aid being sent to Ethiopia and Sudan, whether by us or others, was being stuck in the ports. This was because of the high cost of transporting the aid supplies from the port to the feeding camps. The costs were high because local truckers were ruthlessly and mercilessly operating a cartel.

Bob was determined to destroy the cartels. One of the cartels was being run by the CIA so they could have a foothold in that part of Africa – in simple parlance they were spying but as an unintended consequence they were hampering our aid efforts.

To destroy the cartels he needed fleets of trucks.

To get fleets of trucks he needed money.

He decided the best way to get money was to have not one concert …
but two!

SIMPLE !

CHAPTER 11

LIVE AID 13/7/85

So plans started for the concert. The idea was to have one show in the UK and one in the USA.

I said Bob was excited about the concert – actually that is completely the wrong word. I don't think there was ever a stage before the day or after the event that he could have relaxed enough to enjoy the idea of the concert.

I really don't think I have imagined this next section because I remember it vividly, but at one of our Thursday meetings we discussed whether the USA leg should be in New York or Philadelphia.

Well it was obvious that prestige wise and for artists it should be in New York, but the Mayor of Philadelphia was in desperate need of some good PR. (The ghettos of Philadelphia had been bombed – you couldn't make that up.) So he was making some enticing offers.

Anyhow, after a considered discussion one Thursday, in spite of the mayor's offers, we agreed it needed to be New York. It was an early finish that Thursday, we had started at 5.00pm and we broke up at 9.00pm. I made my way home and sat down to some supper in front of the Ten O'Clock News where I heard at the end of the news the presenter announce that the USA leg of Live Aid would take place in Philadelphia!

In the intervening 60 minutes when the Mayor of Philadelphia had been told we weren't coming there, he made an offer that the USA promoters told Bob and Harvey they couldn't refuse, including of course no charge for the stadium. Things moved fast.

Bob decided at the end of April to do the concert, which was basically ten weeks from July 13th, the chosen show date! Of course not just one concert but two concerts, on two continents – Bob didn't tell Harvey that when he brought him on board!

So we knew that both concerts would take place on July 13th 1985, but there was a small issue ... we didn't really have many artists, or at least not sufficiently big names for the impact that this concert would need to make. Enter stage left ... the hoodwink method again.

When he was trying to persuade people to do the original record Bob made up names when inevitably the artists asked 'who else is doing it'. This time he did the same, 'oh of course they are doing it'.

However, he wasn't really making any progress with The Who and he saw them as critical to the line-up. It had been made clear to us The Who had disbanded and they weren't reforming. You can understand Pete Townshend and Roger Daltrey's surprise (and Harvey's!) when they heard Bob announce from the podium at Wembley, where he was announcing Live Aid, that The Who will be reforming and performing. I think that is developing the hoodwink method to another level – but it worked.

In fact, let me take some time to tell you the extent to which Bob was flying by the seat of his pants when he announced to the world that Live Aid would take place on two continents. He had very close to zero artists, but as an artist himself he knew the psyche of artists. He knew no artist would be the first to agree to do it, and he also knew if an artist thought one of his peers was doing it, they would be affronted that they hadn't been asked.

When Bob reeled off a list of names at the press conference to announce Live Aid this was the actual status of each artist, i.e. NOT signed up!

It is hard to believe but the USA line-up was even worse, and really only fell into place 48 hours before stage time! The politics of the USA show were extraordinary – largely fuelled by the larger than life personality of promoter Bill Graham. Interestingly, more than a third of the artists who performed in the USA were British artists. That was driven by a combination of factors, the Wembley line-up was full, logistics (artists touring America at the time), and it was easier to get decisions from them.

There was an amusing side to the line-up. When Bob was begging artists to sign up and when a manager came back and said his artists wouldn't sign up, Bob would say, "I hope you don't get fired when your artist realises they missed out on performing at the biggest concert in the history of music."

This was ludicrous even for Bob, given he had 11 hours to fill just at Wembley and every minute of those 11 hours was available. But amazingly, within weeks some of those same managers were calling up and saying,

'Great news Bob, my client is going to do the show'.

And equally amazingly, Bob was telling them,

'Sorry mate, I have no room left at Wembley, but I will try and get you on the American show'.

Again, pure genius.

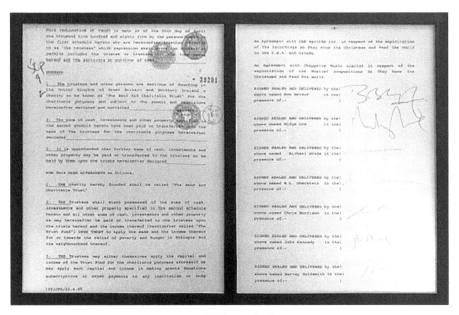

Band Aid trust deed.

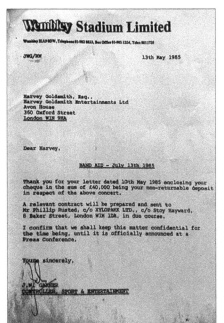

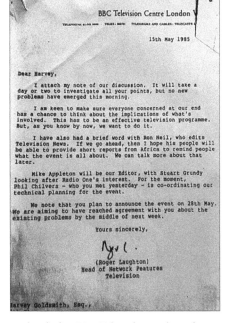

61 days to go before Live Aid ... and only now is Wembley booked – and still confidential.

59 days before Live Aid ... when we hope for an audience of billions over numerous satellites but we have no one to film and broadcast – BBC very positive, but 'IF WE GO AHEAD'.

```
22721  HGENTS G
8958917TLGOLD G
ATTN NICOLE

RELAYED BY TELECOM GOLD LONDON 14:29 TUE, 21 MAY 19:
DGS1065      83  052185  84

REPLY TO:  22721 HGENTS G

FOR THE URGENT ATTENTION OF BILL GRAHAM
----------------------------------------------------HERE FOLLOW
ACTS BOB GELDOF HAS SPOKEN TO AND THEIR CONTACTS:-
PAUL SIMON-  SPOKE TO PAUL -CONTACTS
           DANNY HARRISON AND IAN
                HOBLYN.
BRIAN ADAMS- BRUCE ALLEN
HUGHIE LEWIS- SPOKE TO HUGHIE -CONTACT
                MANAGEMENT.
HALL AND OATES - TOMMY MATTOLA
CARS        - ELLIOT ROBERTS
DYLAN       - ELLIOT ROBERTS AND JEFF
                ROSEN.
POWER STATION-JOHN TAYLOR
JUDAS PRIEST-BILL CURBISHLY.
WILLIE NELSON/WAYLON/JOHNNY CASH-
                MARK ROTHBAUM
BILLY JOEL- SPOKEN TO,
SPRINGSTEEN- JON LANDAU
TEARS FOR FEARS- PAUL KING (LON)
              TEL 437 2777
SIMPLE MINDS-BRUCE FINLAY
PRETENDERS- CHRISSIE HYND
ROBERT PLANT-PHIL CARSON AT ATLANTIC.
ZZ TOP      - NEED TO BE FOLLOWED UP BY YOU.

ANY OTHER ARTISTS THAT YOU THINK WOULD
BE SUITABLE - PLS FEEL FREE TO ASK...
IT IS IMPERATIVE THAT A VENUE IS SECURED ASAP...
1. MEADOWLANDS
2. WASHINGTON
PLS ADVISE AS SOON AS THIS IS DONE
WE ARE STILL AIMING TO ANNOUNCE WORLDWIDE ON MAY
ROGERS AND COPAN ARE THERE ARES JOEL DERA IN NT
```

53 days to go before Live Aid ...
USA telex re; the USA concert – 'it is imperative that a venue is secured ASAP' – YEP!

Bob's life was exhausting. I don't think I was the only person worried about his health, mental and physical. He was sleeping on a camp bed by the phone waiting for artists and managers from the USA to return his calls. He was in agony with back pain. He said himself that he learnt the true meaning of 'bone weary'. I knew I didn't have enough gravitas for this, so I lobbied a long-time friend and adviser of his to suggest to Bob that he took a break for a week. I suggested a gentle and subtle approach, he chose his moment and Bob went berserk. Berserk in a way that showed he needed the break – but the friend, who made the suggestion at my behest, stood firm,

"OK, OK I get it ... it wasn't my idea anyhow, it was KENNEDY'S."

Thanks!

The pressure on Bob was intense, he also said he had never realised there was such a thing as a cold sweat but during June and July he experienced it every night.

And he was completely broke financially. Imagine that!

Bob was largely speaking to the artists themselves, people who weeks ago would hardly have heard of him, let alone taken his call; Led Zeppelin, Paul McCartney, Paul Simon, Bob Dylan, The Beach Boys, Mick Jagger, Tina Turner, David Bowie, and then the idea of Mick and David together.

But it was like the 'Hokey Cokey' – the likes of Paul Simon and Billy Joel were out ... and then they were in! George Harrison for whatever reason was a firm 'no'.

British Airways said they would fly Phil Collins from Wembley to New York so that he could perform in London AND Philadelphia, and they threw in a package of free tickets worth £50,000 for other performers.

I thought at this stage I might take a photo of the Live Aid poster and include it here, but that would be a breach of copyright, but then for these purposes I am the copyright police – so I think I will include it, and then I will threaten to sue me, on the basis there is no such thing as bad publicity!

The poster displayed the artists in alphabetical order, making Adam Ant top of the bill. The eventual line up was unbelievable. Harvey's role was invaluable and the other promoters helped but most artists, or their representatives, were personally cajoled by Bob. Some insisted they performed at the top of the hour which apparently is a much coveted TV slot. Bob promised whatever they wanted, and worried about delivering it later, and if it couldn't be delivered – he blamed someone else.

Again, Bob's autobiography is the place to read about Bob's individual conversations with band members and rock legends. Almost every line

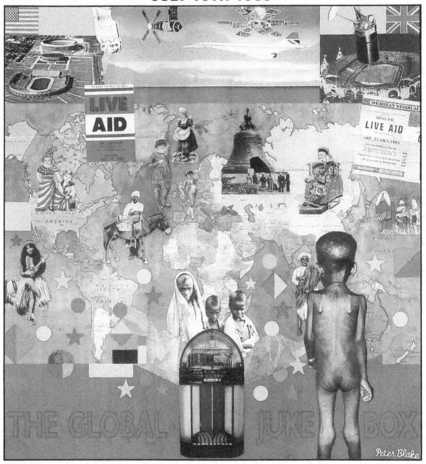

LIVE AID

WEMBLEY STADIUM
LONDON

JOHN F. KENNEDY STADIUM
PHILADELPHIA

JULY 13TH 1985

 THIS POSTER SAVES LIVES

Live Aid Poster, July 13th 1985.

of persuasion ended up in a cul-de-sac before Bob delivered the line that he tried to avoid each time; he begged, and said 'if you do this you will save lives'.

Roger Daltrey, who had been resisting reforming The Who for the occasion, said,

"That's a hard argument to answer Bob."

Bob replied, "It's the only argument there is Roger."

Bob won again and The Who got back together for Live Aid – something which only weeks before had seemed harder to achieve than a global broadcast to 1.9 billion people.

I don't think it's related, or maybe it is, but in years to come Roger Daltrey became a powerful ambassador and fundraiser for Teenage Cancer Trust.

For both shows there were criticisms that there were not enough black artists. Bob's response was that he was putting on the most successful artists he could get, regardless of colour or creed. He was called a racist - another first 'a racist saint'.

He was also accused, by some, of acts of moral blackmail. He was certainly not a racist, and as for the other accusation well …

Inevitably we were working in silos on arrangements and it is only fair to say that there were some things that I learnt after the event that were a surprise to me.

Some of which I learnt as late as 1986 when I read Bob's autobiography, and that has most definitely been a source to refresh my memory now.

I had no idea that in the pursuit of a global broadcast, 'we had a man travelling between Moscow, Peking and Delhi'. Or that for a long time, it looked like being a global broadcast – excluding France!

Three weeks before July 13th the Philadelphia show was a mess. It says it all that at one stage tickets for Wembley were sold out – while tickets for Philadelphia hadn't even gone on sale.

The other issue was that whilst everyone in the UK were doing things for free – in the USA non-performers expected to be paid. Philadelphia cost $3.5 million to put on, whilst Wembley cost $250,000. Fortunately sponsors covered the USA cost.

Positives and negatives came on a daily basis. The fundraising video of Mick Jagger and David Bowie performing '*Dancing in The Street*' generated record royalties for the Trust – but Motown 'couldn't' give us the publishing royalties!

Big name UK acts started to sign up for the USA concert.

Eric Clapton 'in' ... Black Sabbath 'in'.

Not only were bands being asked to perform for free, they had to pay expenses themselves – and sometimes even the cost of cancelling committed shows. As I have said, some UK bands could only get on the USA line-up with the inherent cost of cancelling pre-booked tour dates.

At first those UK acts were filling a barren USA line-up, but then the dominoes started tumbling.

Madonna 'in' ... Joan Baez 'in'.

One of the strangest positives was oddly a harrowing one. A Canadian broadcasting company had to pretty well hold Bob down to make him watch a video they had made of a dying child trying to stand up.

The musical soundtrack was the recording of 'Drive' by The Cars. I have seen that video at least a hundred times, but 39 years later, as I write this, I can't type properly because my eyes are full of tears at the memory of the video.

How did something so terrible, and so harrowing, become a positive? Well it did; in 1985, and also 20 years later in 2005.

As an aside, the songwriter Ric Ocasek who rightly considered the song as 'one of his favourite children' came to feel the song was 'stolen' from him by the video. He was supportive of its use and its catalyst as a fundraiser, but it's original meaning was taken from him and could never be returned. Ric acknowledged that the sacrifice was for a greater good.

When David Bowie saw the video he said he wanted to introduce it at Live Aid and he would sacrifice one of his performances to allow for the time. Everyone begged him not to do so, everyone wanted him to perform as many songs as possible, but he was adamant – it would be his way or no way. No one was going to change David's mind and as on so many other occasions, his instinct was one thousand per cent right.

With all the logistics that were needed, not for just one concert but two, it was important not to lose sight of the fact that the endgame was NOT a successful concert – the endgame was fundraising. The concerts were a means for a successful global telethon and in 1985 that meant telephones and people to answer them.

At first, BBC support services said they would do the UK part of it and could, even in the short time available, provide 20 phones. Bob did not say, 'that's wonderful, that's really kind of you' and from his mute response they garnered that he was hoping for more. And instead

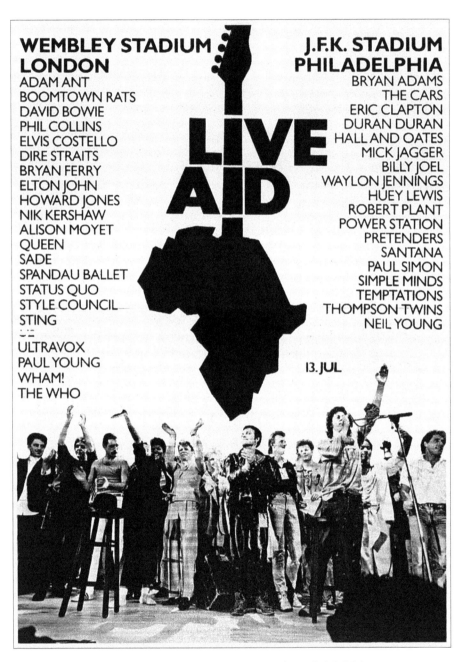

Live Aid, July 13th 1985, performers in London and Philadelphia.

of sulking and saying, 'see if you can do better yourself', they went away, and like so many others, they moved heaven and earth and came back with 500 phones. That was yet another example of the power of Bob!

If there were metaphors of things happening that were out of this world, then the metaphor became more tangible when NASA the American space agency agreed to allow a live television relay from the space shuttle. The captain would introduce an act as the spacecraft passed over Philadelphia and his introduction would finish as seconds later the shuttle passed over Wembley!

Even until the end there was wiggling and wriggling. On the night before at 6.00pm I got a call from a friend on behalf of a major (actually at the time majorish) band. His clients were wondering whether they should be doing the show. I think they were angling for a better slot in the line-up, or maybe insisting on time for a sound-check. There was so much going on that I simply said to them, 'if in doubt, then DON'T'. I was seriously pissed off.

Of course they turned up and were major beneficiaries from their performance. I will take this moment to make the point that no artist did this to help their career. There was no guarantee it was going to be a success – it could have been a shambles. The music press hardly covered it in the week before the show.

In fact, I have just realised that U2 admitted in a Brook Lapping documentary that it was them who threatened to pull out, and apparently even after my call, someone on their behalf phoned Bob at 2.00am on the day of the concert threatening to pull out completely, or at least that is the implication of the Brook Lapping documentary.

When I arrived home that evening I got a call from Harvey. There had been a change of plan – I was to sit in the Royal Box.

You know when you think I am too positive about Bob, just think of that with everything else that was going on he thought that it was wrong that I wasn't in the Royal Box. It had a purpose because I would be five seats from Charles and Diana. Two of those intervening seats would be Bob and Paula, two would be the CEO of Wembley and his wife. After the opening ceremony, Bob and Paula would go off for Bob's performance and we would move up seats. I was there to represent the Trust, and I could answer any questions that Charles and Diana might have. Harvey was going to be occupied elsewhere!

On the day of the concert I actually didn't have much work to do.

Bizarrely that was my first Saturday not working on Band Aid since Bob had barged into my office to engage me ... 'JUST FOR ONE HOUR'.

So, that Friday night before the concert, when I finished the call from Harvey – to be honest I was 'tickled pink'. I gave the wonderful news to Caroline. She stared back at me as if I was stark raving mad. 'What?' I said.

Now this is going to seem like an exaggeration, but her response was very much a reflection of the reality of the time. She was from Derry in Northern Ireland and she pointed out forcefully that if she sat in the Royal Box near Charles and Diana it would be considered fraternising with the Royal Family, and there could be very serious repercussions for her and her family. Yes, she was right and that had not occurred to me for a minute. Only nine months earlier the IRA had tried to kill Maggie Thatcher, in Brighton at the Tory party conference, and they very nearly succeeded.

Caroline and I agreed we would sleep on it.

The following morning we agreed to play it by ear – I would not have difficulty persuading a prominent artist to swap places with her.

Time for a diversion ... as a teenager I had loved and lived music, indeed that was why I wanted to be in the music industry. I had seen the USA film 'Woodstock' three times. It was about a huge music festival that took place in New York state in 1969. My favourite bit in the film was when a helicopter ferrying artists back stage comes over a hill and there are hundreds of thousands of people suddenly beneath them – each time it just took my breath away.

Well to give you an idea that this concert had not been put together with string and elastic bands, Noel Edmunds' helicopter company had agreed (free of charge of course) to fly artists across town from Battersea heliport in south London to a field near Wembley stadium in north London.

In fact, for many of the journeys Noel Edmonds was the pilot. When I heard this helicopter plan I knew this could be my 'Woodstock moment'. I also knew no matter how well this was arranged, and it was like a military operation, that if we got there early enough there would be an opportunity for Caroline and I to be 'stowaways' on one of the helicopter flights.

So we woke up early on the morning of July 13th 1985 to the most astonishingly beautiful day.

In a summer short of beautiful days – God was on our side. Well, it was Him who had knocked on the door of the scruffy Irishman.

In spite of the fact that we lived in north London, and not too far from Wembley stadium, we took a taxi to Battersea heliport in south London.

Of course the atmosphere was fantastic, I made myself known to the flights co-ordinator, and she said she would get us on a flight when she could. I hovered within her eye-line, and I think it was Spandau Ballet she was calling for, but no sign of them. She looked at her clipboard then looked at me. I tried to make myself look bigger and more important, and she nodded her OK for us to board.

We shared the helicopter with Paul McGuinness, U2's manager, and I was on talking terms with him, and subsequently we became good friends. I think the fourth passenger was Paul Allen, the co-founder of Microsoft – we were in esteemed company indeed.

The trip was everything I could have hoped for. After a short time the world famous Wembley towers loomed into view and underneath, not quite the hundreds of thousands of people at Woodstock, but tens of thousands, approximately seventy thousand were streaming towards the stadium.

We landed in a cricket field and a limousine ferried us to Wembley stadium's VIP entrance. The cricket match paused each time a helicopter arrived and restarted when it left.

Bob and Paula were already there, as was Harvey of course, he had probably been there overnight.

Bob looked glamorous but told me in graphic terms that he was very nervous. It's odd, you know I can remember that conversation as if it were yesterday – partly because of the graphic language.

In contrast, I was very relaxed because on the most important day in the Trust's existence I had little to do, no specific responsibilities, I had been doing my bit on the run up to the big day.

Caroline and I hadn't had the follow up conversation about where she would sit.

Someone approached me to tell me what my position would be in the royal line-up. I didn't let on that I didn't know that there was going to be a royal line-up.

So I had no idea that I was in the royal line up ... thank you Bob, thanks Harvey ... truly wonderful.

Fortunately, Caroline was not to be in the line-up but she stood opposite as I lined up – she was chatting with Elton John's wife at the time, Renata Blauel. Bob escorted Prince Charles and Princess Diana down the line. Bob was quite rightly loving it, no sign of nerves now.

The Prince seemed to be comfortable on his own, and he shook everyone's hand, and had a few words with everyone too.

Well if I said earlier that Paula was a flirt (actually it was Caroline that said that) ... well Bob was in his element with Diana, introducing her to everyone – he was flirting and so was she.

I was looking forward to my very brief moment with Princess Diana to share with my future children. Incidentally, they have never expressed any interest - to share with them the charming words we exchanged.

As the Princess and Bob worked their way down the line I was savouring my moment of glory and then as they reached me I could see Bob was smiling mischievously. Bob said, "Your Royal Highness, this is John Kennedy the trustee I mentioned earlier."

WOW! I thought, Bob and Diana had been chatting about me earlier in the very short time they had had together – how good was that? And I waited for her words of praise congratulating me on the role I had played in making all this happen and she opened her elegant mouth and said,

"OH, ... SO YOU ARE THE IDIOT."

Now clearly that needs some explanation. And before I explain, I want to remind you that retrospective vision is a wonderful thing. If I asked you to guess how much a ticket for Live Aid was you might easily guess £100 – but it was in 1985 so you might use common sense to adjust that to £50. Well I just took a deep sigh as I write this. My little tale here will not do justice to the extent that the artists' line-up came together in the last weeks or so before the concert. Big stadium gigs were not the norm in those days, in the way they are now. Well, you can already hear I am on the defensive.

So, many weeks before Diana uttered those memorable words to me, we had, as trustees, discussed what price the tickets should be. I argued forcibly that we needed the concert to sell out – and trust me, that was not a given at the time we were having this discussion. I also argued that we needed a younger demographic, (though it is very likely I had never heard the word demographic at the time). I also pointed out that young people did not have a lot of money – and so my argument was that a full stadium of the right age group was more important than the actual revenue from the ticket sales. I argued the ticket revenue was the smaller picture, because with a global audience of billions you didn't want an empty stadium.

So Bob wanted a ticket price twice what I wanted, and Harvey must have had a very strong view as there was no chance my view alone would have prevailed on the ticket price. Anyhow, astonishingly as it may now seem, the price was not the £50 that Bob was proposing, but £25 – (no please don't deride me). In fact, the actual ticket price was £5 including VAT, plus a £20 donation – a pretty flimsy device at the time to pay VAT only on the £5, and not on the full £25.

Bob and Her Royal Highness Princess Diana bonded over the idea I was an idiot! They both thought £25 was ridiculously low.

As I say, hindsight is a wonderful thing.

So on this lovely sunny day with a packed stadium roaring in our ears, my dear friend Bob had been kind enough to highlight to the Princess that this was my contribution to Live Aid.

I didn't reply, 'well, you are a Princess and I think we gave you and your husband a free ticket – I'll bet you probably weren't working on the tills at Tesco on a Saturday to save up the money for your ticket'.

I think I tried to explain my rationale for a low ticket price, by which time she smiled – delightfully and charmingly I must say – and moved on with Bob smirking from ear to ear.

Of course Caroline asked what Her Royal Highness had said and when I told her she laughed more than Bob. At least there wasn't any danger of Caroline saying, 'you think she fancies you, don't you'!

Anyhow the concert was about to begin, perhaps Caroline liked the Princess's way with words as Caroline appeared to be going to sit with me.

Now to those of my age and background, Wembley was synonymous with the football Cup Final and I was about to go out and sit surrounded by the famous Wembley towers in the Royal Box from which the iconic FA Cup was presented. Indeed only 60 days earlier it had been presented to the winners Manchester United.

I was looking forward to the experience. Well, we were pointed to a dark staircase which apparently led to the Royal Box and I let Caroline go first. As people in front of us emerged into the light it was clear that all eyes in the stadium were looking at that entrance to the Royal Box keen to see the royal couple – in fact, both 'royal couples' Charles and Diana … and Bob and Paula.

I emerged out of the darkness into the light and I swear that a crowd of 72,000 people all cheered as one as I appeared. Well I thought, this is a better reception than I got from the Princess – but even I thought it was a bit over the top … and then I realised … David Bowie was immediately behind me. In fact, maybe I had pushed in front of him!

Well, it was a great feeling being welcomed by the whole of Wembley – whilst it lasted.

So Caroline and I had been told where to go in the front row and we had been given the numbers of our seats. The buzz was just unbelievable, we took our seats and waited for the royal couples. There was a single, empty seat next to Caroline, and David Bowie was in the row behind us. We sat down, we knew we wouldn't have to wait long for the empty seat to be occupied. There was the most enormous roar … who was coming?

It was one single person and I couldn't see who it was because even the Royal Box occupants including David Bowie were standing in adulation. Anyhow, whoever it was, was walking down the stairs we had just come down and seemed to be heading for the front row which was full, but for the four seats for Bob and Paula and Charles and Diana.

Oh, and there was the empty seat next to Caroline … well it was a guy, and this guy had a beard, and I could see him as he excused himself, a bit like at the theatre, as he moved along the front row. I realised before Caroline that it was George Michael and he was going to sit right next to Caroline. I did actually know George, but that's another story, and he arrived and sat down next to Caroline. I introduced her to George … and then there was an almighty roar as the two royal couples arrived. Caroline looked at me with a mixture of 'I am petrified and I have died and gone to heaven'!

Charles and Diana were welcomed by trumpets from a Royal Corps. All eyes were on the Royal Box and Caroline realised that meant the TV cameras were also filming. So she put her hands over her face, as if she was shielding herself from the sun, which was perfectly credible given what a gorgeous day it was. No one else in our box was having a problem with the sun, and anyhow, even if the IRA were tracking Caroline's movements, no one in the Royal Box was looking at her.

Then something Caroline should have foreseen but hadn't – of course the royal guardsmen on stage struck up the national anthem. Caroline was actually pretty neutral on the royal family but it was not a good look for a catholic girl from Derry to be standing upright for 'God Save the Queen' just four seats away from Charles and Diana.

So if you took the trouble to look at the beginning of the Live Aid DVD, then you will see Caroline sort of doing a version of the 'Hokey Cokey' where she doesn't quite stand up and doesn't quite sit down for the national anthem. George Michael must have thought it was an Irish traditional dance, in respectful acknowledgement of the Royal Family but indicating that there was no subservience.

Mercifully, we could all sit down and the show began. We would later brand the DVD, 'The Greatest Show on Earth' – no one has ever complained under the Trade Descriptions Act. Harvey was the great showman – every act had a strict 20 minutes, that was it.

At one time there had been a discussion over whether Status Quo were credible enough to have on the bill, and now here they were opening the show, and what a great decision that was.

It was a truly iconic moment from a band, no longer considered 'cutting edge' – but what better song to start rocking all over the world ... than 'Rocking All Over The World'.

So after that first song Bob and Paula departed the Royal Box, and Caroline and I, with our new mate George, shuffled up to be closer but not beside Charles and Diana. We chatted with George and discovered he was going to go on stage with Elton and perform 'Don't Let The Sun Go Down On Me'. Just such an inspired idea and there were to be many moments of inspiration.

Of course Bob hadn't just gone just to get ready to perform – he had gone to make sure the fundraising was going well ... which it wasn't. After a while George Michael slipped back to sit next to David Bowie and my client Chris Cross from Ultravox slipped into his empty seat intrigued, no doubt, that George and I were so pally.

Everyone in the stadium was having the time of their lives. Every performance was fantastic; the rule was play the hits, this was not the time to introduce your latest single to a billion people.

Bob had discovered that Harvey had a particular modus operandi. If you suggested something that Harvey hadn't done before, he said it was impossible, and then Bob would challenge him with 'why' and excite him about the idea and produce half a solution and Harvey and/or Maurice Jones would complete the solution.

It was this team that came up with the next piece of genius – the revolving stage . Divided into 3 parts – part A, a band is performing on stage. On part B, the next band is setting up. And on part C, the last band is coming off. There were three 'traffic' lights for the performers to see and adhere to. Green = you were in your performance time. Amber = your time is running out, and at Red it meant the stage was about to turn 180 degrees with you on it, so if you don't want to look an idiot – keep to your allotted time!

From noon to 5.00pm the pressure would be enormous but from 5.00pm onwards it would be a little more relaxed because there would be additional time whilst a band performed in the USA.

The potential for things to go wrong was enormous. Imagine if the stage would not revolve around? At one time Bob and Harvey considered bringing in a horse as a back-up in case the revolving mechanics failed.

Harvey the great showman ruled as a dictator with an iron fist and by the end of the day the show was only running two minutes over, quite an astonishing achievement!

All those superstars respected the signals from the Green, Amber and Red lights. No prima donna behaviour, who could consider themselves a prima donna in a gathering like this? If after your performance you wanted to sit in your dressing room and pat yourself on the back then you had to be pretty quick about it because after 30 minutes you were turfed out of your dressing room!

There was no point saying, 'don't you know who I am?'

No point saying I just performed in front of 2 billion people, in front of the largest TV audience in history via 13 satellites to 150 countries, absolutely ... NO POINT.

Once your 30 minutes was up another superstar was moving in!

There were no duff performances. Midge Ure wore sunglasses that reflected the audience and that photo got him on the front page of the Sunday Times. Midge would joke that 'if he hadn't worn those glasses no-one would have known he was there'.

Yes, it was Bob and Harvey's show and with that came huge responsibilities.

Bob performed with the Boomtown Rats and literally stopped the show at the poignant line, '*And the lesson today is how to die*'...' from the song, 'I Don't Like Mondays'.

You can see if you look on YouTube how much Bob loved performing, but as he came off stage he was a troubled soul. The TV audience numbers were at least as good as expected, and the phones were manned, but the audience at home were enjoying the show so much – they weren't taking time to donate which was the sole purpose of the event.

Bob didn't, as was widely reported at the time and ever since, say,

'Give us yer f*cking money!'

However, he did say;

David, Elton, George, Princess Diana – with me in the foreground at Live Aid.

'Don't go down the pub tonight, give us your money instead'.

And when a presenter suggested that they put the donations postal address up on screen Bob did say,

'F*ck the address – put the phone numbers up'.

He was spurred on by the news that the money was pouring in from Ireland, and trickling in from here!

People could pay with credit cards over the phone – but credit cards were not as prevalent then as they were to become. So arrangements had to be made so that the following week, and beyond, people could donate via post offices, building societies and banks.

However, this needed people's euphoria to last from Saturday night into the next week and beyond, and human nature just isn't like that – euphoria and good intentions can evaporate very quickly. But this occasion was the exception and indeed people in the UK and around the world and particularly in Ireland proved that they were exceptional in the days that followed.

You don't need me to run through every performance – just watch on YouTube and there were so many really great musical moments and some important for other reasons, (and the Trust makes money even today from every viewing).

U2 gave one of the great performances of the day. They were not yet global superstars, and yet they were the 'coming' band – but their great performance on that day was nearly their last.

Before they went on stage the other three members of the band reminded Bono, as they had many times before, that they were a rock and roll band – a unit – they were NOT his backing band, so please do not portray us as such. Bono nodded sagely, and they went out on stage to a fantastic reception. For all of their opening song '*Sunday Bloody Sunday*' and for the first six minutes of their next song, '*Bad*', this is a band performing as one. Just sensational chemistry, the crowd loved it, and then the showman in Bono takes over. From where we were sitting it was one of the great moments of the day, the same was true for everyone in the stadium and everyone watching on TV. It was pure genius, Bono dances with a girl, in fact, two girls from the audience. It was magical – for everyone that is apart from his band colleagues.

I loved every second of it on the day, but if you were looking at it from the main stage where his colleagues were, it looks terrible, almost amateurish, and unfortunately Bono had trouble getting back on stage.

So they are not only his backing band, they have to continue playing *'Bad'* for 11 minutes and then have to drop one song as the red light comes on.

When they all go back to their dressing room, apparently and I really don't know who told me this, and I only heard it 10 years later, the band are absolutely furious. They think Bono mucked up their big moment and demeaned them.

That's it – the band are going to break up and a press release is even drafted, but their manager Paul McGuinness suggests it would be wrong to rain on the parade that was Live Aid – and so they hold off publishing the press release for a few days.

Well the band were absolutely correct in what they saw and felt, but the people in the stadium and the TV audience and the media saw it differently – U2 had produced an incredible performance second to none – well, maybe Queen.

Indeed Rolling Stone would look back decades later and run the headline "U2, 12 minutes at Live Aid that made the band's career" – and they weren't wrong.

The 'breaking up' press release never saw the light of day. Thank goodness, think what future delights we would have all been deprived of! But again, in the Brook Lapping documentary, 'Against All Odds', Bono acknowledges, 'the band wanted to fire me'.

Most people agree that the best performance of the day, the best performance among many incredible performances, came from Queen – and no one really expected it. Bob had worked, and worked, and worked on persuading Freddie Mercury to agree to do the show. Freddie was very reluctant – Freddie and the band were going through physical, mental and creative turmoil, but as we know Bob is very persuasive – and charming. He hounded Freddie and the clincher was Bob, one on one with Freddie, Bob saw a chink of interest and went in to close the deal.

"Freddie," Bob said, "it would be madness for you not to be there."

"What do you mean Bobby." (!)

"Well it's your audience." Bob replied.

"What do you mean darling?"

"The whole world."

"Oh yes, I see what you mean."

A piece of rock history was clinched by that exchange and decades later the performance at Wembley would play a pivotal role in helping the film 'Bohemian Rhapsody' make a billion dollars at the box office.

Of course the entertainment value of the show was well beyond 10/10 and the audience was ecstatic ... and then David Bowie introduced the video of 'Drive'.

The whole stadium was stunned into silence and tears.

It was a timely reminder of why the concerts were taking place – not primarily for entertainment but primarily to fundraise – and the video did its job. The video reminded people around the world what they were supposed to do i.e. give money. And that's what they did. The phones rang and people gave as much as they could, and more, and that's really important – people truly stretched themselves.

The Wembley concert drew to a majestic conclusion with really the first faux pas of the day ... Paul McCartney's microphone failing on him ... but Pete Townshend, David Bowie, Alison Moyet and Bob went on stage to offer support, and the microphone started working again.

Then this was followed by a magnificent ensemble version of 'Do They Know it's Christmas' on a balmy July evening with 72,000 backing singers, who actually all thought they were on lead vocals.

The concert in Philadelphia was of course still underway but it was time to vacate Wembley.

What a day – it had been just extraordinary!

The plan now was to head off to Legends night club in London's west end for a party and to watch the rest of the acts in Philadelphia.

I have absolutely no idea how Caroline and I got to the West End but when we arrived we did so with Chris Morrison, my dear friend, my co-trustee and Midge's manager. As a manager he was better organised than us, he had his ticket for the party – but security made it clear that our 'Access All Areas' pass for backstage at Wembley counted for nothing at Legends – but no problem we would wait outside whilst Chris went and got us some passes.

This was certainly not a moment to tell the security guy, 'do you know who I am' – because it was clear he didn't care, he was doing his job and doing it well.

So Caroline and I stood on London's Old Burlington Street thinking of what an experience we had just had. Then a huge blacked out limousine drew around the corner. The security guy waved for it to stop and it did, and the driver passed out the appropriate passes, and as he did so the passenger window was wound down. George Michael leaned out and asked us if we had enjoyed the day, he indicated to his driver to wait and we chatted for a couple of minutes as if we were old friends.

A lovely conversation and we said 'see you inside', he drove on.

The security guard looked at us, smiled and decided that this was evidence enough that we weren't gatecrashers and waved us through to the fabulous party where the main emotion was relief ... intense relief, on such a great day. 'Mission Accomplished', by the time we got home we had been up for the best part of 24 hours and the birds were starting their dawn chorus.

It is difficult to think how Live Aid could have gone better or been better executed. What Harvey and his team, especially Andy Zweck, and Pete Smith, and Maurice Jones, and Bob had done was extraordinary – and even though it went to the wire, in the end the USA team had delivered in handsome style.

As I said, we would eventually describe it when we released the DVD as 'The Greatest Show On Earth' and nobody reported us to the trade descriptions office, thank goodness!

72,000 people at Wembley, 89,000 people in Philadelphia, 13 satellites including military satellites. (The Los Angeles Olympics, just a few years earlier only needed two satellites). An audience of 1.9 billion in 150 countries, 16 hours of music, and a global telethon that raised £80 million. All achieved with just a window of 10 weeks in which to deliver it.

The Black Voice described it as the racist event of the decade!

Of course I had no idea as I drifted off to sleep that I was only about one sixtieth of the way through the Band Aid project – I mistakenly thought I was within reach of the finishing line!

'JUST FOR ONE HOUR'!

What was most impressive for me was people's good intentions did not evaporate over Sunday, and on Monday there were queues around the block at the post offices, building societies and banks – and there were stories of people standing in the queues intending to donate say £20 and being spurred on by others in the queue to donate more.

I have already said I can't even think of the 'Drive' video without being blinded by tears, but there is another story that does the same for me 39 years later.

Interestingly, Bob and I have different recollections – and of course mine is the correct one! The essence of the story is the same in both versions but here I will tell my version.

It's the Monday after the concert and we have gathered in the Band Aid warehouse/office, not really for a meeting or a debrief but just to be all together in the ripples from Saturday.

The phones are constantly ringing and volunteers are fielding any number of enquiries and messages, but someone comes to Bob and says, 'we can't deal with this call Bob it needs to be you'. There's no irritation from Bob, it's just what he does now. The call is from the manager of a building society in Dublin, and he must be surprised how easily he has got through to Bob. I listen to the call on speaker phone. The manager explains his dilemma – an elderly woman has come in and she wants to donate, but she has no spare cash, and she wants to donate her wedding ring of more than 40 years. They want to know should they let her.

NO, NO, NO, my brain is screaming – and yet, I see Bob pause ... he says,

"YES. Yes, but you must ask for her telephone number and tell her that anytime in the next week if she regrets her decision she can come and collect her wedding ring, and then in a week's time you must call her and ask if she has any regrets."

So simple now as a solution – but all that came to Bob in a split second.

Word came back that the woman's face lit up when she was allowed to donate and she asked for soap to get the ring off as she had never removed it since her wedding day.

WOW ... just WOW!

Now ... Bob recalls it as a group of five women from Scotland, but I know it was one woman in Dublin.

Though actually Bob's autobiography has a different version – he says it was a dozen old ladies in Dublin. However, what matters is that my one elderly lady, or Bob's 12 ladies did not come to reclaim their ring(s). It would not even have been a bad story if they did – but she/they didn't.

Sacrifices like that and my fictional 'Beth of Basildon' have been a guiding light for me personally for 39 years. If it sounds sanctimonious, then so be it – we could not waste a penny over the years, or it would be a betrayal of the trust placed in us – so again, no trustee fees, no expenses, no reimbursement of taxis, coffees or even flights, no paid employees.

Subsequently, our commercial arm had to incur some expenses (of course non-trustee) to grow income, but they were paid from commercial income not donations, and the expenses were only incurred if they would drive significantly more income than the expenses.

So after Live Aid our bank account was bulging, and indeed we were earning good interest on the monies we had on deposit.

One day our then accountant rang me to say we need to have lunch.

I said, 'I do not have time for lunch at the best of times but certainly not now'. He insisted it was a subject of great importance and of immense value to the Trust, basically implying, less than subtly, that as a trustee I had a legal and moral obligation to have the lunch.

I am surprised I agreed, but I did.

Over lunch, he explained to me that we were earning eight per cent interest but if we moved all our funds to a client of his we would get twelve per cent interest.

Well, sometimes if things sound too good to be true then they are exactly that.

I said, "I am nervous of anyone offering an interest rate greater than the rest of the market by 50 per cent."

He not only told me I did not need to worry but again suggested we would be in breach of our obligations as trustees if we did not maximise our return on deposits.

But I stood my ground.
The client and bank he was recommending was BCCI ... and they would subsequently go into liquidation.

Imagine the scandal if Band Aid money was lost in that manner!

On 18/8/23, in the middle of the summer holiday period 38.5 years later, I sent 29 emails and received 19 emails on Band Aid projects – so much for 'JUST FOR ONE HOUR'.

CHAPTER 12

1985 - 2005

AT THE BAND AID COALFACE

What a ridiculous chapter heading in the context of JUST FOR ONE HOUR. So Live Aid had been a huge success as an event and as a fundraiser, but now the money needed to be spent and spent wisely.

However, even before Live Aid, I had set myself an important task. It is hard to believe now, but at the very beginning Bob thought the record would raise the very precise sum of £72,000. He thought he could donate that to a well known charity and get back to his music career.

When I told him he needed to set up a charitable trust I knew his £72,000 estimate and his revised £250,000 estimate were going to be miles out. It became clear from an early stage it was going to be many millions, but even I had no idea it would be more like £150 million, or pretty well half a billion pounds in today's terms.

What I did know was that quite rightly, there would be huge scrutiny around the curation and expenditure of the funds. And I left Bob in no doubt that I believed he owed it to everyone who bought the record to visit Ethiopia to see what was needed and where. I suggested Midge should go with the second shipment and I would go with the third.

After the BBC broadcast about the famine that inspired Bob to act, the great British public started donating to the traditional charities. So when the Band Aid record came around those same charities had two legitimate fears. First they feared that monies that they might have received would go to us, and secondly they feared that this music industry initiative would be incompetent and would waste the money.

In fact the first fear was not warranted because the record, and general reporting about the famine, increased charitable giving generally – not just in the short-term, but in the medium and long-term.

In the meantime, the tabloid media were desperate to get Bob to go to Ethiopia, (with them in tow). The journalists frankly admitted they wanted pictures of Bob with sick and dying children. As crass as that sounds it would of course fuel donations to the cause. But do the ends justify the means? Some time later in his philanthropic efforts, Bob would say 'I will shake hands with the devil on my left and on my right to get to the people we are meant to help'. However, he was not there yet and he never gave the journalists that picture they craved.

Anyhow, the charities were quite rightly saying 'what do these musicians know about delivering aid?' Bob was irritated, but they had a point, and it was up to us to establish credibility for our efforts. Bob was growing daily in his new role, and in his incredibly efficient way he had found great contacts on the ground in Ethiopia. One of those contacts was Brother Gus who I think was a Franciscan monk. He and others had told Bob what the money should be spent on, and we were buying those goods in readiness for shipping. It seemed for a short time as if Bob thought that was it – job done.

I was in deep now and I had learnt I had a voice at the table as a trustee. Bob can act like a benevolent dictator to get things done, but unlike a real dictator, he won't shoot you if you disagree with him – but you better have a powerful argument ready to take him on! He must have been aware of this himself, but I repeated what I had said before, 'you have no choice, having taken everyone's money, and having said it will be spent responsibly with no waste, then that means more than just buying wisely'. You have to be able to report that the aid is getting to where it is needed and for that you have to travel there. He looked horrified but he knew there was no choice, and so before he answered, I said again, 'and Midge must go with the second shipment and I will go with the third'.

So Bob went to Ethiopia, and that is brilliantly and movingly described in Bob's autobiography, and in the documentary 'Against All Odds'.

And then Midge went.

The time for my trip was April. I had a one-man business to run and if the one man heads off to Ethiopia then clients are not happy, but I had committed.

So one Saturday afternoon, I am waiting at Heathrow with Judy Anderson, a Band Aid volunteer, to board not a British Airways fully-catered flight to Addis Ababa … but a cargo flight, full with aid supplies.

As we were sitting waiting to board … a surreal moment … I see Harvey Goldsmith heading in my direction. 'That's odd' I thought, 'I didn't know he was joining us'. Well, the reason I didn't know was because he wasn't joining us – he was on his way to China with Wham. They were going to be the first western musicians of their stature to perform there. As I say surreal … 'Hi George' – yes, I knew him from my short time working at CBS Records … 'Hi Andrew' (I knew him less well) … 'Safe Travels!'

So then it was time to head to the cargo area of Heathrow to catch our flight. Well, our pilots did not inspire confidence. They were from the Bob Geldof school of sartorial elegance rather than the well-manicured British Airways style. They were unshaven, scruffy, and with a plane to match.

Wow ... already this adventure was looking like it might be an ordeal. Of course I should have known this was not a catered flight. Judy and I basically had jump seats – certainly not flat beds. Well it is what it is. All aboard for Addis Ababa ... actually no, next stop Athens for re-fuelling.

Fair enough, the plane seems a bit rickety, but I figure the pilots care about their own lives so they must think it's safe.

Now forward planning does not seem to be a great skill of these pilots. For when we arrive in Athens to re-fuel, (it is now the early hours of Sunday morning and we seem to be in a secondary airport) – this airport does not appear to have a 24 hours fuel station. My plan to be back in the office for my Thursday morning meetings is not looking good.

The pilots are not phased that we have to wait until 8.00am – again, it is what it is, and Judy and I sit on the ground by the plane. If there is an airport lounge it is not one we have access to.

At 7.45am the pilots head off to the fuel office, but return 30 minutes later, not bounding onto the plane but with a forlorn look on their faces – it is clear all has not gone according to plan. In fact, in a true indication of the level of professionalism we are dealing with, their credit card has been declined. I didn't even know you would refill a plane on a credit card!

Apparently, not to worry, they have booked us a day room at the airport Hilton hotel and their head office is transferring the money for the fuel. I unhelpfully point out this is a Sunday and the banks are closed. I am assured it will be OK. To be fair, four hours later we are refuelled and ready to take off for Addis Ababa.

If this plane was a car you would wonder if it had passed its MOT and true to form, as we take off from Athens and are rising to cruising height, the red button on the cockpit dashboard with a large triangle and the word DANGER on it, (that you always hope you will not see in action), starts flashing DANGER. The pilot hopes that I have not noticed it as puts his left hand on it, which has two results ... first it makes me think, 'now he has only one hand to deal with any crisis that has arisen' and secondly, his hand is now lit up as if it is the flashing DANGER sign. I nervously ask what the problem is and he suggests it is an electrical fault with the button rather than an actual problem. There is nothing to be gained by me debating this with him, and

I feel considerable relief when the sign stops flashing as we reach cruising height. I try not to dwell on the fact that may only be because the bulb has blown! In fact, I can't be altogether convinced that he hasn't dealt with it by disconnecting a wire! However, we seem to be flying steadily and I figure landing in Addis will be less of a strain on this aircraft.

It's a long journey but we get to Addis safely and head off to our hotel. I remember being surprised that there was a Hilton in Addis Ababa – as Hilton hotels was a luxury chain in 1985.

When I arrived in the capital it was buzzing. Business was good even though there was a famine of biblical proportions up the road!

In fact it was buzzing BECAUSE of the famine – journalists and aid workers were the customers. It certainly felt incongruous that I was able to order a club sandwich and fries!

My mission was to be able to say that I knew that the aid we had brought had found its way into the camps. I knew the plan was that it would be transferred on pallets to a Hercules transport plane with a Red Cross sign on it but flown by the Royal Air Force.

I sought out Brother Gus. He was a remarkable man – he explained to me that in fact the aid I had just accompanied would not be immediately going on a plane, but would join a short queue.

However, he assured me the aid would be in the camps within 72 hours. Aid coming by planes was getting to the camp quickly, but he confirmed what we already knew i.e. that aid coming by sea was stuck in the ports. In the crowded Hilton hotel he introduced me to the head of the air delivery mission. He suggested that I join him on a flight, leaving at 9.00am the next day, to see the camp and witness the aid relief distribution.

The pilots who had flown me out found me and said they were going into a bar in town and I should join them. I agreed reluctantly to do so, but when I got to the bar I immediately regretted it and to their dismay, I headed back to the hotel. We were supposed to be flying out the next evening back to London so I hoped (but had no expectation) that they would go easy on the alcohol.

The following morning I got to the airfield where I saw this huge Hercules plane being filled with food and medicine. The pilot explained to me they were taking it to a camp where it was much needed. We took off and after a few minutes it was as if the ground had totally disappeared from under us. We had flown from a plateau and when we reached the end of the plateau the ground fell into an astonishingly deep valley revealing the incredible beauty of this troubled country.

After a while, I was given a signal that we were arriving at our destination and I was asked if I wanted to help with unloading the aid, and of course I did. To my surprise I was called over for a harness to be put on me. I didn't really understand what was going on, but once I was fully harnessed up I realised to my horror that the back of the plane was opening up. One of the aircrew explained to me that, not surprisingly, there was no airstrip by the camp, so our plane wouldn't be landing.

We would be flying as low as possible and then we would push the pallets out of the back of the plane. He assured me the harness was in perfect condition – but without it I would follow the pallets to the ground, and what medical staff were on the ground had enough to do without having to worry about me.

It was both an exhilarating and frightening experience. The length of the harness to its anchorage had been carefully measured, of course you could not push the pallets off the back unless you went right to the edge. If my kids ever read this they will laugh out loud – as to say I have no head for heights would be a major understatement!

Well, I didn't fall out and as we flew off I saw the whole panorama of the size of the camp. As had already been said many times, it was like a biblical scene – horrific, daunting and frightening. No one spoke much on the journey back. We had just made a journey to a place where hell on earth was playing out!

And then I returned to my Hilton hotel.

I had some meetings to ascertain how aid delivery was going and whether things were improving. It was a simple message, one that Bob had already learnt and delivered to us – aid by plane as I had just experienced was working, but aid by sea was stuck in the ports. Hence Bob's ambitious and extraordinary plan to break the truckers' cartel with a Band Aid fleet of trucks.

OK – I had learnt what I needed from my fleeting trip to Ethiopia, now time to get back to the UK.

Time to find my pilots. I was pretty horrified to find my lead pilot drinking at the bar. I expected him to be off alcohol as he recovered from what I was pretty sure was a drunken night the night before.

Yes he apologised that he was drinking, but he had some bad news. "No fuel?" I asked. Danger light flashing? What now ...

He had been diagnosed with malaria! I took two steps back – he told me not to worry he would be OK to fly and we would fly tomorrow.

This was madness!

So what was I going to do? I found myself a doctor so that I could ask some questions. He told me to my surprise that malaria was not a contagious disease. So the risk wasn't that I would catch malaria – it was that it was a *deadly* disease and that my pilot could collapse at any time.

I think the doctor actually said the pilot's chest might cave in on him, or maybe he meant his lungs might collapse. Not a ringing endorsement, to risk a long flight back to London with a seriously sick pilot.

Who thought I would end up looking fondly on a time when a flashing DANGER sign was my biggest problem!

I went to the bar where I found the pilot was trying to treat his fever with scotch and I told him I would be making my own arrangements for getting back to London. He clearly considered me a wimp and said, 'good luck with that'.

It was the first sensible thing he had said – getting from Addis to London in 1985 was not an easy matter as there were no direct flights.

Fortunately, there was a travel desk in the Hilton hotel so I booked myself a flight, well actually fights ... Addis to Khartoum in Sudan, then Khartoum to Cairo, and then Cairo to Athens ... and on Thursday morning Athens to London.

How was this happening to me? ... 'JUST FOR ONE HOUR'!

So early Wednesday morning I head off to the airport and board my flight which is actually going to Cairo, and only landing in Khartoum for 20 minutes, so I felt myself lucky ... but that was about to change.

I am sitting next to a large gregarious gentleman who is spilling over into my seat. We chat about various things. As the flight is approaching Khartoum the pilot announces that we will be on the ground longer than expected to shelter from a sand storm.

My new friend laughed and says,

"It's not about the sand storm – it means the revolution/coup has started and the flight will be grounded and the airport closed."

I look at him hoping and praying that he is joking, but to my absolute horror, I realise he is not joking and he is now praying to Allah. How is this happening to me? Well if you told me 30 minutes earlier that I would end up in a plane that was flying in a sand storm with zero visibility then I think I would have been physically sick. But as we descended into Khartoum and we were engulfed by such a sand storm I nearly hugged my friend, which would not have been easy because of his size, and felt like shouting 'YIPPPEE' it's only a sand storm – and not a revolution!

Luckily, we landed safely, and even more importantly, took off with only a short delay and headed on to Cairo. I slept – it had been an astonishing 96 hours.

Cairo and my flight to Athens were uneventful. I arrived at my Athens hotel at 10pm and it was not the most salubrious establishment, but my flight was at 6.15am the next morning so I wasn't going to be staying there that long.

I went to check in and not surprisingly the receptionist's English was not good, but he also had a terrible nose bleed, and so was holding his hankie very tightly to his nose, and as he spoke very little English so communicating was not easy.

My passport confirmed to him who I was, and that tallied with the booking he had, so he handed me a key, but with no number on it.

No matter how many times he tried to tell me through his hankie – it was impossible to understand what my actual room number was. Eventually, I persuaded him to write the number down. And I knew the next question was a waste of time, but I asked anyhow – could I have an alarm call? (Of course no mobile phone to put an alarm on.)

So there was every risk that, if I slept at all … I would sleep through my departure time! And 'no' he said, 'an alarm call was not possible'.

Anyhow, there was a fair chance he would have bled to death by the following morning, so I would not be relying on his professionalism to wake me. But I did need his help with one more thing – can I order a taxi for 4.15 am please.

He seemed to say 'no' – but I just assumed it was our communication difficulties, so I repeated my request, and this time very slowly but still same answer … 'no' … but followed by a word that sounded like 'spike'. After pressing the issue a few more times I realised to my absolute horror he was trying to tell me that tomorrow morning the taxi drivers were on strike!

WTF – 'How was I going to get to the airport?' I asked and he helpfully shrugged his shoulders. Again … how was this happening to me? I asked him if there was someone from the hotel who could give me a lift and this was his clearest communication so far … 'NO'.

Well I had just come from the airport, so I knew it was about two miles away, maybe two and a half – so I was going to have to get up at 2.30am and try and walk. So three hours sleep and then a shower with the cockroaches – who were clearly fed up at being woken at that time in the morning – and out of the door at 3.00am. Of course it was pitch black and no Google maps, but I could see the lights of the air traffic control tower so I knew which direction to head in.

I figured it was going to be an unpleasant walk but I had allowed myself enough time. However, I had not allowed for the next problem … my way was barred by a pack of wild dogs. In fact they looked like wolves, but I kept whispering to myself that they were *only* wild dogs – as if that was good news, but it would certainly be better news.

They say necessity is the mother of invention! I could turn back or soldier on. The wolf/dog pack were on a piece of wasteland and on the other side was a street with street lamps which I hoped they would consider a no-go area, so it would be a haven for me.

If…and it was a big IF … I could get there.

So I walked confidently but slowly past them – careful not to make any sudden movements. They barked and they snarled but they stayed a distance until I was nearly at the street, and then two of them came closer yapping and snapping towards me. At this stage I was wishing I had taken my chances with my malaria infested pilot. I decided not to run, because of course I could not outrun them, and for whatever reason they decided not to take a bite out of me. I don't think I am exaggerating when I say that one bite and some blood might have changed things, as these were not just stray dogs but a hunting pack, hopefully of dogs, not wolves!

'JUST FOR ONE HOUR'!

The rest of my walk to the airport and my flight to London passed uneventfully – and amazingly, I got to the office pretty well when I expected to arrive. I knew I had a full day of meetings and my wonderful secretary Lesley brought me a cup of tea and asked,

"HOW WAS IT?"

From 1985 to 2005 I went from being 32 years old to 52 years old. Youngish to middle aged or worse. I got married, changed careers, and became father to three wonderful children. The Band Aid project remained a constant in my life. Some months were busier than others but the project was always demanding, but fascinating.

The 'high' of Live Aid was quite something to come down from – but of course now the real work began, some of which I have described elsewhere. You know, no one challenged the description of Live Aid as 'The Greatest Show On Earth'– but now it was a time for 'Blood, Sweat & Tears'.

One of the reasons Bob had given to us, his fellow trustees, for the concert was that we needed to buy two fleets of trucks. Well as you can imagine we also said, 'WTF' even if that was not common slang at the time.

The problem was that, in Sudan especially, famine relief aid was not getting from the ports to feeding the camps because local truck operators had combined to establish a cartel, which meant trucking costs had increased three-fold. So as a result, food and medicine were stuck in the port because nobody had the money to fund transport for the metaphorical 'last mile'. So Bob and Kevin Jendon, unpaid de facto CEO, had decided we need to buy not one fleet of lorries but two.

Now we had the money to do exactly that.

As of January 2024, the Band Aid project has raised £140 million, the sum usually attributed to Live Aid is £80 million – there were donations, sponsorship monies, ticket income, merchandising income.

One of the interesting initial statistics was that £5 million had been raised in Ireland versus £4 million in the UK. The £4 million was commendable enough, but the Irish population was less than 10 per cent of the UK. What an endorsement for their new favourite prodigal son? Bob had not always been revered at home. Ireland's £5 million subsequently grew to £7 million.

As Bob walked around London people would give him notes and coins! Pushing them into his pockets. But it wasn't just about money, compassion had been ignited.

The public loved it when Bob took on Maggie Thatcher about the EU food mountains. The media portrayed them as opponents but relatively recently I heard from Bob that he would occasionally get a call from Maggie late at night, say 11.00pm, and she would invite him over to Downing Street for a whiskey. He would say, 'but Prime Minister I am in my bed', but she would insist 'this is your Prime Minister asking you' and he would retort that he was Irish, so she was not his Prime Minister. She would be so insistent that he would have to get up, get dressed and cycle over to Downing Street and they would share a whiskey or two until the early hours of the morning. I sat open-mouthed as Bob told me and two others that story.

Maggie clearly respected what Bob was doing and was intrigued by his ability to connect and communicate equally with presidents and prime ministers as well as 'Joe Public'.

There was no doubt that for a time Saint Bob was the most famous person in the world. It was an experience to just walk down the street with him.

At first people couldn't believe it was him, they would largely leave him alone unless they happened to have money to give him, but they would continue walking with their head swivelled round so that they could see him for as long as possible, until they bumped into someone, or something, or tripped over.

Amongst the many issues that Bob berated Maggie over was that the government had taken the VAT on the Band Aid record sales and to his mind made him a liar when he told the public 'every penny they paid would be spent on aid'. Eventually the VAT was returned by a circuitous and supposedly confidential route to additional overseas aid.

Whether it was over whiskey, or by dint of his public persona, Bob made Maggie reconsider her position on humanitarian aid. As Bob said 'not at any stage did she patronise him' and her reconsideration was at least partly influenced by a poll that showed that the Tories had lost a huge amount of support, solely because of their stance on VAT from the Band Aid record. The power of that piece of plastic record never ceased to amaze me .

It was astonishing to watch on a daily basis, as Bob rose in status and intellectually to be the match of any world leader or media broadcaster.

In Bob's book he said that the public seemed to see Band Aid as something which stood for common sense and common decency in a world marked by self-interest and double dealing. Another tenet and guideline to steer us along with 'Beth of Basildon' and 'the lady and her wedding ring'! Bob was even nominated for the Nobel Peace Prize – this was a measurement of his international respect and status .

His energy was now limitless. I would come home and say to Caroline, Bob was on the phone today for 40 minutes on some aspect of what Band Aid needed to be and do. It was astonishing when he spoke, it was as if he was on a TV show with an audience of 10 million, and by the end I was certainly motivated, and was in no doubt of what direction we were heading in as a charity.

In his new role Bob had become more acquainted with the staggering statistic that in 1985 Africa had received 3 billion dollars of aid but paid out 6 billion in interest on loans to the world bank.

You did not need to be an economist or a genius to understand the madness of that situation – but it would be another 20 years work to address this issue ... and that's for another chapter!

Bob's influence on the world stage grew and grew. He openly criticised the Russians' efforts (or non-efforts) in relation to famine and instead of simply ignoring the 'scruffy Irishman' they felt they had to respond.

The American government declared July 13th as Live Aid Day, the bill to make that happen was the most signed bill ever to go through US congress. Even I find these things astonishing to report – Bob brought me back a copy of the signed bill.

Meanwhile, back at home as trustees we had to strategise for what we hoped would be a medium-term future. We had gone from having £8 million to spend to having £80 million to spend.

After much debate, we decided we would allocate 20 per cent to emergency relief, 20 per cent for shipping and transport, and 60 per cent for long-term sustainable projects. We had already decided we would not be operational ourselves, but I did point out that trucks, and ships, and planes felt pretty operational and the idea was that existing agencies would make grant applications to us for funding.

At one time these agencies had seriously resented Band Aid, fearing money given to Band Aid would reduce the donations pot available to them. However, to their surprise, they learnt that the Bob / Band Aid messaging had increased people's willingness to give. The other thing they found was that if Band Aid funded 25 per cent of their project, then the consequent publicity made it easier for them to raise the remaining 75 per cent – and often governments would match Band Aid funding.

But there were two areas in which we clashed.

The first I have already mentioned i.e. that we were, as far as they were concerned, the 'amateurs' – so they thought we should accept their projects without questioning them, and we just weren't very good at that.

However, we did respect their expertise and experience, and certainly never disagreed with them for the sake of it. It was a much better scenario for everyone if the experts and the trustees reached consensus.

The second point was that because of promises made by Bob, and because of 'Beth of Basildon' and 'the lady with the wedding ring', we wouldn't fund ANY part of their overhead cost.

The charities were furious about that. We had explained why we took this stance and pointed out that typically 30 per cent of their funds were spent on marketing and fundraising – and they did not have that cost on monies granted by us for a project. They were not convinced and even started their own cartel of organisations who decided they would not apply for our grants so long as we stuck by that condition. It wasn't their best strategy, as we always had more applicants than we had money to spend, so it was not a problem for us – and one by one members left the cartel and started reapplying for grants.

Bob's autobiography was published in 1986 and in the last pages he is convinced that Band Aid will be wound up by the end of 1986. As I read that I chuckled, as did I as I wrote this chapter - one of two chapters covering approximately 20 years each!

Understandably we were constantly under press scrutiny, but we had nothing to hide – certainly nothing to hide from 'Beth of Basildon'.

At the very beginning, the Sunday Times put their Insight team on the case to investigate what Band Aid was up to. Insight was their team of well-respected investigative journalists. They had the good decency to call us to say that after an intense six weeks of investigation they had found nothing untoward.

Our most ambitious project was certainly our trucking fleets, but it was certainly not easy. I think it was a Monday, as I think Monday was when Panorama (the BBC's highly respected TV programme) was broadcast. We were notified that evening's episode of Panorama was going to run an expose showing that our trucking operation was an expensive shambles. We were disappointed because we didn't think it was but who knew what they had found?

So each of the trustees tuned in at their homes with a heavy heart. I remember after the programme finished calling Michael Grade to say something along the lines, 'that was feeble wasn't it'. Panorama were able to show footage of some of our trucks broken down with food and medicine on the back. This was not the most astonishing discovery of all time, as our trucks were operating in desert conditions and obviously broke down from time to time, to which the response was to get them up and running again. We did not feel that Panorama had delivered any blow – let alone a knock-out blow .

Outside the time scale of this chapter, we woke up one morning to find the BBC news website claiming that Band Aid funds had been used to buy weapons. Of course this was of major concern to us. We were pretty sure it was not true, but this was the BBC and surely they would not make such an allegation unless it was true.

I read the story – again with a heavy heart – and it was to my mind the most feeble piece of uncorroborated journalism imaginable for such an important allegation. If the story smelt of veracity we would have taken it very seriously indeed. Instead, we embarked on a six month journey of complaint about the story. Michael Grade commented that if I had been charging by the hour for this process my bill would have been £500,000.

The ridiculous thing was that, if you complained about a BBC story being incorrect, the BBC were judge and the jury. They were incredibly arrogant. But in the end the medium-level executive responsible for ruling on it showed the integrity to risk his career and uphold our complaint against the BBC. The BBC were forced to give us an unprecedented apology.

That evening, Six O'Clock news started at 6.03pm and the Ten O'Clock news started at 10.03pm to allow for the apology at peak broadcasting and viewing hours!

The apology included an admission that *'the allegations should not have been broadcast'* and an apology for *'the misleading and unfair impression that was created'.*

Over the 20 years that this chapter briefly touches upon there were two attempts to wind up Band Aid's efforts – one unsuccessful and one spectacularly unsuccessful.

The first was attempted in 1992 with a love letter from the Band Aid Team to the public by way of a pamphlet called 'Food and Trucks and Rock and Roll'. It was a message of thanks to the public and a closing down statement. As trustees we knew that some money would continue to dribble in from legacies in wills and from royalties but the expectation was that it would be a trickle and that the story of Band Aid was 99 per cent done, – how wrong we were!

The second was at a trustees meeting on the 25th January 2005 where again we thought we were nearing the end. We even discussed the idea of the rare event of a trustees social dinner as a milestone to celebrate the beginning of the end.

Yet ...152 days later we were staging 11 concerts around the world to an even bigger audience than Live Aid and achieving even more!

CHAPTER 13

PERSUASION INSPIRATION AND LEADERSHIP

THE PIED PIPER

This chapter heading sounds like it is out of a business book you might be silly enough to buy at the airport, but almost certainly will never read.

In November 2023 Bob sent me an interview that Hal Uplinger had done with the USA based Smithstonian Institution.

The interview is a great read but it made me think of two things – they were not new thoughts but the interview put more flesh on the bones. The first thought was really a reminder of what an astonishing technological achievement Live Aid was, and the second was how did Bob get people to do the things they did?

We have already established that God can be a bit lazy and does not do his research, which meant that when there was a famine in Ethiopia he needed sorting out, he knocked on the wrong door and when a scruffy Irishman opened the door, instead of saying 'sorry wrong address, go back to making your music', He/She/Them shrugged their shoulders and left Bob to get on with it.

True, God did make the sun shine on 13/7/85, and on 2/7/2005, and made some amazing coincidences happen, but on the other hand, some would question what role God had in allowing famine, drought, war, pestilence, and a locusts invasion and infestation. Some would question, but I am too old to be risking making an enemy of God.

But God certainly left Bob to do the heavy lifting!

Of course, I saw first-hand the record and the concerts.

I saw second hand the Gleneagles negotiations. But along the way there was an astonishing mobilisation of groups of people.

How did Bob get that to happen?

As we know he did not have a team of staff. He just led by example, and sometimes with eloquent speeches, he touched a nerve with people – actually, not sometimes, frequently.

THE FIRST 6 TRUSTEES : we all had businesses to run, families to bring up and lives to lead. We will soon have given 40 years of our lives at his instigation. You are reading my story and not one of the six walked away. Though one died, may Obie rest in peace. My rows with Bob actually become more fierce over the years. Last week Caroline was surprised to see me on a Tuesday with a bottle of wine and corkscrew in hand – I don't drink during the week. Surprised but sympathetic,

"Tough day?" she said.

"Tough Bob." I replied.

"Ah." she nodded knowingly!

MIDGE URE : Without his songwriting and producing this would not have happened, or maybe it would have been just an acorn, not an oak tree. Once Bob enlisted him to write the song he was not going to escape. He and Bob have traded banter over the years – sometimes barbed banter, now just very funny banter. They are both brilliantly quick witted. They started off as equal songwriting partners in this escapade, but within hours for everything else Midge was left in Bob's slipstream. I think at times he might have resented it, but he could not have been Bob – he would not have wanted to be Bob.

By Bob's own frequent admission, Bob was only home watching the Six O'Clock News because his music career was in the doldrums. Midge's career was flourishing and in 1985 he had a number one solo record and a successful album and tour. Then of course, there is the conspiracy theory that Bob pushed Midge's Ultravox up the set list so that Bob would be on stage while Charles and Diana were still in the stadium. Midge is as engaged in the Trust's work today as he has ever been.

HARVEY GOLDSMITH : He knew what he was letting himself in for when he agreed to help Bob put on a concert. But he did not know he would be by Bob's side at Wembley when they announced a concert that had no acts signed up. Nor that he would hear Bob announce acts that would be appearing that Harvey knew had already said, 'NO THANKS'.

Harvey may have thought he was signing up to do one concert. Not two, on two continents, with numerous satellites and an audience of a billion people. Maybe he thought he had signed up to do a concert in 1986 not 1985. Today, you can buy tickets for a concert in 18 months time.

On 13/5/85, Wembley was booked for a concert 61 days later. Harvey has a strong personality, and a great character, and also a great sense of humour, but he has found himself motivated by Bob to do things that he believed were impossible. I only just realised that all six trustees have a great sense of humour – we have had to!

LORD MICHAEL GRADE : Media aristocracy. He must have wondered at times what he is doing on this board of plebs. What would have happened if he hadn't given us a slot before Top of The Pops to announce the single? The answer is not that 'nothing would have happened' – but much less would have happened. Give yourself a treat, find on YouTube the clip of David Bowie announcing the record wearing our 'FEED THE WORLD' T-shirt, making a cheap run up, look like the most elegant designer fashion wear and so helping us to sell huge numbers of the T-shirt.

CHRIS MORRISON : These days the least active of the trustees but still hanging on in there. For the longest time he was Midge's manager and only got roped in because Midge asked him to ask Bob a question. I was there when he called Bob, five minutes before Bob did not know what a trustee was – and in that call he TOLD Chris that he and Midge were going to be trustees, as if he was doing them an enormous favour. Chris called me straight away to ask what that involved – fortunately, we had no idea!

I chuckle when I think that for Band Aid 20 Chris was charged by Bob with getting Damien Hirst, maybe at the time the most famous artist in the world, to do the artwork for the sleeve of Band Aid 20 … FOR FREE. Chris achieved this gargantuan task and because he had proven himself so successful at this kind of thing, he was then charged with telling the same Damien Hirst (the most famous artist in the world who had indeed created the artwork for free) that Bob did not like it – so we would not be using it. I am glad I swerved that one.

OBIE : Sadly long deceased. A brilliant business man and a cynic. First, as he listened to Bob's plans he would mutter to me, 'there is no such thing as Santa Claus', then as Bob told the trustees of his plans for a concert, Obie said 'KENNEDY – STOP HIM HE IS F*CKING MAD – HE WILL MAKE US ALL HAVE A BREAKDOWN'.

The following day Obie called to resign and I remember the stream of expletives well – shouted down the phone – when I told him I had forgotten to put a resignation clause in the trust deed!

JOE CANNON : Not a trustee, but a sub trustee – he has always worked for the Trust's accountants and has put in thousands and thousands of hours in his own time in many, many roles – but particularly reviewing grant applications, speedily but carefully. He was four years old at the time of Live Aid and he started working for the Band Aid trust when he was 18!

So Bob got five busy men, yes all middle-class, white men – apparently not a good look these days – to work for 200 years between them as trustees. Perhaps, it would be crass to say, we would be free men now if it was armed robbery that we did, rather than saying 'yes' to Bob. Even if I say so myself, a remarkable group of people who have worked together for decades to run the Trust and protect its reputation.

So this was direct recruitment. Maybe I should make it clear that I am using the 'Pied Piper' metaphor in the sub title to this chapter in a positive way. I have just read on the internet that there are many versions of the piper – including one that leads everyone to death by drowning – but even though as trustees we often felt drowning in responsibility, paper and workload. I mean the Pied Piper who is 'a charismatic person who attracts followers.' But a pipe can only be heard by people close by; Bob must have shifted to radio waves to recruit his followers.

Soon after Band Aid, Rowan Atkinson wrote to Bob saying would you mind if us comedians stepped up our charitable endeavours following your example? I have that letter somewhere, but I have put it in that famous safe place. As we know Comic Relief has raised a billion pounds, and has dramatically changed many people's lives, but like us, being accused along the way of being 'white saviours'. Poor Lenny Henry, first of all in the Black and White Minstrels, now a white saviour! I need to find that letter from Rowan, it's a piece of history.

David Bailey, at the time one of the world's most famous photographers, flew to Ethiopia at his own expense to take photos which he converted into a book that raised £250,000 for Band Aid !

Bono came up to me many years ago, shook my hand, looked me in the eyes and said I want to thank you and Bob for showing me the road to philanthropy. If you read Bono's autobiography 'Surrender' you will be astonished by the level and success of his philanthropic endeavours.

And then in 2005, the Pied Piper, Bono and Richard Curtis took on the G8. These were the leaders of the free world with populations totalling about 800 million, but 'team pied piper' claimed an audience of 2 billion for their

Make Poverty History concerts, and only the USA had a population greater than the 185 million signatures that Bob, Bono and Richard took to the G8 meetings.

So the Pied Piper could work his magic on the famous and powerful, but in many ways the most impressive skill was connecting with the ordinary man and woman on the street, and girls and boys in schools, and significant individuals who would go so far beyond the call of duty making personal sacrifices to follow the Pied Piper.

It's difficult now to believe that there was ever a day in his life that Sir Robert Frederick Zenon Geldof lacked confidence, but if you read Bob's autobiography 'Is That It?' you will realise there have been rollercoaster moments in his life and that book is nearly 40 years out of date.

All musicians, especially a lead singer, vacillates between beliefs that they are infallible and times of extreme doubt. In the autumn of 1984 Bob was in the latter place, believing his music career might be over.

How did he pick himself up to make one of the most global events of all time. How on earth did he make people he did not know give up vast amounts of their time to deliver Bob's vision – putting themselves under enormous stress in the process, and nearly abandoning their careers and livelihood for a period of time?

Hal Uplinger is an astonishing example.

Hal became the USA producer of Live Aid but it was not possible to operate in a silo. Hal was not an old friend of Bob's, he was not an old colleague, he was not someone who owed Bob a favour – he was a complete and utter stranger. Who decided Hal was going to put blood, sweat, and tears, not just into making the USA leg of Live Aid a success, but much more importantly – actually make it happen.

In fact, Bob didn't even approach Hal. He met Hal's friend, Mike Mitchell, who astonishingly had an interest in hunger and 'had done some projects for hunger in California'. Hal agreed to produce the American portion of Live Aid and distribute it to the whole world. Hal got involved on May 1st 1985, and the concert happened 74 days later - if you were told that whilst watching a film 'it's time to leave the cinema because it's just too far-fetched' – except that it's true!

First, what do you need most for a concert – a venue, but most good venues are booked at least a year in advance. At least – never mind 75 days! The obvious city for the USA concert was New York, but on such short notice neither the Yankee Stadium, Meadowlands, or Shea Stadium were available.

The good news was that the mayor of Philadelphia had a big PR problem and was trying to make friends, so he offered the JFK Stadium for free.

It was one thing for Hal to be a big believer but he now had to beg steal and borrow. He didn't want well-meaning volunteers, he needed 'the top people in their field'.

Hal had to arrange telethons.

He needed satellites, and for that you had to put down a $25,000 deposit. Hal believes Mike Mitchell put up the money personally – astonishing – a matter of days before he had never met Bob Geldof. As the concert approached, Mike Mitchell like many others was at breaking point, he had no money to pay for necessities for the concert, and had put himself heavily into debt.

Then Hal set up an overflow office in his own house, which as he points out was a mistake, because calls were coming in 24 hours a day. He literally could not sleep – like many of us he did not get a full night's sleep again until after July 15th!

One of his 'top men' was Tony Verna who gave him the important advice 'don't plan a 16 hour show – design 16 one hour shows'.

Hal and Philadelphia were the mother space ship, even the Wembley show was sent by satellite to Philadelphia to go onto the BBC.

And Hal said something which I have said myself many times over the years. 'Just think of the things that could have gone wrong' … but Hal was of the view that if there had been more time – it would have been almost like more time for things to go wrong, or for people to say, 'its not possible' – and I am firmly of that view.

The contract for the Philadelphia stadium was signed at midnight on July 12th … for the concert on July 13th.

And as with Wembley, God was one of the stars – he provided a beautiful sunny day.

What Hal did was beyond astonishing, but when the Smithsonian interviewer tries to congratulate him on a pioneering breakthrough broadcast Hal pushes the praise away and says 'the biggest breakthrough came in bringing the world together for a higher cause'. And he goes on to say the satisfaction for him and his team was bringing together 40 per cent of humanity, the broadcasters and the peoples of the world for the first time. Bob assigned this role to this stranger but the subsequent selfless and self-motivation are just remarkable.

As we know the story of 'when God needed help in Africa, he knocked on a door and when it was opened by a scruffy Irishman, he said you will have to do' – however, Bob was more discerning than God.

Bob only knocked on the doors of the established professionals he knew he needed, and by example, he inspired them to go the extra mile, and then mile after mile after mile!

The astonishing statistics:

Global 16 hour broadcast

13 satellites

22 transponders

Live to 110 countries with a video tape sent to 45 other countries

2 billion viewers

1 billion listeners on radio

13 hours syndicated in the USA, last 3 hours on ABC television network

35 broadcast trailers just in Philadelphia and a field of satellite dishes that controlled uplinks and downlinks

One master control truck

No recording … well that's what everyone thought – but that's another story!

In fact ... a global jukebox!

None of that could have happened without Hal, but Hal is just one example. This concept of persuasion, inspiration and leadership was not limited to Hal Uplinger and his team and Live Aid .

On the recording side, apart from Band Aid and USA for Africa, there were records in Austria, France, Canada, and Germany – apparently 25 in total. Of course Live 8 was not limited to the planned eight countries!

One of the few occasions when Bob's powers of persuasion did not work was when he tried to persuade Bruce Springsteen to perform at Live Aid. Bruce was performing a number of shows in the UK and Bob invited himself to every show and stalked Bruce. He sat at the side of the stage so that the last person Bruce saw as he went on stage was Bob – and the first person he saw as he came off the stage was Bob. And each time Bruce would say, 'Bob I can't do your concert' and Bob would say, 'I know Bruce I understand', but then Bob would be there again the next night. Bob got a partial victory because Bruce donated his stage at Wembley for Live Aid but he refused to perform, because he had long ago promised his new wife that they would be on their honeymoon on July 13th.

And Bob's leadership spawned many other movements;
> Actor Aid
> Air Aid
> Art Aid
> Asian Live Aid
> Bear Aid
> Bush Aid
> Farm Aid - not for Africa, but a momentous charitable project.

Fashion Aid – the top designers of the day put aside their rivalries to stage an incredible cat walk at the Royal Albert Hall. Again at huge personal expense and again raising hundreds and hundreds of thousands of pounds for the Trust.

> Four months after Live Aid, Fashion Aid was glamour personified;
> 35 hairdressers
> 60 make-up artists
> 120 dressers
> 125 models
> Jasper Conran
> Wendy Dagworthy
> Jean Muir
> Zandra Rhodes
>
> With catwalk displays from:
> Calvin Klein
> Giorgio Armani
> Issey Miyake
> Yves Saint Laurent
>
> Celebrity appearances from:
> Boy George
> Jerry Hall
> Kate Bush
> Grace Jones
> Paula Yates
> and according to Wikipedia;
> George Michael, Ringo Starr and Madonna.

And the show closing with Freddie Mercury and Jane Seymour as an unlikely bride and groom. But NONE of this extraordinary list is the best bit about Fashion Aid. I need to double-check this with Bob – please remember it was 39 years ago – but according to Wikipedia all this happened because Bob's radio waves reached a fashion student named Fameed Khalique who created it as part of his degree course at North London Polytechnic.

I would have loved to have been there when Fameed told his lecturers what he had pulled off! But this is yet another fascinating insight into the ecosystem of the Pied Piper, Bob and Band Aid. A student was able to get hold of Bob ... Bob embraced the idea ... and just weeks later it was staged at the Albert Hall in front of 5,500 people, including real royalty, and music and fashion royalty, and broadcast around the world.

I hope Fameed got first class honours for his degree.

When I watched a video of it recently, I was struck by the vibrant colours, and then I remembered Caroline and I in the green room. We had both come straight from work. I was a less than sartorial lawyer and whilst 23 year old Caroline was one of the most beautiful women in the room, even in the presence of 125 models, she was dressing herself on the budget of a nursery nurse teacher. But as I worried about what the models and designers thought of our fashion sense, I realised they had greater things to trouble themselves with!

Food Aid
School Aid which was both educational and fund raising and HUGE!
Sport Aid
To name but a few.

I could write so much about each of the above, but you only have so much of an attention span.

France had been a reluctant participant in Live Aid and a feeble donor – but School Aid became huge in France. Mainly because again one person, Lionel Rotcage, was inspired by Bob, and also because the teachers hated the concept – which meant that the kids loved it. School Aid generally was so important because it brought the concept of philanthropy to such a young audience in a way that interested them.

Then there were more records:
Band Aid 2
Band Aid 20
Band Aid 30

Each time Bob, by radio waves or personal calls, managed to get the most famous artists of the day to turn up at the studio – often at huge personal expense, including cancelling concerts to be there. Band Aid 30 of course included so many artists that had not been born when the journey began.

And if over the years artists thought they had done their bit, or weren't even sure whether it was cool to do their bit, there would be that very persuasive call from Bob. I think I only dreamt it, but I had a vision of Madonna looking at her phone and turning to her manager, and saying, how do you 'block caller'?

I will close this chapter with two contrasting stories of the Pied Piper effect. The effect on some of the most famous people in the world – and the effect on a solitary member of the public.

The single 'Do They Know It's Christmas' was a global success. So many records do well around the world and then do zero sales in America. This was not to be the case for 'DTKIC'. It was a big success in America. It touched a nerve with one of the most famous people in America, the legend that was Harry Belafonte. Bob's radio waves reached Harry.

Amazingly, Harry called Bob and said,

"We are ashamed of what you Brit kids did. We have white folks saving black folks but we don't have black folks saving black folks".

And then he put Michael Jackson on the phone, who invited Bob to attend the recording session for what would become the anthem, 'We Are The World'.

It took place on 28th January 1985 and the Pied Piper and Harry Belafonte seduced the following to participate in what was the biggest gathering of stars ever to be in the same studio, past, present, and I am prepared to bet, the future;

Michael Jackson, plus four siblings!

Lionel Richie

Harry Belafonte

Kim Carnes

Bob Dylan

Dan Ackroyd

Lindsey Buckingham

James Ingram

Quincy Jones

Ray Charles

Stevie Wonder

Darryl Hall
Al Jarreau
Waylon Jennings
Billy Joel
Cyndi Lauper
Huey Lewis
Kenny Loggins
Willie Nelson
Steve Perry
Smokey Robinson
Kenny Rogers
Diana Ross
Paul Simon
Tina Turner
Bruce Springsteen
Dionne Warwick
... To name but a few!
and I nearly forgot the Pied Piper himself – Bob.

The message on the entrance to the studio was 'Check your ego at the door.' And Stevie Wonder warned everyone that if the song wasn't completed in one take, he and Ray Charles, (two blind men), would be driving them home!

It is a party atmosphere and then Quincy Jones asks Bob to address the room. Bob is just back from Africa and he tells them what he has seen – many of the artists are moved to tears.

Bob says,

"I think what is happening in Africa is a crime of historic proportions ... you walk into one of the corrugated iron huts and you see meningitis and malaria and typhoid buzzing around in the air. And you see dead bodies lying side by side with the live ones ... in some of the camps you see 15 bags of flour for 27,500 people. It's that, that we are here for".

Now the superstars really do know why they are here and they are ready to perform like they have never done before.

'We Are The World' is released on March 7th 1985 and becomes the biggest selling single ever, though Wikipedia now says it's the eighth best-selling, physical, single of all time. It raised $80 million, ($222 million in today's terms). The estimated global sales are 20 million. The money was not for Band Aid but a USA foundation with ninety per cent of the funds for

Africa, but with the balance set aside for charity projects at home. We are the world is a new acorn about to grow into a new oak tree.

Quincy Jones told the artists, artists who had achieved everything one could hope for in terms of artistry, success and wealth;

"In years to come, when your children ask 'what did mommy and daddy do for the war against famine?' – you can proudly say 'this' was your contribution".

This magnificent contribution to humanitarian aid is encapsulated in the Netflix documentary 'The Greatest Night in Pop'. I recommend it strongly – an enjoyable evening lies ahead if you tune in.

Then read in his autobiography, Bob's reporting of his experience of 'We Are The World'. It is entertaining and touching as Bob meets his musical heroes who are treating him as an equal or even THEIR hero.

As with our Band Aid record it became common for people to be critical of the song. I just don't get that – neither record is pretending to be something more than it is, a great pop song in each case. In each case great artists, great songwriters, great producers – and a great cause! What is there not to like? That did not stop many critics finding their most brutal language in their own sad role as critics not creators. I have learnt over more than four decades in the music industry that it is much easier to critique than create! The words of the Band Aid single have been put under a magnifying glass over the years – even discussing whether or not there was snow in Africa in December 1984.

For Band Aid 30 the lyrics were updated with two amusing consequences. First of all, the new generation of artists kept singing the original lyrics. Bob said,

"WHAT! are you doing? You have the new lyrics in front of you."

"Bob," they retorted, "we are brainwashed for 15 years – we had to sing your song every Xmas in school!"

Secondly, the Guardian newspaper decided to write a brutal attack on the inappropriateness of the lyrics, without realising the lyrics had been changed in many ways in a manner which addressed their criticism before their criticism had been written!

And it feels appropriate to end this chapter with a story of, and I hope she will forgive me if I say, a 'nobody' who became a 'somebody' – because the radio waves, literally the radio waves, reached her.

There was no point raising all this money if the aid could not get to where it needed to be. Bob had learnt that painfully in his first trip to

Ethiopia and the raison d'être of Live Aid was to ensure we had an effective delivery mechanism. Well, if Freddie Mercury was one of the stars on stage, then Dee Flower was one of the stars off stage.

So I finish this chapter with her story. In many ways it's a simple story, but it shows that the Pied Piper followers were many, and varied, and came from all walks of life.

Dee Flower

So over the last, nearly, 40 years if the Band Aid record was originally a root, it grew into a trunk, and there were many branches off it.

It grew a new branch in 2024 – a musical Just For One Day. The story of Band Aid the record and Live Aid the concert told over two hours. The critics reviews were mixed, as indeed I had experienced decades earlier with Mamma Mia! but every night the audience gave the show a standing ovation. It was also a financial success for the Trust, £250,000 from the initial run at The Old Vic in London and an expected £450,000 from a run in Toronto.

The writer of the story from the play had, with Bob Geldof, wanted to convey the message that the Band Aid story showed that individuals, whether they be big or small, could make a difference. John O'Farrell, the writer, had created a fictional 17 year old girl in a record shop in Weston-super-Mare who made a difference by raising money from using her savings to buy quantities of the Band Aid record and then resell them – the audience loved the story.

On the last night of the show's limited run, by chance I was seated a few seats away from a lady called Dee Flower. My wife's cousin heard her say she was there at the Live Aid concert on the day, and he pointed at me and said, 'so was he'.

We chatted at the interval and I learnt she was more than just one of the audience of 80,000 at Wembley, she was more like the fictional girl in the musical, and more, who had shown in an impressive way that an individual really could make a difference – a significant difference.

Over the years, Bob has talked about the extraordinary things that have happened by chance to put the wind in the sails of the Band Aid story, but he doesn't put them down to the hand of God – he is a confirmed atheist.

Dee Flower was already an unusual woman. She had in a dark age 40 years ago applied for a job on a publication for truckers called

Motor Transport. 'We have never had a woman' she was told. Not put off she said, 'lucky you, you now have a chance to put that right'. The bosses weren't sure – 'not only was she a woman, she had children'.

'What would you do' they asked, 'if your child's school called to say your child had had an accident?' She wasn't going to sugar-coat it, she said, 'I would drop what I was doing and go straight to the school and I would expect my husband to do the same!' In spite of her being bolshie, or maybe because of it, she got the job.

The musical devotes quite a section to the fact that Band Aid needed trucks in Ethiopia and Sudan to get aid from the ports to the refugee camps.

In early 1985 Dee was driving in her car listening to Radio One. They announced that after the news there would be an interview with Bob Geldof. At this stage Bob was certainly the most famous person in the UK and one of the most famous in the world.

The interview was to let the public know how their money was being spent – their money?

Yes, their money – the money they had given when they bought the record. It was always their money ... 'Beth of Basildon' and 'the lady who gave us her wedding ring'!

In his update, Bob said almost desperately, 'we need trucks – trucks to get aid from the ports to the camps.'

Dee could have thought, 'that's interesting', but she didn't, she decided 'I can help with that'. In fact, she was on her way back from a meeting with Mercedes Benz, who made pretty impressive trucks.

But of course she could have had the thought and then done nothing, but she didn't – she called Radio One and said, 'I can help'.

Unfortunately, Bob had left the building!

Radio One asked, 'who are you?' She said, 'I know about trucking' and left her phone number – again there was the possibility for this to come to nothing. The Radio One executive could have just filed it under 'mañana', but they didn't. To Dee's astonishment they arranged for her to meet with one of the most famous people on the planet even though she had just made contact through the Radio One switchboard! Would that happen today?

It was not the first meeting but again to her astonishment, Dee finds herself with her colleague Phil Butterworth Hayes at Bob's house one evening for a meeting. She is introduced to Paula, who is putting Fifi to bed, and they are about to start the meeting when Paula makes it perfectly clear that in their house Bob is not one of the most famous people on the planet when she tells

Bob to get out of the meeting and make sure Fifi brushes her teeth.

By now Dee knows that Bob REALLY needs trucks.

She has asked her boss to let her spend time on the project – he is reluctant, 'Band who? – I don't think so.' She says it will be good for our souls and will be good for our publication. He remains sceptical but cuts her some slack.

Dee knows about trucks. She knows that Mercedes Benz and Iveco still have a line of trucks that they first made in the 1930s. Counter-intuitively, she wants those trucks, not the latest model from the 1980s. British Leyland hear she is doing a deal to buy trucks from those manufacturers and they call her in to berate her for not buying British, after all the funds have come from the British public. She also knew she wanted an African specification, i.e. bolstered suspension, left hand drive and toughened wheels and tyres. This specification would normally have taken manufacturers many months to deliver, but Dee motivated them to make delivery 'immediate'.

British Leyland are surprised when she tells them their trucks are too good, too modern. How could that be a problem – they are computerised – if they break down in the desert no one will be able to repair them. If the 1930s model breaks down it can be repaired with a pair of tights!

This woman in a truckers' world was dictating what was right for the Band Aid fleet. More than a decade before the Spice Girls – this was girl power in action.

Of course it was all unreal, Dee's husband was bemused, and she can still remember her son's face when he answered the home phone, and looked at his mum as he handed the phone to her, and could hardly say, 'it's Bob Geldof for you', knowing his mates at school would never believe him!

Even Dee needed to pinch herself. Having identified the trucks that were needed she then handed the final dealmaking over to Kevin Jendon, de facto ceo – having told the manufacturers that they would have to give a huge discount otherwise Dee would recommend those nice shiny modern ones from British Leyland.

Dee could not have been lacking in confidence when she decided to call Radio One, but Bob's belief in her, (to his immense credit), had emboldened her. She now got on the phone to hauliers asking them to take aid to the Band Aid ships at Tilbury Docks and to planes at Gatwick Airport for free! You won't be surprised to know that she was successful even though, when she first mentioned Band Aid, they still thought it was the plasters. Instead, they were being asked to ship food, medicine, vegetable oil, grain, milk powder, Land Rovers, 500 gallon water tank trailers and high protein biscuits.

Then on May 23rd, Motor Transport publish a middle double page spread about what Dee has been doing – and her previously sceptical boss now thinks she is pretty amazing.

Bob had a lot on his plate, but he made it very clear how appreciative he was of her contribution. She joined a small group of volunteers, her, Valerie Blondeau, Judy Anderson, Penny Jendon, Kevin Jendon, and Ken Martin.

It was the night she met Paula at their house that Bob told Dee he was organising a concert on two continents. When he heard that she was getting some resistance from hauliers, when she wanted them to give their services for free, Bob said, 'promise them tickets for the greatest show on earth'.

She did, it worked, and Bob delivered on his promise but he did more.

Dee was really touched when Bob said, 'of course you will go to the concert as well'. This was a bit like saying Cinderella you shall go to the ball. Dee was even more touched when he said, 'I have got you in the £100 seats', and then he added, 'you will be in the royal line-up and will meet Charles and Diana'. And she did, and then Bob made sure she watched the concert from the royal box. She has pictures of herself a few feet away from David Bowie, and Prince Charles and Princess Diana. And as Dee flicked through the programme she saw her name and was moved to tears.

I only heard this story recently. I know how much was going on in Bob's life in the run up to Live Aid, I feared for his mental and physical health, but he was making sure Dee Flower reaped what she sowed – I have no idea how he found the bandwidth for it but he did.

Talk about 'sliding doors' – what if that day Dee had got into her car and tuned into Capital Radio instead of Radio One – her life would have been different and who knows how Bob's trucking ambitions would have fared!

And to her surprise, at the Wembley concert Dee has a backstage pass. Not only had Cinderella gone to the ball, courtesy of her Prince Charming and courtesy of her invaluable contribution, she had an 'Access All Areas' pass.

Dee sees David Bowie in the distance and thinks she will ask him to sign her Live Aid programme. She saunters up, waiting for someone to stop her, but no one does. She chats to him and asks for his autograph in her programme. Her heart momentarily misses a beat when she hears him say, 'I am sorry' ...he is declining, but NO, he is saying, 'I am sorry I looked earlier but I think they forgot to put me in the programme'.

He isn't miffed, he isn't angry, but just a bit disappointed. 'Oh no,' Dee says, 'I saw you in here' – and the trucker and the superstar spend a few minutes looking for his picture which they find. David's face lights up and he signs – fact really can be stranger than fiction.

And David Bowie leaves Dee to go on stage, to give one of the best rock and roll performances in history, and to introduce a video to a billion people – which is arguably one of the most moving moments ever on TV.

And that is one branch of the Band Aid story, a branch oozing with flowers – and as I wrote that I had no idea what a terrible pun it was!

———————————

The story wasn't completely over. Bob wrote a global best seller autobiography and when Dee bought her copy there she was in the photos. Her kids were impressed, but not as impressed as they were when she showed them her photo in the pop music magazine Smash Hits, with David Bowie, Bob Geldof, Charles and Diana !

And Dee got colleagues involved; Peter Acton started Trans Aid, which whilst it might have a different meaning now, was transport for aid.

It's still going and has had Princess Anne involved and I am told Trans Aid has done wonderful things. Peter also invented a board game called Humanitarian Logistics, not the snappiest of names, but a useful game!

Dee also got Phil Butterworth Hayes on board. He worked on an aviation publication and he helped organise air transport for Band Aid.

So the 'pied piper' turned Dee into a 'pied piper' and the oak tree grew more branches. Strong, firm, useful branches that would help complete the route to where the aid needed to be. The writer of the musical never knew of Dee, but in some ways he was writing 'of her' and the audience would certainly have given Dee a standing ovation!

CHAPTER 14

A TRILOGY OF DATES

This is a subject on which I hope I have not been ambivalent.

Was the 26th November 1984 the best day of my life?

No ... but it was up there with as one of the most important days of my life along with the 10th March 1984 the day I met the love of my life, Caroline. Let me deal with the latter first. In March 1984 I was 31 years old enjoying life professionally and personally and as far from settling down as one can be. Then I went to a party in the glamorous hot spot of 91 Twickenham Road, Leytonstone, London.

It was a normal Saturday night – no reason to think it was anything other than a usual Saturday night party. I followed normal protocol, I went into the kitchen and got myself a beer and strolled into the front room to survey the landscape, before I would return to the kitchen as Jona Lewie sang 'You'll Always Find Me In The Kitchen At Parties'.

In the front room I surveyed the scene and saw a very pretty girl. I can picture my glance like a frozen photo – she was wearing a white blouse and a pencil skirt but most importantly she was wearing the most extraordinary smile.

I made eye contact and then retired to the kitchen as there was a slight complication, as I was there with another girl. Anyhow, I was assimilating the situation and then casually returned to the front room but 'the vision' had disappeared. I later found she had gone, for a long time, to the station to meet her friends.

I carried on partying which is a grand description for having a few more beers. Anyhow, eventually 'the vision' returned and conveniently returned to the kitchen where I seemed to be stuck to the floor as usual.

However, the stickiness didn't prevent me crossing the Lino to say 'hi' – and then 'the vision' spoke. I had no idea what was coming out of her mouth. I could not understand a single word she said – not a word! I thought she was from Liverpool, but then it transpired she was from Northern Ireland, Derry – most certainly not Londonderry – the original Derry girl!

For two hours I tried, mainly unsuccessfully, to understand what she was saying. Later turning to her perspective, as I subsequently heard, she thought we were getting on quite well until at 1.00am she was surprised when a girl tapped me on the shoulder and said, 'time to go'.

That could have been an end of things but the girl tapping me on the shoulder was not a long-term relationship, so I pursued 'the vision' through friends, getting her telephone number, and going out a few times.

I thought things were going quite well and then one night I called and said,

"Fancy going out on Thursday?"

I got the very definitive cold shoulder with that classic line,

"I can't, I am washing my hair."

I was a bit thrown, maybe even hurt /bruised ego, but I threw in an ace from my hand of cards,

"Oh that's a shame, I have two tickets for Billy Joel and his after-show party." I could hear the sound of breaking glass as the shampoo and conditioner went out the window. Maybe I have the Piano Man to thank for a 40 year relationship and 3 kids! Though maybe I would have been washing my hair if I had known what a spirited girl I was engaging with.

She insisted that one day in Derry she got asked out 12 times and told me the Derry men were the best looking men in the world!

She also told me about the Saturday in Derry when as a qualified hairdresser it was nearing the end of the shift and the girls would, as they finished with their clients, start doing each others' hair to prepare for their night on the town.

Now bear in mind this was very much in the midst of 'The Troubles' in Ireland. The door to the salon abruptly swung open and a guy in a balaclava mask came in pointing a gun around the salon.

Unfortunately for him, he went up to 'the vision', (aka Caroline) and pointed the gun at her and shouted, "OPEN THE TILL!"

He took a breath as he waited for his command to be acted on - but to his shock and horror he heard this mad woman, (aka Caroline), reply, "NO."

"What do you mean, no? he said with decreasing confidence.

She replied, "NO ... I am drying my hair, open it yourself."

As I am telling this story I am actually feeling sorry for the gunman – this was most certainly not part of the script!

Caroline subsequently felt guilty, because he then went to another girl, made her open the till and then fled the salon with some pretty paltry fruits of his crime. Derry is not a big place and his balaclava mask was not top of the range so a couple of days later Caroline passed the robber in the street and gave him a withering look. Again I am feeling sorry for him - but the story is not quite over.

A few weeks later Caroline, like most of Ireland, was on a coach to see the pope on his visit to Ireland. On the coach an attractive young man sidled up to her and asked if she would like to go out for a drink. I don't know if it was the 12th or 13th request of the day, but his interest was not completely rebuffed, and he felt he should share with Caroline a piece of pertinent information. 'I hope it won't put you off, but I suppose you should know that my brother is in court next week for the armed robbery on your salon'!

Yes, truth can be stranger than fiction!

But the Trilogy was nothing to do with this. I am trying to make sure I am not creating any ambiguity! I have told this next story so many times that I suspect people roll their eyes. I have even told the story on Ireland's iconic The Late Late Show - gaining me kudos with my Irish cousins.

Bob asked me to do JUST FOR ONE HOUR'S work and I couldn't charge for it and here I am 40 years later doing many hours work every week and undoubtedly having given millions of pounds of my time for free – but do I feel badly done by? Oh my goodness NO, it was and is as nearly as important to me as meeting 'my vision'.

I could start off on a moral high position, and say I have worked to save lives, but I have never spent a second patting myself on the back for that. In spite of the quite correct critical analysis of the achievements of Band Aid I am left in no doubt in very, very simple terms we achieved a lot.

There was a time when the economic progress of Ethiopia was going to be an astonishing success story and then the Ethiopian government managed to snatch defeat from the jaws of victory by engaging in civil war.

However, I have spent nearly 40 years considering grant applications, making the grants and reading the reports of the implementing of the grants – and I have seen on paper and on my visits to Ethiopia the many tangible successes.

In one sense these next few pages are going to be shallow stories of my personal rewards for the contribution I made, but I hope I explain that the satisfaction I got from the work we have done, and continue to do, exceeds the value that millions of pounds of professional fees could have given.

One morning I went into my office in Paddington as I always did. I had left home at 7.00am – I had driven in, parked in the car park, had a cup of tea and a cheese roll at the cafe around the corner, sat down at my desk at 8.00 am and started opening the post!

I needed to be particularly efficient today as I was leaving the office at 11.00 am to travel to Paris to see Arsenal play in a European cup final. I went through the post, and one particular envelope looked unfamiliar, and when I opened it, it sort of looked like an incomprehensible circular.

But as the letter came into focus, and to my astonishment, I realised it was saying 'Her Majesty's Government is minded to recommend to Her Majesty the Queen to award you an honour' and asked if they were so minded would I be so minded to accept the honour?

I cannot tell you what a remarkable experience this was – I was alone in my office reading a not impressive piece of paper which was quite hard to follow and then in the bottom left hand corner was a very dodgy reference number 'JK /2432 /OBE'.

Oh my goodness, I was in line for an OBE.

I will never be able to do justice to what an extraordinary moment this was and I have never thanked Bob appropriately or enough. I really haven't!

At the time, he was probably the most famous person in the world and certainly the busiest, and yet extraordinarily he had found the time to lobby an enormous number of people, including the president of the Law Society, to make this happen.

After Bob, at this time - I was the only Band Aid trustee to be getting this award, not Midge who had co-written the song, not Harvey who has made Live Aid happen, not Michael Grade who had been director general of the BBC. For all of them their time would come and more, but astonishingly Bob had found the time to make this happen.

This was actually a milestone in the music industry at large – it had been a long, long time since the Queen had granted any honours to the music industry, and now a lawyer from a converted Indian restaurant in Paddington was showing the way, thanks to Sir Bob Geldof being just an astonishing human being.

That day I went off to Paris in a daze … but there is a side story. The dodgy piece of paper said don't tell anyone. A previous girlfriend had told me I was born middle-aged and that was borne out by my behaviour. As directed I didn't tell anyone, not even Caroline, and then the Thursday before it would be announced on the Saturday in The Times newspaper, we were (unusually) watching Coronation Street on the TV, and one of the characters, I think a local councillor told his wife, against the rules, that he was going to be awarded an OBE. So I casually dropped into the conversation, over my cup of tea with Caroline,

"Oh, I am getting one of those."

She looked at me as if to say, 'WHAT!!! are you talking about?'

And I said, equally low key,

"Yes I am going to get an OBE."

You know decades later this remains surreal – the son of an Irish republican telling his Catholic wife from Derry that he was about to be a member of the Order of the British Empire as a result of an episode of Coronation Street!

Bob, I have no idea how you found the time, or the energy, or inclination, but even now I find it astonishing that you did this – and if I have never said thank you properly ... THANK YOU.

I can't even remember how, or why, this was a Trilogy, and I realise it hasn't been clear, but I think it was meeting 'the vision', and the 26th November 1984 when I was hired 'JUST FOR ONE HOUR', and the 10th May 1995; the date I realised, I the son of an Irish republican, was going to join the Order of the British Empire – ultimately to be presented to me by Prince Charles at Buckingham Palace.

You know, until I wrote this I had never looked up that date of 10th May 1995. I didn't realise it was 11 years later, but to my mind it makes me love it more. We had all worked all those years with no expectation of even thanks, and somehow Bob had found the time and energy to do that.

AGAIN ... Bob, if I never said thank you – then THANK YOU – from the bottom of my heart!

AND I still don't know why this chapter was called the Trilogy! I can see it's a bit indulgent as a chapter but if you can't be indulgent in your own book when can you?

And I can be indulgent because I am self-publishing this book.

I had the pleasure of co-producing the Live 8 concerts, co-producing the Live Aid and Live 8 DVDs and executive producing the Band Aid 30 record.

After Live 8 Bob, Harvey and I were awarded the honour of Chevalier de L'Ordre des Arts et des Lettres by the French government for our work on Live 8. This is a very prestigious honour, the equivalent of being a 'Sir' in France. And in the same week in Cannes we were given an award as music personalities of the year – again for our work on Live 8. These are very satisfying moments in anyone's life and I particularly relished them.

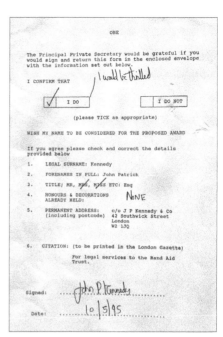

OBE : Offer from 10 Downing Street, May 1995.   My reply ... "I would be thrilled".

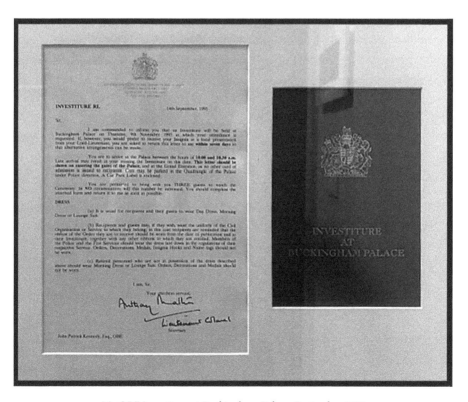

My OBE Investiture at Buckingham Palace, September 1995.

As I near the end of my career in the music industry, I knew I wanted to write a book, just for writing down some experiences which to me were 'pinch me' experiences – 'is this really happening' moments!

So I found myself an agent.

At first he was enthusiastic.

He was particularly enthusiastic about me writing a book solely about Band Aid and Live Aid for the 40th anniversaries. He said I could get 'a big advance'.

And I said,

"I would feel a bit disingenuous about doing that as the big picture is Bob's story."

"Yes", he said "...but Bob won't write it."

And I replied,

"Well, then that would make it even more wrong for me to do it'.

He actually agreed with me – we agreed I would do MY book.

I sent him a couple of chapters. I was encouraged by the reply,

"John, dynamite, really, really, really good."

Subsequently I said, "How confident are you of getting a deal?"

Immediate response, "VERY CONFIDENT – just sorting now."

And then ... complete and utter silence.

Even when I nudged him, so then I sent the email that I knew the answer to – but didn't want to hear;

'Is it fair to say this is now unlikely to find a home?'

And the simple but blunt reply ...

'Unfortunately, no.'

So no financial or editorial help from a publisher ... but then no one telling me what I can or can't do. So there is no one to send this chapter back to me saying in red pen 'SCRAP THIS CHAPTER, TOO INDULGENT, WHO CARES HOW YOU MET YOUR WIFE'!

Well actually, I do!

And I will finish this chapter with the most indulgent of stories, and one which makes a nonsense of the chapter being called a trilogy but ....

When we re-recorded the original song for Band Aid 30 it was to raise money and awareness to fight the Ebola virus outbreak that was devastating a completely different area of Africa to Ethiopia.

When Bob announced the record on The X Factor, (the British TV series), he introduced the video with words which have subsequently taken on a much greater significance. The video had controversially opened with someone dying of Ebola.

Bob said, "This is hard core to allow The X Factor nation to watch this … this is the most anti-human disease, but we can stop it and will stop it." …"IT COULD BE HERE – IT COULD BE A BRITISH PROBLEM."

These prescient words were six years before the COVID epidemic, as we sat in our living rooms feeling safe.

The video was played on the TV programme and in the next few hours the great British public, moved by the graphic images, donated one million pounds – a million pounds in just hours!

The record was number 1 in 69 countries and raised £3 million. There were also French and German versions.

As a fund raiser and as an awareness raiser, this 30 year old song had been wheeled out, updated, and done its job again.

I thought it was time to honour the song again.

So I approached the organisers of the prestigious Ivor Novello Awards and suggested it was time to present Bob and Midge with a special Ivor Novello Award.

I was pushing at an open door and they agreed to present a special anniversary award. There are many awards in the music industry, but for any songwriter this is the most coveted and cherished. We all turned up for a nice lunch at a posh London hotel and the award was announced.

As ever, in collecting the award, Bob had the right words.

Harking back to 1984, he said,

"It struck me at the time that to die of want in a world of surplus was not only intellectually absurd and economically illiterate, but morally repulsive."
…"and when we started, Africa was considered to be the basket case of the planet. Today standing here in front of you, seven of the top ten fastest growing economies on the planet are in Africa – and of those seven, five are where Band Aid operates."

And then I was in for a wonderful surprise.

My daughter was at work and received some texts from a friend of hers who worked in the industry, and was pleased to be at the awards because it always attracted a galaxy of stars, and was an entertaining lunch.

What happened is best explained from their perspective – the friend is Katie and my daughter is Ellie.

They exchanged the following texts;

KATIE : Ellie did you say your dad worked in the music industry?

ELLIE : Yep.

KATIE : Bob Geldof is on stage collecting an award and he just mentioned your dad.

ELLIE : That's nice.

KATIE : Wow, he just spent some time about how important your dad's contribution was to Band Aid, Live Aid and the last 30 years.

ELLIE : Great.

KATIE : You may be surprised to know your dad is now on stage, the room is on their feet in a standing ovation, cheering and applauding your dad and Bob is giving him his Ivor Novello, saying 'you deserve this' ... and your dad then dedicated it to your mum.

In a blaze of immodesty I will set out what Bob said, because it meant a lot then, and it still does.

"This would have never worked, it cannot work, without a man who was born and bred in the industry. John Kennedy was a young lawyer at the start of this, he became president of Universal Music, he then subsequently forced through the EU legislation that allowed our great musicians to enjoy an extended copyright period."

"... John is without question one of the smartest people I have ever met, and I trust him to the deepest pit of my soul and for that he will never get an Ivor Novello Award but I want to give him this one."

There aren't many better moments in life!

CHAPTER 15

THE UNIVERSAL YEARS

So at the end of chapter 6, I explained how I went from running a small, but successful, legal practice in a converted Indian restaurant to being chairman and ceo of the biggest and most successful record company in the UK and CEO of a film company.

It took some adapting, but was simply incredible fun.

In my old role, apart from working very long hours, I would drive myself to work and having parked in a NCP car park, stop in a very basic working man's cafe and have a cheese roll before opening up the office.

Now each morning a chauffeur was waiting outside my house to whisk me to the Polygram office, and if on the way in I decided I needed to go to New York for business then I would ask my secretary to book me a ticket on Concorde.

Instead of five employees I had one thousand across nine different sites and our company turned over half a billion pounds. A learning curve – yes. Pressure – yes. Tiring – yes, but I would not have swapped it for the world.

Our artists included U2, Elton John, Pavarotti, Lionel Richie, Bon Jovi and so many more. Our films included Trainspotting, Four Weddings and a Funeral, Notting Hill, and Mr Bean.

When I first went to the airport on a trip in my new role, a lady from British Airways asked if she could meet me in the Concorde lounge. There she proceeded to, very reverently, hand over to me a Premier Card. This was not just a relation of a Gold Card but something much, much higher. She explained that if I needed to get on a flight, if it was full, a space would be found for me. Of course she didn't quite say 'we will kick someone off' but that's what she meant. If I was late for a flight they would meet me as I arrived at the terminal, and would escort me to the plane, and would even hold up departure for me.

I remember on a few occasions being in the centre of New York on a Friday evening knowing I was on the 8.30pm flight to London, but when meetings finished a bit earlier thinking maybe I could make an earlier flight. I checked the timetable but no 7.30pm flight but one at 6.30pm. Well it was 5.00pm and I was in central Manhattan and it was an hour to the airport and

I didn't have a seat booked. I thought, well why not call the special Premier Card number I had been given? It was answered immediately, 'yes of course Mr Kennedy, if you can get to the terminal by 6.00pm we will escort you to the plane and you will be in seat 1A for the 6.30pm flight to London'.

Of course my wife frequently explained that I got so used to this treatment that I would expect to be treated like a VIP at home! FAT CHANCE of that being married to one of the original Derry Girls! But this lady from British Airways, who was so reverently handing me my Premier Card, offered one very important caveat. 'Mr Kennedy it is important that you understand one thing – this card is not being given to you personally, it is being given to you because you are the chairman of Polygram music and films, and should you no longer be in that role the card expires IMMEDIATELY'.

A very well-known USA lawyer had already advised me it was not a question of *if* I would be fired but *when* I would be fired. Of course he was right, and the British Airways lady was right, but fortunately I like Ryanair and EasyJet, and occasionally I splash out on speedy boarding.

I assumed I was moving from a world of law to an environment of cutting edge creativity, technology and commerce. The UK industry was represented at an umbrella level by a trade organisation called the British Phonographic Industry (BPI) – as chairman of the largest UK music company I partly funded this organization, and of course had a seat on the board. I was looking forward to my first meeting which of course was attended by the heads of all the music companies. I arrived at my first meeting with a sense of apprehension as I was the new boy in town, I went to sit in a random seat and was told,

"You can't sit there, Pete sits there."

"Oh, OK" – I choose another random seat.

"No not there, Paul sits there."

So of course I eventually ask,

"Where can I sit?"

I ended up thinking this feels like establishment bureaucracy set in its way, rather than a dynamic disruptive force.

In my new company we were not getting off to a flying first quarter – in fact, virtually all of our companies were underperforming. Hopefully it was just a spell we were going through but I was trying to get to the root of our problems. This was 1996, chart success was crucial to companies and artists, and for decades record companies had indulged in the practice of chart hyping – an illegal practice that was basically a deception of the public.

To be fair, there was a time when this illegal practice paid dividends, but with the charts now being prepared by new technology it was increasingly becoming a futile practice – but old habits die hard.

I had four record companies in the business of needing chart success reporting to me. The chart hyping was a truly primitive exercise. Record companies would sell their singles to record stores for £1 and then go and buy the records from the stores for £1.99 making a loss of 99p on each record. The idea was that each one of these fraudulent purchases would register as a genuine purchase, and so start moving the record up the charts enabling it to get more radio and TV exposure, and maybe even get a coveted spot on Top of the Pops.

I was pretty convinced this simply didn't work anymore, but as the newcomer I knew I had to tread carefully, but I only had so much patience.

So, first a meeting with the four relevant managing directors and our sales director. All of those, and indeed all of our competitors, pretended chart hyping did not exist – it was never to be mentioned – so you can imagine I got their attention when I said,

"Right let's discuss chart hyping."

I was not for turning,

"Do any of you hype the charts?"

Stunned silence ... no eye contact ... everyone studying the empty writing pads in front of them.

"OK" I say, "For the moment, let's assume this is not the ex-lawyer taking a moral stance - I know you are all doing it and I can see in your accounts the huge sums you are spending – for the moment my position is not one of morality but just that you are all f*cking useless at it – just look at our chart positions, you are achieving nothing but going back and doing the same thing, again and again, achieving nothing."

I continued,

"I will not mention this again for three months and then we will revisit this again, and if I still think we are wasting our time and money I will end chart hyping."

They couldn't help laughing at that – good luck with that – to be fair to them it had been ingrained in the industry for decades.

Three months later we reconvened. I could demonstrate that they had made no progress. I said,

"Right, I advise you all to go clean because in one month's time the proverbial is going to hit the fan."

So one month later I attended the monthly BPI meeting which commenced at 9.30am. We worked through the agenda to 12.40pm and many were preparing to head to the door for their business lunch.

The chairman said,

"Right – any other business?"

The answer was always 'no' because everyone wanted to head off to lunch.

To everyone's surprise I said,

"Yes, just one item – chart hyping." I could feel in the room, 'WTF'! A couple of people who were already at the exit returned to their seats.

"Mr chairman," I said, "May I propose a motion – *This organisation deplores and condemns the practice of chart hyping.*" 'WTF'!

The chairman was stunned, "Er, er, er, who is proposing the motion?"

"I am." I said.

"OK, who will second the motion?" ... nobody.

So, I said, "Mr chairman, can I suggest you second it."

"John that would be unusual."

"Yes Mr chairman, unusual but not unconstitutional – I presume you agree with the motion?"

"Of course, of course!"

"OK then, rather than start with all those in favour, can we ask for a show of those against."

Everyone wanted to raise their hand, but knew they couldn't.

"Motion carried!" I suggested. 'WTF'!

And I continued, "I have a second motion Mr chairman." 'WTF'!

"I propose, *This organisation agrees that if it finds any evidence of chart hyping it will call in the Metropolitan Police to investigate.*" 'WTF'!

By the same process it was carried without opposition. 'WTF'!

"Mr chairman, one last motion." 'WTF'!

"In the event this organisation finds that one of its members has engaged in chart hyping in view of the unacceptable fraudulent deception of the public it will encourage a prison sentence for everyone involved in the practice."

Motion carried by the same procedure.

Simon Napier Bell, the manager of Wham and journalist, wrote; 'From that moment the decades old practice of chart hyping in the UK was over.'

The chairman of the BPI told me that normally if he called a record company chairman it would take two or three days for them to get back to him, but for the next two months his calls were returned in five minutes! They were worried they had been caught hyping!

On 31st August 1997 I went to check out of my hotel in Corsica where I had been holidaying with my family. As I paid the bill, the lady on reception asked,

"Are you going back to the UK?"

I said, "yes" and she said, "A very sad day for the UK."

I thought how odd – in fact, how rude!

But as I went back to our room I of course wondered what she meant. I turned on the TV to see the news about Princess Diana's fatal car crash. Oh my goodness, yes, a very, very, sad day for the country.

When I went into my office on the Monday at a very early stage I was contacted by Elton John's manager. Elton and Diana had had a rollercoaster relationship, but a month earlier at Gianni Versace's funeral, Diana had been seen comforting Elton. Of course Elton was devastated by the tragic news of Diana's death and had contacted his writing partner, Bernie Taupin, to rewrite some of the lyrics from their huge hit *'Candle in the Wind'* – the new lyrics were very moving and poignant.

I was being contacted as chairman of Elton's record company, did I think it was a good idea to release the new version, and if so was it possible to do it quickly. Of course I thought it was a great idea and we would pull out all the stops to get it out quickly, but I said it was very important it should be a charity record as no one should be seen to be profiting from such a terrible tragedy. I have little doubt that Elton would have given his royalties away anyhow but I was now suggesting that our company would not make a profit on the record. Elton's manager thought this was a great idea and appropriate. When I told my bosses, the chief financial officer was less appreciative, suggesting 'couldn't we take a lesser profit' – 'No, I said No!'

It's astonishing how soon after Diana's death the funeral was, the following Saturday, with all that we have seen in films and The Crown about the Royal Family's behaviour it seemed to be much later.

At the time we agreed to put out the recording, it was NOT the plan that Elton would sing the song at the funeral, but I was confident it would be a huge commercial success and raise money for charity – at this stage we did not know what charity! Sounds a bit Deja Vu of my first day on the Band Aid Team! The new version became known as *'Candle in the Wind 1997'*, or more poignantly *'Goodbye England's Rose'*.

This was a very sad week but of course with the most astonishing tide of emotion coming from the public for The People's Princess.

We were busy making arrangements for the release of the single, we heard through the grapevine that Richard Branson's Virgin Records was going to put out an album as a tribute to Diana. To be fair, he like Elton was apparently also a friend of the princess, and in fact I have just read on Wikipedia that he was the person whose idea it was to redo 'Candle in the Wind' – I have no idea if Elton would agree with that but maybe it was.

I got a message one day that week saying Virgin Records have asked about arrangements for us to send over the master tapes for the new version of 'Candle In the Wind' for their album.

What? I ignored it.

As you can imagine, Elton was grieving and by now it was clear he would sing the song at the funeral. I decided I would wait until Elton or his manager asked me to make it available for the album.

I actually did not think it was a good idea. It was clear this song had touched a nerve with the public, the new version and the performance were shaping up to be an iconic piece of history and a huge charity fundraiser. I did not think the impact should be diluted by it also being on an album.

Even if I say so myself we produced a very tasteful package. There were two songs, 'Something About The Way You Look Tonight' and 'Candle in the Wind 1997' – there is a picture of a rose and the line;

'In loving memory of Diana Princess of Wales.'

Like millions, or more likely billions, around the world I watched the funeral service.

As the service finished my mobile phone rang, it was Richard Branson – I was very surprised as I had just seen him on TV at the actual service.

"John," he said, "I must have Candle in the Wind for my album."

I said, "I don't think that's a good idea, but of course it's not my decision, and Richard this is not the day or time to discuss it."

Richard said, "But I need a decision now, as the album is about to be manufactured."

I replied, "Richard I won't have this discussion now – in fact, it would have to be Elton's decision and I am certainly not going to contact him today." Richard was charming as he always is but clearly very, very annoyed.

As things unfolded the record sold 33 million singles around the world – I have a gold disc commemorating that. Of course the money took some time to come in, but then Elton and I took a cheque for £33 million to Kensington Palace. The cheque was payable to THE DIANA PRINCESS OF WALES MEMORIAL FUND.

I am a huge Elton fan, as an artist and as a human being - I intend to finish this book with a very simple Elton story.

He has had quite a life, as is shown by the biopic Rocketman, but he has ended up in a wonderful place as an artist, as a businessman, and as a family with David and their two sons.

He does of course get credit as a humanitarian and an activist, but I have never felt the credit is equal to his astonishing achievements. What he and David have done in the fight against AIDS around the world is astonishing – there is a book to be written about that – the sums raised are mind-boggling, but the activism and awareness work beats even that.

No number could be put on the lives saved by the Elton John AIDS Foundation – never mind Saint Bob, it should also have been Saint Elton!

One of the more entertaining ways in which Elton and David raised funds was a party every May at their home 'Woodside' in Windsor, Berkshire. For a long time, Caroline and I had the good fortune to attend every year. These were astonishingly, stylish affairs packed with celebrities, but the one which stands out in my mind is the very first one because it was the most intimate and for me particularly memorable for one faux pas and one great incident!

But just before that story, I need to explain that having given up my solid safe business of 12 years to run Polygram music and films I suddenly found myself in unexpected and uncharted waters. I had made my decision to make my move based on three things; Alain Levy had wanted me onboard, my boss would be my friend/client Roger Ames, and a good solid contract. Then in 1998 the Universal group decided to takeover Polygram, and after a very short while it was clear Alain and Roger would not stay – they had other options. In theory I would be chairman of the new UK company but that was by no means a certainty, my future was in the hands of the new incoming CEO for Universal Music International, Jorgen Larsen, and he was giving me mixed signals. There wasn't much I could do about it, Caroline and I had our third child on the way, I had a great parachute clause in my contract so 'Que Sera, Sera'.

So in May 1998, I was working hard and enjoying myself and actually pinching myself about the experiences I was having as part of my work duties. On a balmy night I found myself with about 200 others in Elton and David's garden at Windsor for the first, ELTON JOHN'S WHITE TIE AND TIARA BALL. This was to become an annual event, all astonishingly stylish, but none to beat this first one to my mind.

It was celebrity packed and everyone's neck was sore from making sure they wouldn't miss anyone famous. I was standing with a group of say four guys and four girls, and there was a group of super models a few yards away. The guys were looking at these beautiful girls and fully understanding why they were called 'supermodels' and why 'they did not get out of bed for less than £10,000 a day'. However, the girls had a different perspective and had noticed that one of these young ladies had less than perfect skin – to my mind making much more of it than was warranted or was kind.

As the discussion continued, I could see in the distance my new boss approaching. He himself was a very sophisticated man who spoke eight languages fluently - his wife was very elegant, and apart from also being an accomplished linguist, was a descendant of the Wagner family – for them watching the 15 hours of the Ring Cycle was pure bliss. They had both been very nice to me, but in the next few weeks Jorgen would decide to hire me or fire me, so it was a slightly uncomfortable dynamic when they came to join our group – only slightly – I welcomed them and introduced them to the group, some of whom they already knew.

Almost immediately the much maligned supermodel walked past and every male admired the wonderful dress she was wearing which again made it clear why she was a supermodel – at this very moment my new boss's wife said, 'oh my goodness look at her skin'.

Dear reader … it's best at this stage if you are sitting down.

In what is not a text book approach to charming the man who is about to decide on your future career, or his wife, I find myself saying,

"Well, I would not kick her out of bed to let you in."

I can recall it so clearly – of course today I would be fired for it with no parachute payment, and even then I remember trying desperately to see if I could suck the words back into my mouth. I remember again so clearly the absolute astonishment on my boss's face and his wife's, but most of all the mutual colleagues faces.

Caroline was seven and a half months pregnant and it is a miracle she did not go into labour.

And I had not had a single drop of alcohol!

To her absolute credit, Ms Wagner laughed out loud and took it in great spirit, and I would say it broke the ice between us – to my mind we got on quite well from that moment onwards, but I am sure most will consider that being me and rose-tinted glasses. I can give an explanation but I accept it is that – an explanation, not an excuse.

As I grew up I was one of six children – and as with most families in the 1960s, life revolved around a room where you ate and watched TV. My sister Pat was working for a record company and would have been the more sophisticated of us, and my brother Maurice was a bit of a lad about town.

On more than one occasion sitting in front of the polluting coal fire, a number of us would be watching 'telly' when Pat would say about a female character something like 'look at the state of her' and Maurice would say, 'well, I wouldn't kick her out of bed to let you in' – so inappropriate in so many ways – but there it was in my memory and god only knows why I dredged it up in such a sophisticated location but I did!

Today those 12 words would have cost me all my termination payment, but as it turned out weeks later I wasn't fired, I was anointed as the CEO of the new enlarged UK company and my contract was extended.

But now let's go back to that balmy evening in Windsor.

It was time to go in for dinner – we were not all sitting on the same table – dinner was to be in this huge marquee – the tables would have done justice to a royal wedding reception and everyone was dressed in tails and tiaras. One of our guests was our good friend Carolyn – I once got myself into trouble by describing her as 'Caroline's friend Carolyn' at which she said, 'am I not your friend?' Like all of us she was milking in this magical setting and evening – there really was nothing to match it.

And at that moment, Carolyn saw Michael Douglas and Catherine Zeta Jones glide past to sit at Elton's table – this couple at the time were at the peak of their Hollywood royalty status.

Carolyn said to me,

"Oh my goodness, I am going to make sure I say hello to Michael."

To her mind they were both guests at the same dinner party so they were already on first name terms.

I explained to her that was not how things worked – when one was lucky enough to be invited to an event like this it was very important to leave celebrities alone. I was pretty sure she took it on board.

However, after champagne, lobster, caviar, white wine, red wine, and dessert wine, my advice seemed to fade from her memory. I saw Carolyn push back her chair, and even if I didn't realise the significance of that my wife Caroline did, and took the view – blow that, if Carolyn was going to meet Michael Douglas then so was she. I watched them make a beeline for Michael, certainly not in a subtle way, but undoubtedly enhanced by being two beautiful women in their finest evening wear.

I was left standing on my own. After about 10 minutes, I thought I would head over. As I did so, I could feel a very strong vibe from Carolyn and Caroline who were indeed chatting away to Michael, that basically was emitting – 'stay away we are doing just fine without you'.

So I took this onboard, and paused a good distance away, and as I did so I suddenly heard very loud,

"Oh my goodness, John how fabulous to see you." – at which point Catherine Zeta Jones came over and gave me the most fantastic hug.

It was lovely, and certainly got Michael's attention, who dumped Caroline and Carolyn, came over to myself and Catherine, proffered his hand and said,

"I don't think we have met."

To say Carolyn and Caroline were miffed would be an understatement – to explain – I had represented Catherine when she signed a record deal with Sony. The three of us had a lovely chat, and at the end Catherine said,

"John, we must have dinner."

To which Michael said, "Yes John, we must."

The unforgettable evening finished at 3.30am with the sun trying to rise in the sky and the birds singing with every guest leaving with a goodie bag worth thousands of pounds. SUCH STYLE!

So now I was working for Universal. Universal was owned by Seagram which was owned by the Bronfman family - the move for the Seagram family into the media world had happened at the behest of Edgar Bronfman Junior, a smart, sophisticated man.

Soon after I had been anointed to my role, he asked if I could see him urgently – to my mind if your boss's boss, who owns the company, asks to see you urgently, then the answer is 'Yes of course, when do you want'.

So I went to see him in his townhouse, there he gave me a copy of a letter from U2's lawyers basically saying that their contract with Polygram / Universal was in restraint of trade, so they would be terminating it.

I would not say he was at his wits' end – but he was nervous.

I said, "Let me read the letter."

It was well written and their declaration that the contract was invalid was supported by advice from an eminent UK barrister.

After I had read it for the second time, Edgar said, "What do you think?"

I replied, "I don't want to sound immodest but I am an expert in this area, and I am not convinced by their arguments."

He asked me for percentages. I replied,

"It sounds like they are prepared to litigate and obviously we would get our own legal advice, but litigation is an unpredictable arena, but I think you are 80 per cent OK."

He said, "That gives me some comfort, but I have just paid 10 billion for this company, I could not take even a 20 per cent chance of losing our biggest and maybe coolest and most credible act."

I smiled and said, "The band, their manager, and their advisers are smart – they know that and that is exactly why they have done this and done it now!"

Then the words, "John I need you to sort this for me."

No pressure then!

But fair enough, I was the well remunerated chairman of the company that U2 were signed to. As I left the office, Edgar added,

"And I need you to 'sort it' – QUICKLY."

Again, fair enough.

So the next week I headed off to New York on Concorde to meet the band's attorney. I was criticised for not making him come to me, and for not fielding our lawyers rather than me the chairman of the company, but I knew my adversary quite well and I preferred this dynamic. I wanted to cut through the bullshit and didn't want messages through intermediaries to get misquoted and cause problems.

I said, "Allen, I come in peace – I think your argument that you can walk away from the contract is bullshit, and if your actions damage the company's share price that leaves your clients quite exposed if a court agrees with us, but I come in peace."

Allen was not in a rush and for a few hours we sparred with no real progress, and then he said, "Let's resume tomorrow."

I said, "OK, I will get one of our lawyers to meet with you tomorrow – I have a business to run so I am on the last flight to London this evening."

He was shocked, "You are leaving this evening?'

I said, "Yes."

In the next two hours we sorted out 90 per cent of the deal we would eventually sign, and we did the final 10 per cent a week later when I did the same thing Concorde in – last flight out that evening.

It was a good deal for them, cleverly strategised by the U2 team – a relatively small price for Edgar to not lose the gloss on his 10 billion acquisition – a win-win in the spirit of compromise, but with an even greater cherry on the cake. In that year we would release, not one, but two U2 greatest hits albums in an era where such releases were hugely profitable. That year our UK company had its most profitable year ever and it would be a long time before that profit was exceeded.

I went to Dublin to meet the band and celebrate the new deal. They were charming and welcoming and whilst I gave them a substantial cheque they gave me a signed drawing by Peter Blake of three great Irish writers, including James Joyce. I was very touched and I tell my kids that cost more than a Picasso.

The new deal worked for everyone and of course Edgar stayed in harmonious business with one of the greatest bands of all time – one that is still signed to Universal today and no band has ever stayed together for longer!

During the 1990s Christmas was a very important time in the music industry. I have often driven people mad with my summary of commerce in the music industry, 'if you have hits you will be successful and if you don't you won't'.

My chief financial officer at Polygram did not really understand why, with to his mind no relevant experience, I was the chairman and his boss. He was one of those guys who loved those books you see at the airport about being a success in business. He cut me a bit of slack for my first six months and we finished 1996 in a perfectly fine financial position – not gangbuster but fine. At the beginning of 1997 he tried to put me on the spot in one of our management meetings with, 'what is your strategy for 1997?'

He was horrified by my answer, 'my aim is that we have four albums in the top 10 for Christmas.' He was dismissive – 'that isn't a business strategy'. But he was wrong – we were the market leaders – a huge percentage of sales took place in December; this was a time when people would give CDs and DVDs for Xmas. Most record retailers lost money up until the middle of November and then made their profits in the last six weeks of the year.

I knew if we had four albums in the top 10 during December we would beat our financial targets, if we had three albums then we might match our financial targets, if we only had two then we would be in 'Dire Straits' – if you excuse the pun. Our CFO hated this approach, he wanted life to be more complex than that.

As a record company our relations with record retailers were crucial, but even if we cultivated great relationships if we didn't have products that they and their customers, i.e. the public, wanted then the relationships could

With U2 ... 'Concorde diplomacy shuffling concluded'.

Sir Peter Blake limited edition print – a present from U2.

not help us. There were always tussles between us and the retailers about commercial trading terms . One area was that we gave them 30 days to pay us, but then a game would go on whereby they would drag out the 30 days, and a lot of time and energy was wasted and tension created whilst we chased for payment.

So I said, I am actually going to give you 60 days to pay but if we haven't been paid by then, then an automatic block goes on shipping product to you – no one will chase you, there will be no internal discussions. The 60 days was generous and the new system worked.

Then one January my new CFO, (I had to get myself a new one as the old one was convinced I didn't know what I was doing, even though we kept matching or beating our financial targets), came into my office with a frown on his face and said, "We have a problem."

"What's that?" I said, "We had a very successful Xmas, what problems could we have in January – all is good with the world."

He replied, "It seems as if Virgin Retail are not going to pay their outstanding bill." (I think it was £10 million)

I said, "Fine, as you know if they don't pay on time, we don't ship any more records."

"No" he said, "it's not just not paying on time, it's about not paying at all."

I said, "Is there any explanation being offered?"

He replied, "No, they just said Richard Branson will call you."

Well this was very odd – Virgin Retail was owned by Richard Branson – there was a time when some people thought 'he was not a very good businessman but a great PR manipulator'.

Well the 'doubting Thomases' about his business acumen were completely wrong – he has amassed great wealth as an entrepreneur, and in particular when he sold Virgin Records to EMI for a billion it was graphic evidence of a business acumen that some said didn't exist.

In any event he was also a genius at public relations.

I didn't really know what was going on – my gut instinct was that he wasn't paying because he couldn't pay for cash flow reasons, but I had no evidence that my gut instinct was correct.

What I was expecting was for him to take the PR lead and I tried to think what his move would be. This was a time when the media thought CD prices were too high, and so I thought it would be quite clever of him to say he was making a stand on behalf of music fans by taking on the largest record company by not paying them until they reduce prices. But he didn't play that card – he just didn't pay us – I presume we stopped supplying him and started proceedings.

I knew Richard – as a music business lawyer I had had numerous dealings with him – he was always fun and charming. I noticed he had a clever trick – he knew me, but he knew a lot of people, so I might be in a meeting with someone at Virgin Records, and he would join the meeting greeting me as a long lost friend, but almost certainly having said to the secretary sitting outside, 'remind me who that is in with Simon and Ken'.

I don't take that as insincere, just a clever trick to jog his memory.

He could be terrier-like, I was in my office on the 20th December 1989 – I was still a lawyer – it was our office party that afternoon, and so effectively the last day before Xmas. I was in a meeting with a client – I had a golden rule I didn't take any calls when I was in a meeting with a client – they had booked an appointment and to my mind they had my attention exclusively and without distractions. A rule that my long serving and long suffering secretary was only too familiar with, and knew that I strictly adhered to. Half way through the meeting to my surprise my phone rang. My secretary, Lesley, said, "I am very sorry John, it's Richard Branson insisting that he speaks to you now."

I was irritated and surprised because the newspapers that morning had been full of the fact that Richard was marrying his long-term partner on Necker Island that day – also it must be 6.00am there.

I said, "Lesley, please tell Richard I will have finished my meeting in 30 minutes and I will call him then."

Ten seconds later the phone rang again, it was Lesley profusely apologising and also laughing – she said,

"It's 6.00am there, he has promised his wife he won't make any business calls today – she gets up at 6.30am and if she catches him on a call she will call the wedding off."

I didn't believe a word of it, but you had to admit it was a good story – I apologised to the client in front of me and took the call.

Richard profusely thanked me for taking the call and for having saved his wedding day – of course you had to smile. He then launched into how his label Virgin Records had to sign my clients, Smith & Mighty, and there could be no greater indication of Virgin's vision, belief and commitment to my clients than the fact it was the only call he would be making on his wedding day and calling at 6.00am, and he was putting his marriage at peril by risking the wrath of his bride to be. It was a great pitch and his coup de grâce was that his bride to be was a huge music fan and there was no better news he could give his bride on her wedding day than the news that Smith & Mighty were signing to Virgin – I wanted to clap with admiration.

Unfortunately the dye was already cast, the artists and manager had already decided that they wanted to sign to London Records, but I said,

"Congratulations Richard on your big day, have a beautiful day – I promise to pass on your passion to my clients." And of course I did.

As I put down the phone – I laughed out loud – you had to admire his style and charm.

As it turned out, not having the band sign to Virgin may have been a lucky escape – it was an expensive deal, the album took a long time to make and was a critical, but not commercial, success – but I know from experience, there is no point offering someone like Richard that comfort – he would just have said 'if they had signed to Virgin they would have been global superstars'.

As an aside – one of the great things about the music industry is that, like boxing, it can take you from rags to riches and fame. I never went to Smith & Mighty's flat in Bristol but I was told it was not luxurious, and here they were being pursued on his wedding day by one of the richest and most famous people in the world from a Caribbean island that he owned – I am not sure you can get many greater contrasts than that!

And now back to Virgin Retail refusing to pay us millions that were due to us.

When my CFO came to tell me that Virgin weren't going to pay us, my CFO reminded me it was Tuesday. The reminder that it was Tuesday was a bit of banter. My job was stressful, but not like going down a mine stressful, or what I always describe as real world stress like – not like not being able to pay your electricity bill stressful. I had 1000 employees and we had a business turning over £500 million with profits of about £85 million. For that job I was handsomely rewarded, but I was out most nights and most weekends, but I did have one of the best jobs in the world, but I still, like most people, hoped for stress-free weekends with my family.

Anyhow I digress. One day I said to Pete my CFO – only half joking – let's say it's Friday afternoon and it's 4.00pm and we are sailing into the weekend and some bad news reaches your desk. I want you to take a view – is it something where I can improve the situation – if yes, tell me IMMEDIATELY – if it's something I can't do anything about, tell me about it Monday morning.

He looked unsure about this strategy – he said, "Give me an example."

I said, "If we need U2 to deliver their next album in July, but you hear they are going to deliver it in September, and we have it in our financial planning for 10 million copies, then tell me Monday. Because if I call up Bono on Friday afternoon and tell him he needs to buck up his ideas, he is going to tell me to f*ck off, and anyhow it wouldn't be a good idea, because it means the album isn't ready, so trying to get it delivered in July would not be smart."

Pete got the idea, even if he thought it wasn't very professional, and in fact a derogation of duty, but I am not sure he practiced it because that would have meant that he bore the brunt of the bad news over the weekend, whilst I slept like a baby. That seemed unfair given our respective salaries – better to download it to your boss who after all got paid the big bucks for soaking up and dealing with these problems.

Anyhow all of this was irrelevant, because as Pete had pointed out, it was a Tuesday.

I was mystified as to why Virgin were not paying. This wasn't a bill which could be open to dispute – they ordered records, we delivered them, they had sold them, now 60 days later they had to pay us.

As I say, I believe the sum was about £10 million.
At first the promised call from Richard did not materialize, but then on a Friday, Richard called me, 'would you come and see me on Monday'. I was tempted to go all alpha male and say, 'no you come and see me, you are in the wrong' – but I agreed to have a coffee with him at his home in Holland Park. In fact, I preferred to be on his home territory – in fact, the timing proved to be fortuitous.

I turned up Monday morning at his beautiful Holland Park villa.

It was an odd meeting. Richard at the best of times can mumble or even bumble – it is not a sign of poor intellect or even nerves it's just a mannerism which can be confusing, as you know you are engaging with a very successful man – sometimes it is a Performance. It was also odd because he would not say why he wasn't paying, but did imply that we would eventually get paid, but wasn't saying give me a certain amount of time, it was inconclusive. No mention of Singapore Airlines. Anyhow, a nice cup of coffee in an elegant house with a very interesting entrepreneur was an enjoyable start to the week.

Just before I got up to leave, I said,

"Richard I saw you on TV last night."

"Oh yes." he said. On Sunday evening, Richard had launched or re-launched his bid to run the National Lottery.

He said, "I think I have a good chance of being successful."

"Well," I said, "I believe the decision is made by Chris Smith, the culture secretary."

"Yes," he said, "it is."

I said, "By pure coincidence I have a meeting with him tomorrow on something else – and by way of polite conversation, he will ask me how business is, and I will mention our little problem, and I may or may not say, imagine if you awarded Richard the National Lottery and someone won £10 million but didn't get paid."

"You wouldn't, would you?"

By now, either correctly or incorrectly, I had formed the view that the Virgin empire had cash flow issues, and that the solution to those issues would be the conclusion of current negotiations to sell 49 per cent of Virgin airlines to Singapore airlines.

One Friday evening I am at Stansted airport with my family, about to fly on Ryanair to Derry. My phone rings, 'unknown caller'.

"Hi John, it's Richard."

I am about to say 'Richard who?' when I realise it's this Richard.

"Hi" I say.

He says, "I have decided to pay you." – not 'now I can afford to pay you'.

He says, "What can I do to get you most kudos with your bosses for having wrestled the money from me."

I laughed and said,

"Kind of you to think like that, but the simplest fastest bank transfer is all I need – actually I am as pleased for you as I am for me – I take it the Singapore Airlines deal has gone through?"

No response to that – just ... "thanks for your understanding"!

About this time, Richard was being knighted, and to show there were no hard feelings, he invited me to his post Buckingham Palace party at The Roof Gardens in Kensington which he owned, and in fact where I had had my wedding reception. At the party we engaged in conversation, not about our tussle, but about dyslexia because I knew he was dyslexic and so is my son. We discussed that some of the world's most successful people currently and in history were dyslexic. This very successful, entrepreneurial, business man explained,

"That it certainly hinders me in areas of finance, and I struggled with the concepts of gross and net profit, but my accountant told me to think of all the money coming in as a sea of money, and think of a fisherman's net being hauled in. When you haul it in lots flows out of the net, but what's left of the haul is yours – that's your net profit."

Well I thought, one way or another, your brain had adapted to help you build a fortune – good for you.

Years later my brother Michael met Richard at a party, and said to Richard,

"You might know my brother – he works in the record industry."

Richard said, "What's his name?"

"John Kennedy."

Richard laughed and said, with no hint of anger or resentment,

"Oh yes I know him, not only is your brother the only person who threatened to bankrupt me, he also tried to stop me getting the National Lottery!"

"Oh dear," my brother said, "Sorry."

"Oh no …" Richard said, "I deserved it."

It was a fantastic job running a record company – no two days were the same. Networking was important and three days a week I would stroll from my office along the river to the River Cafe which then, and now, was considered London's best restaurant. What a life.

One particular Tuesday in 1998, I was having lunch with two of our most important artist managers. After a very enjoyable and convivial lunch we were parting company, and just as part of the usual small talk as we went our separate ways, one of them asked me if I had a busy day. They were a bit taken aback by my answer;

"Well, I am having a baby at 5.30pm."

Of course this was not strictly true, Caroline was having the baby by virtue of a pre-planned caesarean procedure. I left the River Café at 3.30pm, hospital 4.30pm, Grace born before 6.00pm!

After the success of 'Mamma Mia!' many other artists wanted their music catalogues turned into a theatrical musical. 'Mamma Mia!' was patronisingly described as a jukebox musical – it was not meant by the critics to be a compliment but the public loved jukebox musicals. The format had effectively been created by Judy Cramer, but over the next 25 years, tens and tens of artists, producers, directors, followed her format, some more successfully than others – but Judy's format has certainly created billions of pounds of box office receipts.

'We Will Rock You' was a huge success with a story woven around Queen's catalogue of fabulous songs.

Then one day, very, very early in that evolution Cat Stevens, now known as Yusuf Islam, invited me out to lunch – another pinch me moment. He had chosen Nobu the trendy Japanese restaurant as our venue. He turned up in the most beautiful beige Armani suit – I was not expecting him to look so fantastic – I suppose because decades earlier he had rejected the rock star life to pursue his life as a Muslim.

Not that the two were not compatible, but he had chosen a different road, certainly a less high profile road other than the profile and debate prompted by his decision. He was a charming host and he told me that he had been told that I had provided the investment for 'Mamma Mia!' – I explained it was a bit more complicated than that – but yes.

He wanted to know if I/Universal would fund his musical. I was excited, I said almost certainly yes, his catalogue and his lyrics were just perfect for the format – in fact I enthused that I could hardly think of a more perfect candidate. Then I could see he wanted me to pause in my enthusiasm. He explained that he did not want to use his back catalogue, he wanted to write new songs and he wanted to use the musical as a vehicle for the audience to be morally educated. It was more important to him that the audience left the theatre educated and wiser, more than entertained.

I hope I was polite but I do suspect I was blunt. In two minutes I went from being ready to write an investment cheque to having zero interest. It's a simple fact of life that for most artists their best song writing is at the beginning of their career, and I felt that the risk of investing in Yusuf's incredible existing catalogue of songs was much, much less than investing in a body of work that had not yet been written.

Also my abiding memory from seeing 'Mamma Mia!' more than 20 times in three different continents was the show finishing with the whole audience on their feet giving a standing ovation and singing *'Waterloo'* and *'Dancing Queen'*. They had been entertained from the first note to the last and I didn't believe audiences, at least for this type of show, wanted to be educated or maybe even preached to. I could see that Yusuf was not going to change his mind, and I understood that, and that was how it should be. So one of the greatest songwriters and I parted company, me with a heavy heart for what might have been!

As an Irishman my father's hero was John F. Kennedy – the name was not one of the reasons – it was because a Catholic of Irish heritage had become the president of the free world. In years to come, so many would feel similarly about Barack Obama – probably even more passionately. Even as a 10 year old I was devastated by President Kennedy's assassination, but my father felt it even more deeply. It happened on a Friday night and early on the Saturday morning, very unusually my father came into my bedroom and asked me to go with him to the American Embassy to sign the book of remembrance. I wasn't a teenager, but like a spoilt teenager I would not get out of my bed. A terrible, terrible thing, my father had rarely asked anything of me and this meant a lot to him. He had also asked my younger sister and she had readily agreed. She came home with a brand new tennis racket!

More than 30 years later, in my role as Universal chairman, I find myself at a very sophisticated party in Manhattan. I look over the other side of the room and see John Kennedy junior and muse as to what my dad would have thought about me being in the same room as him. Someone is amused by the fact that there are two John Kennedys in the same room and feel we should meet. I would never have been so bold but they actually bring him over to me! He was astonishingly charming and incredibly good looking. I felt I could sense the eyes of every woman in the room looking adoringly at him. He did not rush to end the conversation and move on, he was just so engaging. I knew I was going to name drop this experience many times.

The following evening I was at another party in Manhattan central library – let's call it networking rather than partying. I was chatting to a group of people and suddenly I could see I had lost their attention – they were looking across the room at someone who was clearly a sufficient celebrity that they were impressed that he or she were in the room. And then I could see a look of bemusement on their face which at the time I did not know was bemusement that the celebrity was crossing the room towards them. I felt a tap on my shoulder and turned round to hear John Kennedy junior saying,

"Please excuse me for interrupting, John, but I just wanted to say how much I enjoyed our chat last night and I hope you are enjoying this evening." Completely unnecessary on his part – I was gobsmacked and the people I had been chatting to were very impressed with the company I kept!

After Universal purchased Polygram I struck up a relationship with a husband of one of the main Bronfman shareholders. He and his wife were by no means convinced that the foray into the unpredictable music industry was a good thing for the Bronfman family fortune, but it had happened and they had to live with it. My new friend was not alone amongst outsiders to think he could spot talent and recognise a hit. I had learnt over the years that hits can come from the strangest of places, so I always tried to keep an open mind. In October 2001 he asked if he could come and see me – I said of course – he came to my office, I offered him a coffee, and he asked me if he could play me some music. He played me three perfectly good quality songs by a female artist. I said,

"They sound good, but we would need one of our companies to want to sign and champion the artist, so I would need to circulate the music to our various managing directors."

He put his hand on my arm and said,

"But I wanted to ask you if you thought her name would be a barrier to success."

I said, "I doubt it, but why do you ask?"

"Well …" he said, "her surname is Bin Laden – it is Osama's niece."

He looked at me and said, "I can tell from your reaction you think it's an issue!" I nodded!

Whilst I was at Polygram/Universal we started the revival of the talent TV show which was to become a huge business for decades, almost all of it under the stewardship of the very smart and talented Simon Cowell, but we set it on its way.

I took a meeting with a TV executive from Australia. They had created a TV talent show in Australia and the winning artist had been successful and they wanted to bring the show to the UK. To the executive's surprise I said,

"Yes I am in, let's do it."

Unfortunately when he then went back to his UK TV partner they wanted to shop the deal around the various record companies, but I made it clear I wasn't interested in getting to a deal that made the venture too risky. Anyhow, I decided I would stay in the competition for the deal for a while, I knew my competition was Simon Cowell. I was feeling I had bid as much as I was prepared to bid, when one day I got a call telling me if I very slightly improved my offer it was my deal – the requested improvement was so slight that I realised that, for whatever reason, Simon had pulled out. Now I had to persuade one of my record labels to take on the project as I was head office not an operating label. To my surprise I could not garner any enthusiasm, and then at the last moment Paul Adam, from one of our labels Polydor, put his hand up for the deal. He ended up on prime time TV and he, and his boss

Lucian Grainge, and their label Polydor, did an incredible job resulting in the first winning band, Hearsay, selling millions of singles and millions of albums in days, not weeks, or months. The series then also produced Girls Aloud for Polydor.

I have no idea why Simon Cowell withdrew from the bidding war, but I have always assumed that missing out on that original success and seeing Paul Adam on TV spurred him on to create his global franchises; Pop Idol, American Idol, and of course The X Factor. We did very well out of Popstars but his success eclipsed ours by a very long way!

I have already said my job involved networking, but what better place to network than Buckingham Palace – the Queen and Prince Philip threw a cocktail party for the music industry. As I arrived I bumped into Jazzie B, a former client of mine at JPK and Co. Jazzie is a great songwriter, one of the coolest legends you will ever meet, but just a great guy who does a huge amount of charity work with young adults. There he was at Buckingham Palace dressed elegantly in a fabulous suit with his dreadlocks trailing down his back. 30 minutes later I found myself saying to Her Majesty The Queen;

"Your Majesty, I don't believe you have met Jazzie B."

"No I haven't." she said.

And I left them heavily engaged in conversation as one of his most memorable lyrics came to mind, 'back to life, back to reality'! As I bumped into Prince Philip – who said to me, "and what do you do"!

It was a strange job to describe as work, but it was of course a large business turning over £500 million a year and employing hundreds of people, so of course it was stressful, (but of course not being able to pay your gas or electricity bill is more stressful), and on an almost weekly basis there were magical moments.

Since I was 18 I had been a huge Van Morrison fan and now I was chairman of his record company. Weekends often involved me going to see our artists perform.

One Saturday I went to see Van perform and I joined him for a drink after the show with his then girlfriend Michelle Rocca, a former Miss Ireland. It turned into a long drink and it was surreal, and not for the first time in my music career, I wondered what the young 18 year old John Kennedy would have thought of this experience. Van told me in confidence that he had been awarded an OBE which had not yet been announced and then he said haven't you got one of those – I said I did. I ordered a bottle of Dom Perignon, certainly at the time Van's favourite tipple, and we toasted his honour – and I then find myself advising one of the greatest musicians ever what the protocol process and event would be around his visit to Buckingham Palace.

After this it was time for another bottle – fortunately I had a driver – and as the Dom P flowed I got up the courage to ask him a question I knew I should not ask, and would not have asked but for the Dom P, and should not be asking in front of his current girlfriend.

"Van," I said trying not to slur, *"Have I Told You Lately That I Love You* is one of the most beautiful songs ever written, who is 'you' – who is it written about?"

I could tell from the stare I had crossed a line, he said,

"I never answer that question."

Fair enough and I move on. A while later through a haze I hear someone say, 'one more bottle for the road.' Yes I say, this time certainly slurring – what a job – no one was going to query on my expenses; '4 bottles of Dom Perignon' with Van the Man.

Well, we drink the bottle dry and it's the early hours of the morning and we are saying our goodbyes and Van looks at me and he says one word that I don't really understand and he says it again. I look bemused and he says again, 'the song' – and I realise that he is explaining who *'Have I Told You Lately That I Love You'* was written for.

I was fascinated with his answer but I will respect his confidence. For me what was already to my mind one of the most beautiful songs ever, just got even better – it worked brilliantly on a spiritual and romantic level. We were to spend other evenings together but none as memorable as that.

I really enjoyed my time at Universal, and there simply isn't enough room for more stories, but all good things must come to an end.

Before Apple and Spotify saved the music industry it was a tough financial climate for the industry, and even Universal needed to make savings – by this time I was number two in the world ex USA and Canada. The master of the cost savings plan was my boss, the number one, and so not surprisingly he thought I should go rather than him.

I was well treated and I had negotiated my own contract so I was entitled to generous severance terms. We shook hands on the deal but 24 hours later I was offered a job representing the whole of the music industry in their lobbying group.

It was an interesting role and in that role we secured the extension of the copyright period from 50 to 70 years, a measure that was worth billions to record companies and artists.

A few months after I left Universal, my wife Caroline said,

"Do you still have that life insurance policy?"

At Universal I had a policy that paid out four times my salary if I died – I laughed and said,

"No, that went with the job."

And then I said, "But which would you rather have, me alive or a payment under the policy?"

She paused for a moment and said,

"Well, it would soften the blow"!

CHAPTER 16

MAMMA MIA!

So it is now the second half of 1996. A few short weeks ago I was running a legal practice in Paddington employing five people. Now I am chairman of the biggest record company in the UK and a successful film company. I can have, if I choose to do so, a chauffeur and my default means of travel to New York is Concorde.

I am responsible for four major record companies, a music publishing company, the most successful record club outside the USA, a distribution centre, and as I say a film and video company. 1000 employees and a turnover of half a billion pounds. Daunting and exciting.

I remember one week which was not so exceptional. I flew on Monday to Bologna to have dinner with Pavarotti in his home town Modena and then flew back Tuesday morning to join Elton in the studio to hear his new album, which we would pay him many millions of pounds for. Wednesday evening was the premier of one of our films. Thursday evening was Wembley Arena back stage to meet Michael Hutchence, one of our major artists. An uncomfortable experience for all of us as he was accompanied by Paula who of course I had known for years as the wife of my dear friend Bob Geldof. Our meet and greet was as swift and superficial as it was possible to be.

I had taken over the role from my friend and client Roger Ames. To my surprise my new desk had more paperwork on it than I had on my desk as a lawyer. For two months I carried it with me wherever I went. I learnt that 50 page documents could be navigated by reading the executive summary of three pages – with my legal training it was counter intuitive for me to ignore the other 47 pages, but necessity is the mother of invention, so I learnt that less can be more – the three pages would suffice.

A lot of the paperwork was dreary, but in there were many film scripts which I learnt were almost always 120 pages long and of course whilst they covered the full spectrum of great, average and downright bad, they were almost always enjoyable to read because I knew someone would need a signature from me if we were going to fund them.

All the film scripts were sent to me by our film company Polygram films.

In amongst all this paperwork was a document which seemed to be an orphan – it wasn't from the record companies or from the film company – it had emblazoned on the front page 'Summer Night City – a musical'.

I opened it and read it, and soon learnt that it was a proposal for a musical based on 28 ABBA songs. It is very important to remember two things; not only were ABBA at this time the opposite to cool, their success was inevitably very much in the past – they had split up a long time ago and in record terms they were a catalogue artist.

Anyhow, I loved what I read – it immediately seemed to me the type of thing we should be doing, we owned the recordings and the songs – if it worked, the potential synergies were huge.

So I asked Roger about it, he said, 'Ah that's been around for ages, it's something the music publishing company may or may not do - ask David Hockman about it'.

So I did. I liked David, a true gentleman who had done two of the best deals in the history of the music industry. He had purchased the Elton John and ABBA recording and songs catalogue for what today is an incomprehensibly small price. To his credit, at a dinner at the Bibendum restaurant in Fulham, he begged Elton and his manager not to sell their catalogues as they would regret it. Eventually this sound advice was coming under 'no good deed goes unpunished' – because Elton and his manager John Reid were ready to walk out of the restaurant saying, 'Well if you don't want to buy them then someone else will'. David persuaded them to sit down and said, 'Yes we will buy them and we agree your price'.

David gave me the low down. He said 'Summer Night City' was the brainchild of a lady called Judy Craymer who had been trying for 10 years to get it financed. She was represented by Howard Jones (a very successful music business lawyer who I knew well). David suggested I give Howard a call. So I did and arranged to meet up with Judy at Howard's office.

There is an apocryphal story that when I met Judy, that as part of her pitch, she stood on the table in her trademark high heels and acted and sang part of 'Summer Night City'. Sadly that is not true, but even without that one does not forget the first time you meet Judy Craymer. At the time she was 38 years old and oozed glamour – given she had had the idea for the show 10 years before, she was 28 when she came up with the idea after working with Tim Rice and Björn and Benny on the musical 'Chess'. Since that first meeting she has become more glamorous, more fun, and extraordinarily successful, but at the time success had not yet arrived.

What was there to not like about Judy, her enthusiasm was infectious. We chatted about the project.

I asked, "What would it cost to put on?"

"£6 million," she replied.

I asked, "Why weren't Björn and Benny just funding it themselves?"

"They would only do it with a partner," she replied.

"So they would put in money?" I asked.

"Yes, they would put up 40 per cent if we put up 60 per cent," she said.

"OK," I said, "let me think."

Judy said, "Let me help you with your thinking, I want to put on a workshop of the project.

"Great." I said – but she said,

"I want you to pay for it."

"How much?" I said.

She said, "I will send you a budget."

I left the meeting with plenty of food for thought – not least £3.6 million worth of food for thought. I may be the chairman of the biggest and most successful record company in the UK, but the most I could spend was £1 million without my bosses approval. My immediate boss was, as I have said, my friend Roger Ames. As a boss Roger had a devil's advocate type of management style – this often meant that you often didn't know what his view was about what you were discussing, because an oft repeated refrain was 'are you sure about that?'

That didn't mean he disagreed but he wanted to be sure you were confident in what you wanted to do. He pointed out, what I did not need reminding about, that £3.6 million was a lot of money. I of course agreed but reminded him many albums cost £1 million these days, and if this worked it could create a global franchise, and the synergy of record sales and publishing income could be huge.

"Yes, he said, "IF it works".

And then I suggested we would spread the cost over five years so it would only be a hit to profits of £720,000 a year.

"Oh no," he said, "it gets expensed in one go when it opens."

That was probably sensible, but it meant that in that year it was likely the full £3.6 million would be a cost to the profits I was supposed to deliver, because even if it was a success we wouldn't get the benefits in that year, they would take time to flow through.

I tried to argue that his international division should invest half the cost as, if it worked, they would sell lots of ABBA records and they owned the ABBA recordings and songs catalogue – his face suggested 'nice try' but 'NO'.

So we left it that I would mull my decision and go and see the workshop. I think it's fair to say Roger was not going to stop me doing it, but wanted me to be convinced enough that I would say, unequivocally, I want permission to invest £3.6 million!

GULP!

So I went to the workshop which was in Brixton. Judy was clearly good, she had an audience of about 60 people and of course a number of musicians and singers. I was going to say Björn and Benny were there, but if they were, I am not sure I got to say 'hello' because I remember my first meeting with them as being at the Covent Garden Hotel – but more of that later.

Actually I think they were there, but busy, and as I slipped away before the end we didn't get to meet. David Hockman was there, as was David Munns who worked with Roger Ames, and was a big supporter of the project both then and in the future.

A workshop is of necessity a pretty basic affair – I enjoyed it but it didn't really influence my decision that much. I had been doing a lot of mulling. £3.6 million was a lot of money, but I was carrying out a risk/reward assessment in my mind. I had a business plan to look at which told me how many weeks at x per cent of 'bums on seats' it would take for break-even. But again that didn't really help even though any business school would tell you that would be what I would base my decision on.

This is how my thinking was going. Judy's concept, which would subsequently rather disparagingly be described as a jukebox musical, was unique. It had never been done before. I knew how successful greatest hits albums were and I personally loved greatest hits albums. This was putting a greatest hits album of one of the greatest artists and songwriters of all time (even if they weren't in mode at the moment) on stage with what I thought was a clever story wrapped around it and whilst the costs were high a theatre ticket brought in higher revenues than a greatest hits album.

If it worked in the UK we would sell lots of ABBA records, and if it worked in the UK we could roll it out around the world, just as Andrew Lloyd Webber did with his musicals, and we would sell ABBA albums around the world. I looked at the pages and pages of audience projections and put them to one side. I wasn't brave enough to put them in the bin and simply decided if I am wrong about my view of the potential for this we will lose £3.6 million. If I am right the sky is the limit!

I went back to Roger Ames and said,

"I want to do it."

And he said, 'If you are sure, then fine'.

I had no experience of negotiating theatre musical deals, but fortunately our director of business affairs Clive Fisher did, so I briefed him and then called Judy. 'Your 10 year wait is over – let's do this'.

She was of course thrilled – 'Summer Night City' was heading to the stage. It hadn't occurred to me it was a very strange title for a play based on a Greek island – I had bought in hook, line and sinker to the overall concept – the detail was for Judy, Björn and Benny.

I said, 'before I sign I want to meet up with Björn and Benny to see the whites of their eyes and to hear of their own conviction'. But of course whilst I was putting in £3.6 million of company money, they were putting in £2.4 million of their own money, so they were putting their money where their mouth was, so I knew of their conviction before I sat down with them.

Negotiations were progressing even without our meeting, and dinner was arranged at the Covent Garden Restaurant near the Covent Garden Hotel in London where they were staying.

I have never taken for granted how lucky I have been in my career and this evening was a 'pinch yourself' evening. As a lawyer I had met many big stars and I already had in my relatively new career as a chairman, but I was about to spend the evening with two of the greatest songwriters in history; two of my heroes (along with my heroine Judy) and I was in a position to press the green button to bring their dream project to the stage – what could go wrong?

Well … a LOT is the answer.

I turned up at the restaurant expecting a warm reception, they were my heroes, but I was helping their dream come true after 10 years of waiting, so I expected an atmosphere of celebration. I could not have been more wrong. They were as cold as a Scandinavian winter. We were strangers not friends, but I knew something was very, very wrong. Judy didn't rush to my rescue because of course she was on their side. I tried to ignore the atmosphere, and had an aperitif, and we ordered food, but this was clearly NOT a celebration.

It was so bad by the end of the first course that I was thinking of making my excuses and leaving – I had no idea where that was going to leave 'Summer Night City', which had been scrapped as a title for the working title, (at least for my files), 'ABBA - the musical' – but I was not only uncomfortable but actually offended, because I had done nothing wrong in my mind other than bring belief and £3.6 million to their project that frankly after 10 years was languishing in purgatory if I did not invest.

But apparently unbeknownst to me I HAD done something wrong.

I must have said, before I suggested I leave, 'is something wrong?' and Benny silently pushed two pieces of pink paper across the table at me. He in particular was completely 'pissed off'.

I looked at the pieces of paper – which I still have – and couldn't at first understand what they were.

The company I was chairman of and that was making the investment was called Polygram – I had no idea but that day the lawyers for both sides had had a discussion about billing credits for the musical, and Björn and Benny clearly thought our requests which I didn't know about were over-reaching.

The two pieces of paper were their mock-up of what the credits would look like if we got our way. It was a masterpiece of sarcasm, it suggested the musical would be called Polygram with an acknowledgement that all the ABBA songs had been co-written by Polygram, Benny and Björn and that Polygram had co-written the story, and it would be performed in a Polygram theatre!

The mock-up had, as I say, been done on two pages and I am sure I didn't notice at the time but on the second version their depth of feelings were illustrated by the chilling credit, 'Music and lyrics by Polygram and Stig Anderson'.

Stig Anderson, their ex-manager, was NOT their favourite person!

I was stunned … I was actually completely in the dark, and I knew they wouldn't believe me if I said I had not spent a single second thinking about credits, and what was worse this over the top performance left me no wiser about what we had asked for or what they wanted.

What is interesting is they were so angry that they were clearly prepared to risk the whole project, because this wasn't really how intended partners should behave, and dare I say about my heroes who I now consider friends, it was prima donna / childish behaviour. I have now known them for more than 20 years and never saw anything close to such behaviour again – in fact it would be difficult to find more modest charming guys.

I guess we had been at the table a painful hour by now … where do we go from here?

It's the only time I remember in my life Judy being silent, she was either in awe or fear of them on this night, not a modus operandi that would last for long.

So what to do next?

I said, "First of all you will just have to believe me that I knew nothing of our requests and if you don't believe me then I don't see how we could work together because we would go into this with you thinking I was trying to steal credit for your immense creativity and talent, and that would be such a terrible start that it would be best not to start. Secondly, tell me how you envisage the credits."

They told me and I said, "Fine."

They said, "What do you mean fine?"

I said, "Fine, those will be the credits."

They looked at me both quizzically and suspiciously - I said,

"You have my word."

And put the two pink pieces of paper in my pocket.

I think the evening recovered, but anyhow our relationship certainly did as we never had a cross word after that, and I produced the two pink pieces of paper at the party to celebrate 20 years of Mamma Mia!

I showed them to Benny first who had no recollection, but said,

"Come, let's show Björn."

We went over and Benny said,

"Björn that's your writing isn't it?"

It was a party and the lighting wasn't great so Björn had to really focus.

"Yes," he said, "it's my writing."

And as it dawned on him a big smile came across his face, and in a Scandinavian way, he said,

"We behaved rather badly that night didn't we."

I nodded and laughed and gestured to a room full of people 20 years on and said, "It worked out OK!"

So the credits were written in stone in the form requested by Björn and Benny, and the contracts were signed, and the hard work began, not by me, but by Judy, Björn and Benny, and their creative team and cast. As the creative team honed the concept and chose their cast, there was little for me to do other than release our investment in tranches and make supportive noises and attend the occasional rehearsal. 'Summer Night City' was ditched as a name, as was 'ABBA - the musical' because this was not the story of ABBA, this was a completely different story but weaving the story around ABBA songs – and now it was called 'Mamma Mia!'

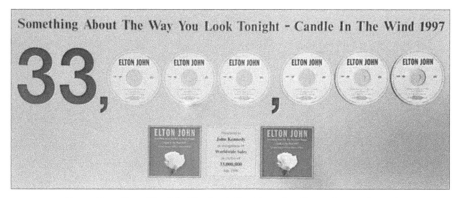

'Something About The Way You Look Tonight – Candle In The Wind 1997'

With Björn and Benny – a fantastic, creative partnership and collaboration with 'Mamma Mia!' – the musical.

One of the two 'pink pages' from my first meeting with Björn and Benny.

Björn and Benny – 3 million sales presentation.

NOMINATION

ANTOINETTE PERRY AWARD

Best Musical

MAMMA MIA!

Producers: Judy Craymer, Richard East and Björn Ulvaeus for
Littlestar, Universal

2001-2002

The American Theatre Wing, Inc.
and
The League of American Theatres and Producers. Inc.

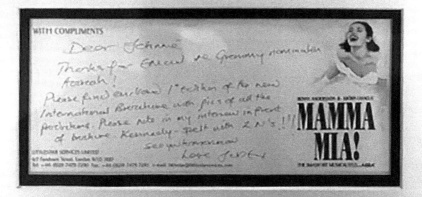

Tony Award for 'Mamma Mia!' – Best Musical, 2001-2002.

Within our group of companies the ABBA catalogue was with Polydor Records, which was run by Lucian Grainge, now Sir Lucian Grainge, and now the most important person in the global music industry. One day he came into my office with some good and clever news. He and Pete Waterman had pitched an idea for the Brits TV programme and the idea had been accepted. The suggestion was that that year's Brits would close the show with a number of artists performing a medley of ABBA songs. As Lucian said, 'that should help ticket sales' – yes it certainly should – it would be difficult to think of a better advert just weeks before the show was to open.

As with any new production, tensions were high as the opening night approached. I went to a few rehearsals – I loved what was happening on the stage but it was impossible to get a feel for the show in the stop-start dynamic of rehearsals. As the dress rehearsals approached there were concerns, and a couple of the dress rehearsals were postponed which I actually think made the front page of the Evening Standard newspaper – publicity, but to my mind unwelcome publicity. Then the first dress rehearsal – Judy fundamentally disagrees with me on this and to be fair she should know, but I felt the first time the show was played in full in front of an audience that audience helped mould it into the wonderful work of art that it became. I think they laughed in unexpected places, and I watched the cast adapt to that, and as a result there were more funny moments – maybe it took itself less seriously – Judy would not be impressed with that suggestion, but that's the way it seemed to me and a wonderful piece of theatre just became more entertaining. The Brits performance added to the ticket advance orders and we all awaited the opening night with great excitement.

There was now a sense of irony about the credits dispute with Björn and Benny as Polygram music had been bought by Universal music so any branding for Polygram was irrelevant and simply slipped away.

And so the first night arrived – what Judy, Björn and Benny and their creative team had done was remarkable. The show starts on a beat of music that would make you jump out of your seat and to my mind you are entertained from beginning to end – a clever story, and 22 of the best songs ever written, a dynamic stage, and great choreography .

The audience absolutely loved it – and instead of just the cast bowing to the crowd there were musical encores. But for a long time no 'Waterloo' – but then that was added, not so much by public demand, but as a cry to Björn and Benny from the creative team.

And then to the after show party. Judy had been an athlete in her younger years, I have no idea how good (but I believe pretty impressive) she was, but she would win the gold medal in the throwing a party stakes!

It was spectacular.

And a theme came out which to my shame I had not noticed before – the producer Judy, the director Phyllida Lloyd and the writer Catherine Johnstone were all women – as a gesture to the on-stage story they designated themselves the three dynamos – they were breaking ground as a pioneering female team, full credit to them.

And then as the party-to-beat-all-parties begins to wind down, as for every theatrical opening those in the team await the arrival of the reviews. I think it's fair to say that everyone expected good reviews because the audience reaction showed they had given it 5 stars. But talk about raining on the parade; the reviews were brutal – I think a one word summary would be that they thought it was 'cheesy'. This was a shock to us all, but something we were going to have to get used to. I think I went to about 10 opening nights around the world and I don't think it's an exaggeration to say I don't remember one opening night good review. And again, a typical critic's review would be, *'I have no idea why anyone thought this was a good idea, I found it absolute torture, but in fairness I should say everyone else in the audience seemed to be having the time of their life!'*

Very few books, films or plays survive bad reviews but 'Mamma Mia!' did. It had something more important than good reviews – it had great word of mouth – the critics and the theatre elite were culture snobs but the public were not. It became a wonderful, virtuous circle. The news around the opening, in spite of the reviews, had put ABBA's music back in the spotlight. There was great tabloid coverage and radio stations started playing ABBA again – the start had been the Brits performance but the publicity of the opening had literally put ABBA centre stage. 'Mamma Mia!' was a hot ticket! I allowed myself a sigh of relief – it looked like we would make our money back, then we could enjoy the profits – or so I thought.

Judy and I had lunch to celebrate but she had another agenda. Where are we going to open next? I asked whether Broadway would take the show and she explained to me that Björn and Benny weren't ready to take the show to Broadway, and may never be ready because of their terrible experience when they took 'Chess' to Broadway. So Judy explained the best plan would be to open next in Canada, specifically in Toronto, and she wanted me to go there with her to meet promoters - I readily agreed. So feeling pleased with myself that the show was a success, and soon our investment would be recovered, I headed off to Toronto with Judy and 'Mamma Mia!'s general manager Andrew Treagus. We had arranged to meet a number of promoters and after two days of meetings it was clear that we had a number of interested parties. As we retired to the bar at the end of day two, I was thinking all was going well and I said to Andrew and Judy as I drank my local beer,

"OK, I suppose it's a case of which one will pay us most for the show?" They looked at me as if I was mad – "Pay us? What do you mean?"

I said, "We have a hit, a number of people want to put on the show in Toronto, what's the best deal we can get? We are in the driving seat!"
They deflated my balloon pretty effectively by explaining to me that wasn't how it worked.

We would put up the money for a Canadian production, which they would put on in their theatre, and they would pay us a percentage of ticket sales. 'Oh no' I thought I had gone to the roulette wheel with £3.6 million and after the show's success in London that money was on its way back to me (Universal) – but 'oh no' I now had to reinvest that money at the roulette wheel that was Canada.

And I learnt that was to be the story as we ventured to other countries. Judy and I went to Australia to see how the market felt for a 'Mamma Mia!' launch. I don't think it's a story we have imagined but on the British Airways flight to Australia Judy drank the first class cabin dry of Dom Perignon. It seemed to me obvious that we would open in Sydney but after a trip to there and Melbourne all factors pointed to opening in Melbourne, so we did.

There was no doubt the show was a huge success. Over the years, I went to opening nights in Toronto, Sydney, Melbourne, Hamburg, Amsterdam, Chicago, San Francisco, Los Angeles, Tokyo, and many more. Each time the critics were the same – they hated it, but often would add in bemusement that everyone around them were having the time of their lives.

Tokyo was an interesting experience for me, by now I knew every line of the play, but of course knew no Japanese, but I knew when a funny line was coming up and so, whilst I couldn't understand the Japanese words being used to deliver the line, I was relieved to find the audience laughing in the same places.

As you can see there were now dates in the USA. This was a carefully planned strategy by Judy. In spite of the proven success in many parts of the world, Björn and Benny remained wary of New York and Broadway. Toronto had been chosen knowing that some New Yorkers flew to Toronto for a weekend of theatre, and then a USA touring production was sent on the road. All of this was giving us an indication of how the American public felt about 'Mamma Mia!' – they loved it.

Of course all these opening nights were run by Judy, and I think Björn attended most of them, Benny was a rarer visitor but always a welcome addition. It was in San Francisco that we all returned to the hotel to find the bar closed. We weren't getting anywhere by saying 'do you know you have music royalty in your bar waiting for a drink' – so Benny went to his room and brought down the contents of his mini bar so that we could toast another great opening night – the words 'f*ck the critics' were a frequent refrain.

The American touring production was an inspired idea as a piece of market research and Björn and Benny were beginning to contemplate Broadway. I had given my word that when they were ready I would be ready. However I was not on as strong ground as I had been when I gave my word. Since then the company I was chairman of Polygram had been bought by the entertainment giant Universal. After some shenanigans I had been made chairman of Universal, but my friend Roger Ames had left and my new boss was a very cultured Dane. His wife was actually a descendant of Wagner. Jorgen certainly did not 'get' 'Mamma Mia!' but to be fair I think he would have been supportive – but this roll of the dice was now 60 per cent of 10 million dollars and our head office in New York would have to give approval.

One of the things you need for a successful business is decisiveness when it comes to decision making. It was once said of one music company that 'their indecision was final' – it was not intended as a compliment. If you are looking for a decision you never like 'no' as an answer, but no answer is worse than 'no'.

So Björn and Benny were sure they wanted to open on Broadway but I couldn't get a decision from New York. It was about to be embarrassing, so I got the head office chief financial officer on a call. Nick I said,

"These are two of our most important artists, the show has been a success, I am in a difficult position." He was not moved by my entreaties.

So I said,

"Nick, you cannot sit on the fence."

(I could almost hear him thinking 'yes I can')

I said,

"Please either say yes, or confirm I can invest the money personally."

There was silence the other end – he said,

"You would invest personally?"

I said, "Yes I would ."

He said, "OK, I will recommend to the board that we go ahead, you will have an answer in 48 hours."

They came back and gave the go ahead. I wondered for a while if I had played my cards differently could I have persuaded them to not invest and let me invest. I would have made a handsome return but there were scary times ahead, they already caused me sleepless nights, but with my home at risk as well then ...

It is neither cheap nor easy to put on a show on Broadway. Unions remain a powerful force in the world of American theatre, but then Judy is a powerful force and found strategic partners in New York.

The Broadway opening night was set for the 18th October 2001. It is unlikely that anyone reading that date now will have thought, 'oh no, poor John, Judy, Björn and Benny' but if I remind you that on the 11th September 2001 the twin towers of the World Trade Centre had been destroyed in a terrorist attack you will understand that there could not have been much worse a time to be opening a show on Broadway. There were so many more important issues. New York went into lockdown, for all intents and purposes the city was closed. In the ripples of one of the greatest and most significant tragedies to hit the western world it seemed trite to be even thinking of the consequences for our now unimportant show.

We agonised over whether we should postpone or even cancel – there were no easy answers.

The decision was made to carry on but anyone who didn't have to come into Manhattan simply wasn't coming, who could blame them. The city had an understandable cloud of tragedy, sadness, mourning and fear over it – this was not the time for a musical comedy. Rehearsals continued in the way people need a distraction, and although no decision was made to postpone or cancel it remained a possibility.

I am not in a position to talk about what Americans, and New Yorkers in particular, were going through but I happened to be in Boston on 9/11 and I got an email from my 11 year old daughter in leafy, safe, suburban Highgate, London, thousands of miles away telling me she was frightened, so imagine the impact for all those more affected.

Maybe we just drifted into going ahead because no decision was made to postpone or cancel, but the decision to go ahead was made by Judy and the impresarios putting on the show.

I arrived in New York on the day of the show. Björn and Benny were of course already there, and I arrived to a moving tale about Benny having been in a pizza place the night before when he realised that a group on the next table were twin towers fire fighters. He engaged with them and tried to sense their mood about whether it was good or bad that a piece of light entertainment was about to open on Broadway. They were all for it – Benny hesitatingly asked them if they would like to come to the show – they would.

The show opened and was a big success with the audience – Judy threw yet another of her spectacular opening night parties. I can't remember what the reviews were like.

In the early hours of the morning we returned to our hotel, not to bed but to the bar. The firefighters joined us – Björn and Benny entertained us from the piano and the party rolled through the night. At 6.00am I left the bar with Benny. As we passed reception, to Benny's surprise, I asked the concierge for my suitcase – Benny looked at me quizzically.

I said, "I am off to the airport – we will both wake up in a few hours time with a hangover – but I will be back in London."

He seemed impressed with this logistical planning.

The press coverage was huge. This was not a city disapproving of a glamorous opening night – everyone was desperate for good news. It didn't matter what the critics thought, an event had happened.

Indeed the mayor of New York credited 'Mamma Mia!' with opening up New York again – if that was true what an achievement.

'Mamma Mia!' ran on Broadway for 14 years and became 'one of the most popular shows in Broadway history'.

So after that faltering start in that Covent Garden restaurant, 'Mamma Mia!' had become the second most successful musical ever – only being beaten by 'Phantom of the Opera'. It had played in so many different countries with 10,000 plus performances and taken a billion dollars at the theatre box office, and of course would lead to two great films which took another billion dollars at the cinema box office.

Judy became rightly feted as an astonishingly successful theatrical and film producer, and Björn and Benny seemed so invigorated by this new career that they looked younger each time I saw them, but took it all in their stride remaining modest, understated gentlemen, apart from when they composed those two sheets of pink paper, which I have now framed for posterity!

In April 2024 we celebrated 25 years of 'Mamma Mia!' – at the party I saw Björn for the first time in a while, we hugged and he looked at me, 'any regrets?' I laughed.

Later from the stage, Judy announced that 70 million people had seen 'Mamma Mia!' I think that means the theatrical production and the films, but what an astonishing number.

Thank goodness we worked out our differences in that Covent Garden restaurant.

Of course success has many parents, but just as I was finishing this chapter I came across a 'Mamma Mia!' programme created for one of the landmark productions, maybe the 5th or the 10th anniversary – I don't know, but in the programme Judy is asked,

'Has creating such an incredibly successful musical been easy?'

Judy answered,

'NOT AT ALL! There was a lot of apathy towards the project at the beginning, and investors were hardly beating down our door! I was lucky to convince John Kennedy at Universal to come on board (after performing the entire show for him in his office all by myself). He has been a great champion of the project ever since.'

It's strange, it's a reassuring reminder that the story told in this chapter really is fact, not a figment of my imagination!

CHAPTER 17

LIVE 8

On 25th January 2005 a strange thing happened in the world of Band Aid – we had a trustees meeting.

For the first six months of Band Aid we met Tuesdays and Thursdays, each time for at least four hours, and then for six years we met on Thursdays again for four hours. I suppose there must have been breaks for holidays but those days were pretty well religiously adhered to. Then after six years we set into a pattern of dealing with issues by email and even if we say so ourselves very efficiently. If we received a grant application it was not unusual for us to approve it in 24 hours or even less.

We did on a few occasions – as we should – have visits from the inspection team from the Charity Commission and they didn't like that we didn't meet very often, but they struggled to come up with a compelling answer as to why it was better to wait four weeks for a monthly meeting than to make a decision in 24 hours. We said we were willing, ready, and able to meet when required but we dealt with issues as they arose, wherever it made sense to do so, and usually it made sense to deal with things sooner rather than later.

But January 2005 was a momentous occasion. 2004 had been a big fund raising year – we had raised £3 million from Band Aid 20 and about £7 million from the Live Aid DVD. In each case we had recovered the VAT paid by the public – from the government.

We knew we would be active for a considerable time spending these wonderful sums, but I for one felt our days of new fundraising activities were done.

We also had £6 million from the Tom Hunter Foundation in a complex arrangement – but more of that elsewhere.

These were astonishing sums 20 years after we had started.

The minutes from that 25th January meeting show we had not only run a great charitable organisation for 20 years but we had operated it as an impressive profitable business based on intellectual property.

Would it be immodest to say that not only God had knocked on the right door but so had Bob when he selected his co-trustees – yes it would be, so I won't say it!

And then Michael Grade asked what was a fair question; was there any pressure to celebrate the 20th anniversary of Live Aid with another concert? I nearly choked on my coffee – god forbid – what a thought – I was thinking we were done with new projects and now this suggestion.

As there was a meeting there were minutes of the meeting and you can see the various positions.

Chris Morrison put it very succinctly as far as I was concerned – he feared the enormous expectation of matching the original Live Aid concert. I agreed with that and said, 'a concert may detract from the main issues of 2005, i.e. the political issues surrounding the G8 and the write-off of third world debt.' I have no idea where I had got that perspective from but that's what I said.

Harvey had various ideas for how a concert could happen including the first concert at the new Wembley Stadium. Bob states that, 'he would be reluctant to hold another event but would be prepared to do so if it would achieve something.' Harvey was clearly keen on a Live Aid 2.

Bob then goes on to say, 'the purpose of the Trust should now be to push for change as opposed to fundraising and that any event should be left for someone else to organise.'

The minutes simply say, 'JK agreed.' In truth I am surprised I did not stand on my chair and shout AMEN and HALLELUJAH.

The work I had done in 2004 in connection with Band Aid 30 and the Live Aid DVD had been like a full-time job and I already had a full-time job and a young family!

But any sense of relief was to be short lived. If I didn't know at the time, and I don't think I did, Bob already knew there was going to be Live Aid 2 – even though the discussion was minuted as follows;
'It was agreed by all that a Live Aid 2 would be inappropriate at this stage.'

Bob actually said, that 'simultaneous concerts in the G8 countries would not be a good idea.'

I have read the minutes of this meeting as I write now in July 2020 – they conclude with;
'It was agreed by all that a Live Aid 2 would not be planned at this stage ,but may need to be discussed at a future meeting.'

I naively thought that was an end of the matter. Trustees meetings were as rare as rare could be – even now we were only 24 weeks from the 20th anniversary of Live Aid – I was confident the clock would run down and there would be no Live Aid 2. NAIVE? … doesn't even come close.

I wasn't the only one, as he left the meeting Michael Grade said,

"This is a landmark year, our fundraising days are over, let's have a trustees social dinner to mark that and our 20 years."

It seemed like a great idea as we no longer socialise.

And after everyone had left the meeting, Bob sat with me and he said,

"What are you going to do if there is a movement for another concert?"

I said, "We can say no."

He said, "So stop people raising money for good causes?"

I said, "Bob by a miracle for 20 years we haven't put a step wrong – we have been under incredible scrutiny and we have weathered that scrutiny. We have a legacy and a heritage, we should preserve it not risk it – sometimes something can be a step too far. In its simplest terms I believe it's impossible to emulate Live Aid, and if we try and FAIL we will diminish the memory."

I added, "I am happy for us to be an activist organisation pushing for change but not another concert."

I continued, 'If others want to do it we can licence the Live Aid name to them, we get a licence fee of a percentage of gross revenues – they do all the organising and all the logistics, and they keep all the net sums after we have been paid our licence fee.

And then he looked at me and he said,

"Bono has this idea ... the concert opens with Paul McCartney conducting U2, and Paul and U2 are in Sergeant Pepper outfits, and at noon they open with ...IT WAS 20 YEARS AGO TODAY."

"OH NO." I said.

I knew no one could fight an inspired idea like that!

I still thought 'it will all just go away' but I hadn't allowed for the triumvirate of Bono, Richard Curtis and Bob.

A couple of weeks later on a quiet Wednesday evening in February my phone rings. I do not have caller ID – I answer and hear,

"Kennedy can you be at the Rangers Lodge at Hyde Park, London tomorrow morning at 10.00am?"

I gather that it's Bob and say, "OK" – without asking any questions.

I don't know if I am a glutton for punishment or naively thought I would go along with this as it's too late now anyhow. What I was not doing was relishing the prospect – I wasn't tired, I wasn't bored, but I really feared for damaging the legacy.

So I turn up at the lodge at 9.30am – I get out of my taxi – to my surprise

I see Bob is already there, he often runs late. I go over to the people carrier that he seems to be the driver of, and as I approach, I see Richard Curtis (one of our most successful ever film producers and the co-founder of Comic Relief) in the passenger seat and he says,

"Hi John ... welcome on board."

I know immediately I have been hi-jacked / kidnapped.

There has been no follow-up trustees meeting to discuss whether there should be a Live Aid 2.

But something was clearly happening and clearly the plan was that it should happen at Hyde Park.

At this stage there wasn't much flesh on the bones. I suspect Bob had told Richard I was reluctant, so Richard went on a charm offensive, and he can be, and is, very charming and engaging.

Richard explained the idea was to have a concert in Hyde Park – this was not a fundraiser, but the intention was to raise awareness for the Make Poverty History campaign, and to put pressure on the G8 when they met in July – simple!

And of course the reason Bob had been able to say with such conviction that there shouldn't be a Live Aid 2 was because this was going to be Live 8 as a nod to the G8! ... SEMANTICS.

We were going into a meeting in the park's lodge to discuss plans. I assumed we would go and sit round the table and have a cup of tea with whoever was in charge of Hyde Park.

However, we entered a room with about 60 people – Bob, Richard and I sat at a trestle table – it was more like a town hall meeting than a friendly chat. I had no idea who these people were, but I began to realise they were the fire brigade, the police, the ambulance service, the park's maintenance people, the people who ran Hyde Park, Transport for London (or whoever their equivalents were at the time) – and god knows who else.

I realised they had had more than 15 hours notice.

This motley crew were all united with one message – it was absolutely impossible to put on a concert in Hyde Park of the scale that was envisaged at all, let alone in the very few weeks there were to the suggested date! It just wasn't realistic or safe.

They were loud, forceful, passionate and convincing. I doubt if there is anyone else in the world who could not only have stood up to this cacophony but then been ready to take them on.

Bob said, "Make no mistake, this concert is happening – this meeting is not about whether it happens … just about HOW it happens."

And then he said something which made me sick to my stomach – he said, "Let's just accept that things will go wrong – it's very likely someone will have a heart attack and die – that's not a good reason for not doing this."

I couldn't believe what I was hearing, it sounded to me like a very good reason for not doing it. I was scared stiff, what would our legal responsibility as trustees be, and what about our moral responsibility, that was even worse. I think I thought, 'he has gone mad' but I suppose it was not the first time I thought that.

The meeting was not productive, though various dates had been mooted, but there was only one date Bob and Richard wanted … July 2nd, the Saturday before the G8 summit, hosted by the UK at Gleneagles in Scotland. Well there was an easy answer to that – it simply wasn't possible as the park was already booked by the Prince's Trust and Capital Radio for their annual Party in the Park concert.

The meeting ended with everyone present, apart from two people Bob and Richard, convinced that the concert was not happening.

As we left, as was his general modus operandi, Bob was now late for another meeting so there was no time for a debrief. He rushed off – I did have time to ask Bob,

"Does Harvey know anything about this?"

"No, Bob replied, "I don't think he will want to do it!"

"BE IN TOUCH!" Bob shouted as he drove off.

As he did so, I thought of his relatively recent quote dismissing any idea of another concert, 'son of Live Aid can never have the impact of the original'.

I realised all my reservations about another concert were nothing – and rightly so against the team of Bob, Bono, and Richard Curtis. As Bob drove off I didn't realise that by July 2nd at midnight I would be glad that I had been outmanoeuvred – but I would be.

I presume what happened next was that Bob started lobbying Number 10 to get the bosses of all those who were at the meeting on board for a concert in Hyde Park on July 2nd. Bob had a great relationship with Prime Minister Tony Blair, but the truth was that Tony was at least as scared as he was thrilled at the idea of his G8 summit being hijacked by Make Poverty History.

At this stage there were 108 days to July 2nd, only 78 of those business days.

Not immediately but very soon after my modus operandi for Live 8 started.

I was chairman and CEO of a global organisation with extensive travel commitments so I very much had a day job.

My three children were aged 7 to 15.

My wife's middle name was 'understanding'.

Not quite 24/7 but certainly 7 days a week.

I always insisted on sleep, but for the next 15 weeks sleep would be midnight to 5.30am – it's not terrible with one glass of wine at 11.45pm to clear my head so that I could sleep.

Monday to Friday I would go into my office at 7.00am having done an hour and a half's work at home and in my taxi there. I had two friends / secretaries who I personally paid for to type up emails that I had dictated the night before – they would go off to their day job at 9.30am.

I bumped into one of those secretaries, Laura, recently and she told me, 'I realise it was not a prime reason for Live 8 but that work you paid me for helped with my debt relief – I cleared all my debts and even got a pair of shoes!'

During the day my wonderful assistant, Lesley, who had been with me before Band Aid would juggle her day job with her Live 8 volunteer role.

The first job was to persuade the Prince's Trust and Capital Radio to give up July 2nd for Live 8.

Bob and I went to see them both at the Prince's Trust head office by Regent's Park – I had my elder daughter in tow for work experience! Bob's language was unusual work experience for a 15 year old.

Charles Dunstone was the spokesman for both organisations. He was sympathetic and co-operative and it was clear they would stand aside if we covered their cancellation costs. As their planned events were only weeks away those costs were not surprisingly significant – I think the figure was £350,000.

I was not surprised when I heard Bob say 'deal' – we will pay them but I knew we were now running at a loss of £350,000.

So it had been a successful meeting and the starting pistol was well and truly fired. The date was to be July 2nd and there was to be a concert in each of the eight G8 countries to put pressure on the G8 leaders, at their gathering at Gleneagles on July 6th, to play their role in 'making poverty history'.

That was the campaign mantra; 'Make Poverty History', a slogan created by Richard Curtis who was as passionate as Bob in his activism on behalf of those who had nothing.

Of course I did not know whether to laugh or to cry – Live Aid had been two concerts ... now there were eight, and the regulatory world, the media world, and the health and safety world was considerably more complex than it had been 20 years before.

In fact the eight concerts became eleven!

I do know, because I have a copy of the letter somewhere, that one of Bob's first self-allotted tasks was to write to the (then) new pope, Pope Benedict inviting him to open Live 8 telling him 'it would be good for his career'. It was astonishing cheek but actually correct – Pope Benedict for his whole reign was perceived as a bit of a cold fish – Live 8 would have given him the opportunity to engage with a demographic that he would never usually have access to. I remember laughing when I read Bob's letter, but actually it would have been wonderful for everyone – sadly the pope didn't share Bob's vision and declined the gig!

It's not normal behaviour to walk into your friends flat and find him writing to the pope, but literally the next time I visited Bob he was writing to ex-President Bush junior. They had met during Live Aid and had become good friends. I may have told this story before but it bears repetition – when Bob took President Bush a copy of his book, the President picked up the weighty tome and said to Bob,

"Oh my goodness, who wrote this for you?"

and Bob replied equally quickly,

"That's interesting Mr President, I was just wondering who would read it to you."

Anyhow, as I say, as I entered Bob's flat he was writing to his dear friend. I asked if I could read it –'sure' he said. It was a light-hearted but meaningful missive, which showed Bob's deep respect for the former president, especially for what he had done for Africa in the past, and he was asking him to use his influence for the future. I asked Bob for a copy – he was very surprised because this writing to world leaders was at least a daily occurrence. He ran me off a copy and I have it in a safe place – I must find that safe place. It was a great piece of prose, but what I found most significant was that the media world would not have thought of Bush as a friend of Africa – but here was Bob the man who would most know the truth of that, sincerely praising him for what he had already done.

I don't know how I am going to deal with mid February 2005 to 2/7/2005 without boring any reader with detail and minutiae but I will find a way or park it!

The eight concerts did not need micro-managing but they did need supervision, and if they had a problem they came to us and many of them needed cash.

These were not to be fund raising events but that did not make them any cheaper to put on.

Money was a very, very, real issue – we didn't have ANY ... just as simple as that.

I don't know if Bob didn't think about financing, or he just figured it would be OK, but it was not obviously on his agenda.

During COVID Bob was going stir-crazy, and he was clearly going through his loft or garage, and would send me copies of things I had sent him 15 years before.

We were a band of six trustees, but during Live Aid and Live 8 it was really Bob, Harvey and me.

Things were unfolding, not by the hour, but by the minute. Email was a great asset in 2005, except that Bob would not use email, so I had to post to him something that would otherwise have gone to him by email.

I am sure every morning the postman would put about six envelopes through his letterbox from me. Some of the envelopes contained multiple emails – he hated these missives.

He called Lesley, my secretary, and said, 'stop posting them to me!' I don't know if he hoped she would put them in the bin and not tell me, but that was not a likely scenario for the highly professional, efficient, and above all loyal, Lesley.

She of course told me of his request so I wrote another annoying note;
Dear Bob,

I know you don't want to be kept informed, sometimes I wish I wasn't informed, but you are Chair of the Trustees – you have legal and moral responsibilities, and it is part of my role to keep you informed.

I will continue to send you my missives, I know you recognise the envelopes – I can't stop you putting them in the bin unopened.

Well during COVID I learnt that he didn't put them in the bin, but he put them unopened in the loft or garage!

Now, during COVID he started opening them and scanning them, and returning them to me with numerous, often rude, comments.

Bob Geldof

10th May 2005

Dear Bob

Lesley – of course – got your message about not copying you in on things because you bin them. I have no problem with you binning them but:

A. You are a Director of Bracetone Limited.

B. You are a Trustee.

C. You are the most important person to be kept in the loop.

We have to send you these copies. I imagine these envelopes are distinctive, so when you get them you can put them straight in the bin without reading them if you choose to do so.

If you have trouble identifying the envelope we could even write on the front of every one "Heading For The Bin".

One day you will complain there is something you don't know about and whilst I know you hate email it is great at keeping a load of people informed.

Best wishes

Yours sincerely

John Kennedy

53 days before Live 8 – Bob has told my personal assistant to ask me to stop writing to him keeping him in the loop about Live 8!

16 days to Live 8 – tensions running high; 'I thought yesterday was the worse day but today has got worse.'

Gmail

(no subject)
1 message

John Kennedy <john.kennedy@lfpl.org>   16 June 2005 15:49
To: Harvey Goldsmith

Harvey

I thought yesterday was the worst day but today has got worse.

Feel like piggy in the middle.

You are fed up that Bob has given a press conference. Bob is fed up because I said that because he said he hasn't given a press conference.

Apparently everybody is fed up with the article in the Daily Mirror about artists being banned.

No steps are being made to reduce the list of artists by 4 artists - I know that is not your fault, you want it done.

All I can suggest is you Bob and I meet with the park people and say we need to light the park and finish at whatever time allows the 4 artists to play.

I know you don't want this, but what choice do we have.

You say the show is not progressing.

We don't have the time to lose.

If given the commitment you have made to the park it is too embarrassing for you to be at the meeting then Bob and I need to do it.

I don't see what else to do.

John

Copy Bob c/o Andy Barber

One of my favourites was when he said, *'now reading these I find it astonishing that Live 8 ever happened, not least because many of them are you begging me to make a decision within 24 hours, and as I never read them I never gave you a decision, so you must have made all the decisions!'*

I sent a one word reply, 'YEP'.

Then one day during COVID he called instead of scanning / emailing – he had just read one particular missive more than 15 years old.

He said, "What is this about – me, and you, and Harvey, losing our houses?

"Bob," I said, "one day I realised we had £10 million worth of expenses and no income, and I remained surprisingly calm, but wrote to you and Harvey, saying Live 8 is trading insolvently, and as we three are directors then we are personally liable, and so that means all our assets including our homes are at risk.

"WOW!" he said … only 15 years too late!

"Bob," I said, "that was a low point but I thought it was the floor, because at least we have the ticket revenues from Hyde Park, but then I was driving my car listening to the radio, enjoying some respite from the madness that was Live 8, when on the news the announcer said that Bob Geldof had just announced that the Hyde Park concerts would be free concerts!"

WTF.

I continued, "Bob, you may remember you had been lobbied by O2 that if you made it a free concert, whereby everyone applied for their free ticket – as a lottery – with a paid for text message, you would make much more money from the text messages than you would get from selling the tickets … well, unfortunately they were simply and massively wrong, leaving us with a huge hole in our budget – actually the income column was not showing a hole it was showing zero!"

Sponsorship income had been a huge help for Live Aid and now 20 years later the global sponsorship pot was much bigger and now we had eight concerts instead of two.

If only life was that simple.

Peter Blake had again come up trumps for us and had created a fabulous Live 8 poster showing the leaders of the G8 countries with the strapline 'The Long Walk to Justice'.

This reflected that Live 8 was not about fundraising but lobbying the eight leaders of the free world to do the right thing at the Gleneagles summit.

To my surprise this meant that the leading brands; Coke, Pepsi, McDonald's, etc. did not want to be seen as sponsors for an event in opposition to eight premiers of their biggest world markets.

So attempts at raising sponsorship deals …100

– and results …zero.

This was a major set back.

And in the meantime, costs were mounting and requests for financial assistance were pouring in. We were facing financial meltdown. Somehow with my one glass of red wine at 11.45pm I still got a night's sleep.

Then at an incredibly late stage I got a breakthrough – in fact two break-throughs.

Caroline had insisted that Live 8, or no Live 8, I had to take a night off to go to a friend's birthday dinner.

I was sort of enjoying the evening but I was certainly distracted, then I got a message 'could I urgently call the chairman of EMI Records' – would tomorrow do? Apparently not – so I stepped out of the dinner and in the next 10 minutes negotiated a deal for the rights for the eight Live 8 DVDs.

The Live Aid DVD had been released by Warners and was a huge success – I had expected that they would want the Live 8 DVD, but they were not being generous with their offer.

The chairman of EMI was a friend, colleague and one-time competitor of mine. He asked what it took to get rights, not just for the London concert and the USA concert, but all the concerts. I paused for thought and suggested what I thought was a reasonable figure – he said, 'if I say yes do we have a deal?' I said 'yes' – he said 'yes'.

I went back into the restaurant and ordered a bottle of champagne. Of course that's incongruous given the cause, but I was paying for it myself, it was a friend's birthday and I could feel my family home tottering less towards disaster, so I did not feel guilty or hypocritical!

We had just achieved millions of pounds towards our expenses.

Then, almost the next day, I got a call – 'did I have time to meet Nokia to discuss a possible sponsorship deal?' I pretended to check my diary, and said, 'it wouldn't be easy but I would make time'.

I then got hold of Harvey to see what front of stage branding I could offer, and Harvey insisted on coming to the meeting – not unreasonable.

The Nokia team were very nice professional people but they had a long list of demands for a sponsorship package. As they listed their demands Harvey kept shaking his head and saying, 'no way'.

I suggested to the nice Nokia people that maybe my colleague Harvey and I should have a chat outside to try and find some common ground.

We went outside – I said to Harvey,

"I have a request."

"What's that?" he said.

I said, "I would like you to head off down the corridor, take the lift and head back to your office."

To his credit, he laughed and to my surprise he said ... "OK".

I went back into the Nokia team, they were surprised to see me alone. I said, "Harvey sends his apologies, a problem with the Berlin concert that needs addressing – you know how the Germans are."

The Scandinavians nodded in agreement, 'yes they knew how the Germans could be'.

I said, "Let's go through your request list again."

We did – and I agreed to 90 per cent of it.

It was a great package for them, including front of stage branding, and exclusive tracks on their phone until the DVD was released.

So they said, "Yes, that's a good package."

And then the elephant in the room ...

"What would we have to pay for that package?"

Again I paused for thought, and said a figure which with the EMI DVD monies and text income would take us to break-even.

"That's a big figure" they said.

"Yes," I said, "this is eight big concerts."

They said they needed 24 hours to see if head office would approve – I said, "Fine, take 48 hours, but after that it will be too late to deliver the package.

They came back within 24 hours and said, 'DEAL'.

It was ridiculous that for an event like this we had only one sponsor, but I have explained why the household names were not prepared to get involved.

In the week before the concerts a friend I had met more than 30 years ago contacted me and said TopShop might be interested in a sponsorship deal – would I go and meet their chairman Philip Green – of course.

And so ensued one of the most unpleasant meetings of my life.

In he stormed, "What do you want?"

"Er ... actually, you asked to see me."

"Oh yes, that f*cking concert."

"Well, I suppose you could call it that."

"What's the deal?"

"Well, we can be creative but you could have joint branding with Nokia either side of the stage – very visible in a broadcast to billions of people."

"Well that's interesting ... OK ... but I wouldn't pay you until after the concert," he said.

"Well I am not sure I can agree that Sir Phillip."

"But what If you don't deliver what you say you will deliver?"

"Well we would be in breach of contract."

Then I had a brainwave;

"Sir Philip, we both have a good mutual friend Richard Caring – we can put the money into escrow and if on the Monday morning after the concerts Richard says we have done what we contracted to do the money is released to us – if he says we haven't it's released to you.

Well I knew he and Richard had been friends and business partners for 30 years. So I didn't expect to hear ...

"I don't need no f*cking Richard f*cking Caring to be meddling in my business ... why don't you just f*ck off out of my office.

I looked at him with complete disgust and disdain, said nothing, and left. As far as I was concerned we were done.

It seemed very odd – what a great demographic for TopShop – but who would want to do business with this man?

As I left his office, he had shouted after me 'we will call in the morning and tell you if we are in or out'.

The following morning his office called to say 'they didn't think it was a good fit for TopShop'.

As I say, it was odd, but I was relieved rather than disappointed – it would not have been a partnership made in heaven!

There was one further development which I still remember fondly. I think there were three Nokia executives I had done the deal with – they were of course VIP guests at the London show.

At one stage during the day I looked at the Italian concert and not only did I see no branding for Nokia but I saw a Nokia rivals branding. I went to find my Nokia friends – as I found them my phone rang and I said to them excuse me – and they heard me saying, 'well if Beyoncé won't go on stage I can't make her ... yes she can have those two approvals but not those three – if she goes on she goes on!'

I apologised to my Nokia friends and said 'I wanted you to hear from me that our Italian partners have not only not honoured our deal but have given your competitor branding I wanted you to know on Monday I will call you and discuss how much we should refund you.'

I was surprised when they laughed – they said, 'John relax do you really think we will sue Band Aid for breach of contract, we won't ask for a refund, enjoy the day.'

Somehow that meant a lot in the moment – an awful lot.

So we had saved our houses. We got to break-even and by continuing to wheel and deal, even though we weren't trying to fund raise, by Monday after the concert we had made £12 million profit – even now I don't know how, but I have the figures somewhere.

We put all the figures up on our website within 24 hours – I must try and find out where that extra £12 million came from.

Because of email the Live 8 organising story is much more documented than Live Aid, many thousands and thousands of emails are in the ether and physically in storage.

I have a good memory – it was a continual rollercoaster.

Harvey and Bob were frequently at loggerheads.
My home is in an area of terrible phone reception. Wi-Fi at home is OK. One evening at 10.00pm I realised I had missed a call from Harvey. I had a voicemail message which I eternally regret not keeping.

It was expletive laden with the 'f' word and the 'c' word making frequent appearances.

The gist was that I should tell that 'C' Bob that Harvey was resigning, because that 'C' Bob was impossible to work with … DO NOT TRY TO MAKE ME CHANGE MY MIND … DO NOT CALL ME. DO NOT UNDER ANY F*CKING CIRCUMSTANCES CALL ME … I AM DONE … DONE.

Well I thought, 'that's pretty clear'.

I decided to go for a 15 minute walk for some fresh air and to clear my head before resuming work until 11.45pm having my glass of red wine, going to bed and seeing what tomorrow brings.

As I returned from my walk there was another missed call from Harvey, again with a consequent voicemail message;

'WHAT THE F*CK … WHY HAVEN'T YOU CALLED ME?'

I brought forward my glass of red wine and went to bed!

Of course the USA show was a big deal – they were organising it independently, and with an arrogance that resented me asking for any updates – I particularly wanted a financial update.

They were vague but assured me it would make a profit, but this was not the quality of governance that we required. When pressed they told me to stop worrying, it would make a million dollars profit – that would be fine this was not a fund raiser, but in due course we would need audited figures.

And then on Wednesday June 29th their confidence evaporated – they had a cash flow crisis, they needed a loan of $800,000.

They knew I would not be an ally because of their arrogance, and lack of co-operation and communication, and because I had only just got my house back on safe foundations – so they lobbied Bob and Harvey who lobbied me to make a loan until the following Monday after the concert.

I reluctantly agreed, but only so long as Bob and Harvey understood this loan was NEVER coming back – not for the first time in my life I was accused of being a cynic.

The money was transferred.

Even with everything going on, on the Monday after the concerts I emailed the USA;

'Congratulations on a great show, look forward to repayment of our loan today as agreed.'

The producer must have called in his secretary and dictated an email to his finance guy John 'XYZ' with words to the effect;

'Tell Kennedy he will get the money by the end of the week – I know he goes on holiday tomorrow, when he gets back he will have forgotten all about our loan.'

Unfortunately his secretary instead of sending the email to John 'XYZ' sent it to me!

I replied, *'No I won't forget!'*

Live 8 poster - designed by Sir Peter Blake.

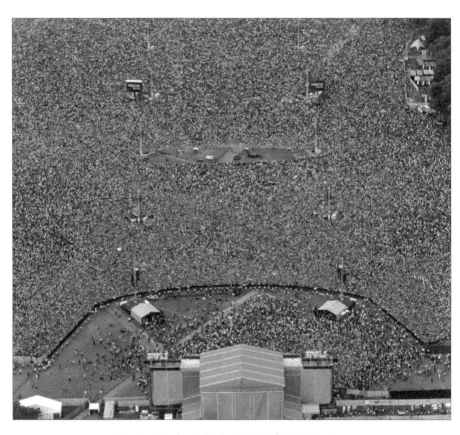

Live 8 : Saturday 2nd July, 2005, Hyde Park, London.

CHAPTER 18

LIVE 8 : THE DAY ITSELF

I have said before about Band Aid and Live Aid that if we had known what we were letting ourselves in for we would have been too scared to do it. We just started in the shallow end and waded in – and as it got deeper and more challenging we just tried to ensure we kept our heads above the water.

As I got up on the morning of Saturday July 2nd, the thought that largely three of us were responsible for 11 huge concerts around the world with an audience of billions was both frightening and daunting.

After a breakfast at my usual Saturday morning cafe I headed to Hyde Park. There had been disagreements with Harvey along the way, but it would be an astonishing understatement to say that neither Live Aid nor Live 8 could have happened without him.

As I met him at Hyde Park it was reassuring to see him so calm.

Harvey – I owe you an apology and here it is. When we released the Live Aid and Live 8 DVDs, the credit was Executive Producers Bob Geldof and John Kennedy. It was correct that Bob and I did the work and got the DVDs out (along with Jill Sinclair) and Harvey wasn't involved in that – but they were his concerts without which there would have been no DVDs. So it was both pathetic and crass not to give him proper credit and I know he was upset and offended – HARVEY, I AM SORRY! ... REALLY SORRY – IT WAS CRASS!

It was great to walk around the venue as it sat there waiting for the gates to open. The stage looked great and, as with Live Aid, we were blessed with a beautiful day of sunshine – that is pure luck – imagine how different the mood would have been if it rained all day. No matter how great the cause and no matter how great the performances you would never get over the adverse effects of the pouring rain.

Harvey was as I say calm and collected, but there was a deep tension between him, and myself, and Bob.

The simple problem was we had too many bands and not enough time – in fact a strict curfew. Laura, one of the girls who had come to the office every morning at 7.00am to help make all this happen, joked we were looking at 'party in the dark'!

LIVE 8 CONCERT
RUNNING ORDER
SATURDAY 2ND JULY 2005 - HYDE PARK

Act	Time	Songs	Artist
1	14:01:00	0	Trumpeters Fanfare
2	14:01:30	1	Paul McCartney + U2
3	14:06:30	3	U2
4	14:26:30	3	Coldplay
5	14:46:30	3	Elton
6	15:06:30	3	Dido
7	15:26:30	3	Stereophonics
8	15:46:30	3	REM
9	16:06:30	2	Miss Dynamite
10	16:26:30	2	Keane
11	16:46:30	2	Travis
12	17:06:30	3	Annie Lennox
13	17:26:30	2	UB40
14	17:49:30	2	Snoop Doggy Dog
15	18:09:30	2	Razorlight
16	18:29:30	3	Madonna
17	18:49:30	2	Snow Patrol
18	19:04:30	1	The Killers
19	19:14:30	2	Joss Stone
20	19:34:30	3	Scissor Sisters
21	19:54:30	3	Velvet Revolver
22	20:14:30	3	Sting
23	20:34:30	3	Mariah Carey
24	20:54:30	3	Robbie Williams
25	21:14:30	3	The Who
26	21:34:30	3	Pink Floyd
27	21:59:30	4	Paul McCartney
28	22:16:30	1	Finale

'Live 8 London' Concert Running Order.

And even though Harvey didn't know it, the problem was going to get slightly worse!

For all that Bob Geldof has achieved in his life the thing he cares most about is being a musician. It is the thing that excites him most and what he would really have liked was a long and globally successful music career. Just after Live Aid, acknowledging his eloquence intelligence and charm, I said,

"Bob you know you could make a very well-remunerated career as a chat show host – rotating between the UK, Europe, USA and Australia."

He looked at me and said,

"You don't get it do you – I just want to be a musician – simple as that". There were some who suggested he shouldn't have performed at Live Aid because he was more of a statesman than a musician. It wasn't a prolonged debate and it is now impossible to contemplate the event without his memorable performance with the Rats, and then him on stage with Paul McCartney, and then the finale.

But fast forward 20 years and everyone involved thought he shouldn't perform at Live 8 – everyone except him and me.

Remember how much the statesman role had been magnified over the 20 years and Live 8 was a political statement about raising awareness to make poverty history. Most felt – strangely to my view – that the musician Bob was not a good look versus the statesman Bob, who would join the G8 presidents and prime ministers at Gleneagles the following Wednesday. I really didn't get that – to me the musician and the statesman were joined at the hip!

Harvey was adamant he had too many acts and Bob the musician did not warrant taking up a slot that could be given to someone else and there was a curfew .

Richard Curtis's role in Live 8 was in many ways as important as Bob's, so I thought I would lobby Richard in the days running up to the concert. I did not get the support I expected – Richard agreed with the view that it was more important that Bob was seen as a statesman than a musician. I was surprised.

I was nearly giving up, but I knew how much this meant to Bob so I persevered. I can't now remember who my co-conspirator was – maybe Jill Sinclair, but somehow behind Harvey's back a not listed space was targeted for Bob's appearance.

I then rang Bob and said,

"Bob you know Harvey doesn't want you to perform, and to my

surprise Richard doesn't think it's a good idea, because it detracts from your role as a statesman, but I have conspired to get you an opening where you will have to jump in and just perform, but you mustn't tell anyone – and you need to know that Harvey has said you will perform 'over his dead body' and that if you try to perform he will unplug you."

Bob laughed and said,

"Thanks J, but re; the secret bit, maybe I should have told you ... you are on speaker mode on my phone and I am sitting here with Richard Curtis and others."

Silence from me, followed by "OH DEAR!" and then a feeble,

"Hi everyone".

Well, Richard didn't shop us to Harvey and on the day to Harvey's dismay, all of a sudden, Bob was on stage. I simply cannot tell you, because I can't remember, how the subterfuge as far as instruments and musicians worked but it worked. Harvey understandably was apoplectic – he simply didn't have a spare ten minutes, and even if he did he felt Bob the musician was not a deserving case.

Bob loved it and so did the crowd - Bob acknowledging he was not given a slot! "I know it's a cheek, but I had to play on this stage."

And in the middle of '*I Don't Like Mondays*' he does a reprise of the Live Aid moment where he sings "*The lesson today is how to die ...*" and then he just stops the music for that line to just hang in the air – and the crowd goes crazy.

He leaves the stage to rapturous adoring applause and cheers – saying to the crowd, "Thanks for letting me do that".

I thought it was a necessary development in the day. Certainly for Bob it would have been a tough situation to reward all his hard work by depriving him of what he wanted most – Bob performing – it was not listed in the programme. I just went to check whether I am exaggerating all this – but no, I have the set list framed – 28 slots, none with The Boomtown Rats or Bob Geldof against it.

But I did know where Harvey was coming from.

The whole day was astonishing and again Harvey's organisation was incredible. I watched the concert from a combination of the stage and the pit in front of the stage. I had my family there who were having the time of their life. My son Conor was 12 and had an autograph book in hand, but he was spoilt for choice as to which superstar to seek out next. He was keen to get

Snoop Dogg's autograph, and he did, but one star was clearly out of bounds as he had not one but four security guys around him. My eldest daughter Ellie challenged my son to get his autograph. Conor liked what was effectively a dare –he was nimble and small, he ducked under the security guards and rudely pushed his autograph book in front of his target who had no choice but to oblige. Conor ducked out again and said to his sister "Who was that?" – she sighed and said, "Brad Pitt"!

Ellie herself had her own story. As the concert approached, I asked 15 year old Ellie how many tickets she wanted for the concert – I nearly fell off my chair when she replied, "None - I don't want to go."

I was stunned and said sarcastically,

"What are you going to do instead – go to Brent Cross?"

"Yes" she said, "it will probably be deserted." She was serious.

I said, "This is going to be one of the biggest and most famous concerts in history."

She replied, "But you don't have any bands that I like!!!"

Well this was good market research. I got on the phone to Harvey and Bob and relayed the story – they took it on board more than I expected. There wasn't long to go and the line-up was packed but we all started racking our brains as to who would appeal to Ellie's demographic – who was big enough for such a global audience and who was available?

It wasn't easy to adjust at short notice but one big addition was The Killers – a great addition. The lead singer of The Killers, Brandon Flowers, loved their appearance so much he said,

"Only a gig on Mars could better it."

When he was interviewed for a documentary on Live 8, he was told of Ellie's role in getting the band on the line up – he loved the story, and wrote and signed a message, *'Ellie will you marry me?'*

As you can imagine that's a message framed and treasured by Ellie.

When the DVD was released the inside flap had the following:

9 concerts (it was actually 11)

1000 artists

2 million spectators

3 billion viewers

One message;

Make Poverty History.

Live 8 : Hyde Park, London, 2005. My daughter Grace watching Bono on stage.

Backstage my daughter Ellie with Sting.

Bob with my daughter Grace.

Richard Curtis with my daughter Ellie and Olivia.

Kofi Annan with Chris Martin, back stage at Live 8, London.

Bill Gates.

Midge Ure.

Paul McCartney.

Snoop Dogg – with my son Conor gazing in adoration.

Live 8 : Hyde Park, London, 2005.
Bob on stage.

That speaks volumes – but so many astonishing things were going on. Apart from Brad Pitt – Bill Gates, Kofi Annan the head of the United Nations, and of course, Angelina Jolie were back stage in London.

We had the famous photographer Brian Aris as the only designated photographer back stage –but I had brought my camera and was clicking all over the place. Brian summonsed Bernard Doherty our PR guru and, not recognising me, tried to get me thrown out.

"Brian!" Bernard said, "That would be difficult!"

As I walked amongst the back stage crowd I heard two well-known industry figures chatting – one said to the other, "I bet Geldof, Goldsmith and Kennedy are making a fortune out of this!"

IF ONLY!

The Hyde Park concert started in spectacular style – the idea that had made me realise that the concert would happen – Paul McCartney opening the concert with U2 with them singing,

'It was 20 years ago today! We hope you will enjoy the show!'

They weren't all dressed up in Sgt Pepper outfits – but the brass section were. There could have been no better opener.

The stage looked spectacular and at the top was, 'We don't want your money we want you' – so very different from Live Aid, but the correct approach, and a powerful approach.

There is nothing to be gained by me going through every performance. The crowd loved everyone – superstars to just stars – but then what is there not to like about U2, Madonna, Paul McCartney, Coldplay, Richard Ashcroft (introduced by Chris Martin, 'as the best singer in the world singing probably the best song in the world', – and an artist who I now have the privilege of co-managing), Elton, REM, Annie Lennox (my favourite performance), Snoop Dogg, Sting, Mariah Carey, Robbie Williams, George Michael, The Who, and Pink Floyd – and that isn't even the full list.

And let's not forget Nelson Mandela from Johannesburg telling everyone, "Sometimes it falls upon a generation to be great. You can be that generation."

And in Philadelphia – Beyoncé, Bon Jovi, Destiny's Child, Stevie Wonder. One rainy weekend day, treat yourself to watching these performances and indeed the Live Aid performances on our official YouTube channel – once you start watching, it's hard to stop.

Sting from my ringside stage position.
Live 8 : Hyde Park, London, 2005.

Robbie Williams.
Live 8 : Hyde Park, London, 2005.

Roger Daltrey and Pete Townshend of The Who.
Live 8 : Hyde Park, London, 2005.

Live 8 : The beautiful Birhan from the 'Drive' video introduced by David Bowie at Live Aid.

But it was none of these that were the star of the show, but an unknown 24 year old girl.

Just as it had been at Live Aid – the Canadian broadcasting video of the famine in 1984 was played again to the backing track of '*Who's Going To Drive You Home*' by The Cars – hundreds of thousands were silenced and this time the video focused on one face from the harrowing pictures ...

And then paused.

And with that Bob – or was it Madonna – or maybe both, walked out on stage with a beautiful Ethiopian girl that he introduced to the crowd as Birhan.

"20 years ago, some of you weren't even born, this young girl was in that video and had ten minutes to live – but because of what you or people like you did 20 years ago, she survived and has just got a degree from agricultural college!"

"DON'T LET THEM TELL YOU THIS STUFF DOESN'T WORK!"

It was a very powerful and moving moment – if there were cynics in the 200,000 crowd their number diminished significantly.

At 5pm, UK time, the concert in Philadelphia started with Will Smith as the opening master of ceremonies! Bob stood on stage and said 'hello' to Will – then to Rome, and Rome then cheered Berlin who cheered Johannesburg who cheered Ontario who cheered Philadelphia – Tokyo who had started the day had understandably gone to bed.

All this was being achieved again by the stellar power of the BBC – their technicians were unsung heroes as they had been at Live Aid.

And as he opened Philadelphia, Will Smith delivered a message that I believe (but don't know) was a Richard Curtis brilliant communication.

"*Every three seconds in one of the poorest countries in the world a child dies from extreme poverty. Every three seconds.*"

He clicked his fingers in a slow rhythm to mark the timing of each death. Every three seconds somebody's son, somebody's daughter, someone's future is gone.

Dead.

With a stroke of a pen eight men can make a difference and end the misery of millions of people.

Unscripted the crowd of nearly a million people started clicking their finger every 3 seconds.

ASTONISHINGLY POWERFUL.

Live 8 : London, 2005. The crowd from the stage in dark as the 10.30pm curfew approaches.

And always lingering in the background was this huge problem. We had a curfew – an astonishingly early curfew, and as things were running the curfew if enforced would mean Robbie Williams and Pink Floyd would not appear. The curfew was a very strict 10.30pm – dictated by the emergency services and transport for London. Their genuine concern was that any later than that and half a million people would not be able to get home and would be left sleeping on the streets of London – with no bedding or toilet facilities. It was a fair point and was a far cry from the all-night tube of today.

But now the alternative fear was 500,000 people reacting and rioting if the concert was unplugged before Pink Floyd (whose reunion would bring to an end 20 years of not speaking to each other) and Robbie Williams and The Who performed.

Harvey had warned us – he wanted less acts, certainly less Bob. He had wanted to start earlier but as he would say, Bob and I would not listen – he understandably worried throughout the day.

And then out of nowhere a fairy godmother arrived!

We literally did not know what the solution was.

There were so many people back stage – so many world famous names, but two names more UK-famous than globally-famous were to play an important role. Matthew Freud the PR entrepreneur and guru, who also happened to be Rupert Murdoch's son-in-law, was a long-time supporter of Bob and Band Aid. Matthew was there just to enjoy the concert – I don't know whether it was Bob or I, or possibly both who mentioned the curfew as a real issue probably in response to the simple question,

"Is everything going OK?"

He didn't seem to react – but to say Matthew is well connected would be as big an understatement as you could get. He appeared to have come with Tessa Jowell, the Culture Secretary – he was in conversation with her and then came over to me and asked some more info about the curfew.

I explained the legitimate and sensible view of the emergency services and Transport for London about people sleeping on the streets of London. He asked what is your view – I said we get that, but this isn't a football crowd – it's a happy crowd – if you deprive them of Robbie and Pink Floyd then it will be a mess. But if you give them both those acts, the fans will go home happy – some will walk, some will get cabs, some will get night buses, and if they have to, others will simply wait for the morning tube to start – these are not the old and infirm! Matthew nodded and went back to Tessa who went to see the curfew powers that be – it was clear I was NOT allowed to join them.

They were gone about half an hour and Matthew – in true Matthew style – returned and just said, "It's sorted."

I asked for a bit of clarification – he said,

"No one is going to pull the plug."

Matthew had persuaded Tessa to be our fairy godmother!
I relayed the good news to Bob and Harvey – both were pleased and relieved, but there was a bit of Harvey that was furious that we had lucked out!

Thank goodness for Tessa. Robbie was astonishing, then The Who, and Pink Floyd – a magical piece of musical history, and then Paul McCartney and the finale.

But as these last three slots unfolded the drama was not over . . .

Bob had been adamant all along he wanted 500,000 people in Hyde Park – the location for the stage would only allow for 200,000 – but what did it matter given the three billion TV audience, but it mattered to Bob.

Irrationally, given how much we had to deal with – he decided that if we couldn't have the 500,000 by the stage then 300,000 would watch on big screens elsewhere in the park.

"Really, Bob?" I argued, "Is that necessary – we don't have the money for the screens, the loos etc."

Well apparently, yes it mattered a lot – but the Hyde Park officials were having none of it – I was almost relieved, and Harvey understandably had washed his hands of this second site – he had enough on his plate.

As I had done before, I made the mistake of thinking it would go away. Then a couple of weeks before the concert a call from Bob,

"JK 2pm tomorrow, some building in Whitehall, you and me and the minister with responsibility for the parks."

I turned up on time – Bob was late – the Minister was Baroness someone (usually people are upset if you can't remember their name - I doubt if she will be). As we waited for Bob, she and I had tea and biscuits but she warned me the meeting was a courtesy – there would be no second site, there was nothing to discuss – she convinced me.

Bob arrived, and after pleasantries, she thanked Bob for coming but gently explained it was not possible to accommodate another 300,000 people and big screens on a second site – she made the mistake of adding it wouldn't be safe.

Bob pounced ready to attack and maybe not maim but simply bully – he pulled a notebook and pointed to a telephone number.

He said to me, "John, do you know whose number that is?"

"No Bob, I do not."

And then he proceeded to converse with me in front of the Baroness.

"John, that number is the personal number of the Head of the International Olympic Committee and John, as you know on July the 6th he will announce which city has won the bid for the 2012 Olympics".

I was struggling to see the relevance.

"John" he said, "What do you think he will think of London's organisational skills if I have to leave this room and call him and tell him that the Baroness here can't put 500,000 people safely in Hyde Park – do you think he will then be announcing Paris or London as the winner on July 6th?"

I couldn't believe what I was hearing – I actually thought I was going to be physically sick and I didn't want to be a party to this threat.

Bob was threatening to sabotage the UK's bid for the Olympics – I also saw the blood drain out of the Baroness's face.

"Let me get back to you", she glared and left the room.

I was shaking – "Bob please tell me you would not have made that call."

He replied, "I knew I wouldn't have to."

"But Bob, you haven't answered my question" he still didn't answer – and I am ninety per cent certain he wouldn't have made the call – but only 90 per cent !

But that was the cause of the new drama. Bob got his site – somehow we found the extra money – I don't think there were 300,000 people there but there were a lot.

And thinking of his ruthlessness with the Baroness – and then let me tell you that with everything that was going on at Live 8 – he took the trouble to find me to tell me to go on stage for the *'Do They Know It's Christmas'* finale – but added, 'for God's sake mime, don't sing anywhere near a microphone!'

But that never happened. Harvey was also trying to find me to tell me,

"Well you and Bob have really f*cked up now!"

Either through spite, or omission, the powers that be that ran Hyde Park had not extended the curfew at Bob's other site – they had pulled the plug on the big screens. Harvey was in absolute panic and was deadly serious – he said the huge crowd at the other site were now running here to watch the rest of the concert and he genuinely feared a riot or a stampede, injuries or even deaths. He did frighten me – my wife and younger daughter had headed off home, but my son and elder daughter were still here. So I decided I had no choice but to forget going on stage for the finale and find them, which I did.

Fortunately, Harvey's worst fears were misfounded – but I do believe they were legitimate fears – so I missed being on stage for the finale, but I was relieved there was no riot and no stampede, no injuries, and a friend offered to take Ellie and Conor home – they were tired.

I went backstage – it was quiet, but I found a new friend.

As with Live Aid my work was largely done by the day of the concert, but I had one important task. The digital download world for the music industry was still finding its feet – or at least the legal world was.

In an effort to pay for the spiralling costs of the concert, a tech wizard friend of mine Barney Wragg and I had decided we were going to get the opening song by Paul McCartney and U2 available to buy within one hour of the end of the performance. Barney was the brains making this happen – I was just a facilitator – but we did it, which actually warranted an entry in the Guinness Book of Records.

Now backstage in the early hours of the morning I was having a beer with Paul McCartney – as you do – I told him that the performance was now available to buy on the internet and had been since about 1pm.

"Did you do that?" he asked.

"I did." I said.

And was stunned to see him put down his beer and give me an almighty hug.

"Thank you" Paul said, "That's the first time any of my music has been available legally on the internet".

Wow, the whole day was amazing but a hug from a Beatle – how do you ever beat that!

(Though the following year at the World Music Awards - I did present Ringo Starr on TV with a lifetime achievement award without mentioning the Beatles which amused him – especially by suggesting there was a whole generation for whom his most famous role was as the voice of Thomas the Tank Engine! However, he only shook my hand – no hug!)

Heather, (Paul's wife at the time), dragged Paul off home – even though he didn't want to go, and I sat at a trestle table on my own and had a beer. I was just thinking about the day but was conscious someone had joined me – I wasn't the only one who was 'Billy No-Mates' – Roger Waters fresh from his Pink Floyd reunion was also flying solo.

We clinked beer bottles – said what a day and gently talked about the last 12 hours. After a beer it seemed like time to head off – I had no idea how I was getting home but started walking into Hyde Park and amazingly bumped into my young cousins from Ireland who were my guests for the day. We headed off in the direction of home and then my phone rang – it was Bob,

"Where are you – Richard Curtis and I are in one of the portacabins having a beer come and join me" – so we did.

For a man, who for the last 12 hours, had 3 billion people hanging on his every word it was not a glamorous occasion, but became a touching one. As we came through the door, Bob shouted to the room,

"Here he is – the man without whom Live 8 could not have happened".

I think this may be the second time I have quoted this but how lovely that at this moment he should say that – what a finish to a wonderful day. He then gave me a long hug,

"Couldn't have done it without you," he said, and then again to the room, "This man is the rock on which Live 8 was built."

It made all the blood, sweat, stress, and tears worthwhile!

———————

In every moment of poignancy some will find humour or cynicism. On the Wednesday following Live 8, on stage in Edinburgh, Bono repeated the mantra, *"Every time I click my fingers a child dies."*

The apocryphal story is that someone called out,

"Then for f*ck's sake stop clicking your fingers."

If it had happened I think the crowd would have engulfed him – they were so moved by the message.

CHAPTER 19

THE DAY BEFORE LIVE 8 : 1/7/2005

I had finished this book and was about to shout 'PUBLISH' when I felt the final version of this chapter was not right and I should start from scratch.

Even I don't want to remind myself what life is like the day before you are responsible with two long-term friends and collaborators for 11 concerts around the world which will be broadcast to an audience of billions of people involving 1,000 artists.

Harvey, Bob and I had become friends over the years, we had incredible shared experiences. It was not of course one long permanent honeymoon. There were many difficult bust-ups and big falling outs. We would eventually make up, but without ever really making up, but actually just moving on.

Over the nearly 40 years it is Bob and I who have mostly engaged and discussed the issues that evolved along the way. Bob frequently describes me as the Band Aid CEO, he of course is the chairman. For Live Aid it was Bob and Harvey in the driving seat and for Live 8 the three of us. Harvey has been very engaged as a trustee throughout as indeed have all trustees. Midge was heavily involved in the Edinburgh concert that was staged on the Wednesday after Live 8 to coincide with the G8 summit and with proximity to Gleneagles and of course co-wrote and produced the magnificent song which was the acorn from which the oak tree grew.

As I have said a few times, at all times I had a day job.

It would be fair to say in January 2005, having had a mega fundraising year in 2004, I thought we were near the end of our journey and we would move into cruise mode as we spent those monies now in our account.

I should have learnt over the years to expect the unexpected but I thought the unexpected was behind us.

I have explained already how Live 8 came about and now on this Friday, 1/7/2005, it was 24 hours to lift-off.

There were many things to juggle but we had become pretty good and agile at dealing with issues as they arose.

I started the Friday knowing we had one huge, seemingly insoluble, issue – the 10.30pm curfew at Hyde Park. I expected that issue to be what would take up my mind during my waking hours.

The Hyde Park authorities were going to turn off the power at 10.30pm, no matter who was performing, and no matter who had not yet performed.

Early in the morning there was a different 'bump in the road'.

The goodwill shown by artists' record companies and their representatives to the trust and to the concerts was remarkable.

If you are going to deal with a thousand artists then you need to decide at an early stage, as I did, that all artists are equal. You simply cannot enter complex negotiations with one thousand artists.

Life was more complicated than1984 and so we needed every artist to sign an agreement for the rights we were granting others to fund the costs of the concerts.

So we prepared a draft contract which we believed was reasonable and fair and gave us the rights we needed but no more. It had to be a document that we could credibly say was reasonable and could be signed in the form that was presented to the artist and at the same time was acceptable to the artist's record company.

In return for a signature it was a sometimes said, and sometimes unsaid, driving mantra that all artists would be treated equally; the minnows, the stars and the superstars. Though really almost every artist was a superstar.

Over the two weeks before the big day I was given updates as signed contracts came in. Mega stars who would have normally dictated the terms of their appearance in minute details, including extreme detail of what food and wine and treats MUST be in their dressing room, simply signed the agreements and sent them back. As with 1985, no artist was doing this for the promotional value, they were doing it for the cause and every artist would have been out of pocket by paying their own not inconsiderable costs. As far as I was concerned we were not paying anyone's expenses, we simply did not have the cash to do so. I did subsequently find, actually to my disappointment, that on a TINY number of occasions a costs contribution was made. I simply don't know how that was authorised or paid for – I don't know but I don't think any such expenses were authorised by Bob, or Harvey, and certainly not by me.

As well as deciding that the Hyde Park concert would be a free concert Bob had declared the other concerts in the G8 countries free concerts.

So the first 'different bump in the road' came from Germany. A major local artist was saying they did not want to grant rights for a DVD, but also wanted to be top of the bill. To me this was not a difficult issue to deal with. It was simple. The German concert was costing a million euros to put on.

With no ticket sales our income was about 60,000 euros. To partly fund the costs of the concerts we had sold rights to DVDs of the concerts. So I sent a missive that the artist should be advised, respectfully and politely, that the financial ecosystem did not allow for an artist to appear top of the bill but not grant DVD rights. The matter was resolved satisfactorily.

However, there was a much bigger bump in the road ahead.

Much bigger.

Unbeknownst to me over the previous 10 days a rights issue had been unfolding in relation to Pink Floyd.

I want to make it clear Pink Floyd and their advisers were doing nothing wrong. Throughout their career Pink Floyd had carefully protected their rights in their performances and were simply seeking to do the same for Live 8. However this careful protection and curation of rights was a modus operandi for many of the artists appearing, but fortunately for us those artists had persuaded themselves that they could make an exception for Live 8.

This is not a tale about heroes and villains, this is I hope a relatively interesting story about a tussle over rights.

Actually it is a story about heroes – Pink Floyd had agreed to reunite for this concert – they had agreed to put their differences aside for a great concert and a great cause – THAT is heroic behaviour.

I imagine our lawyers dealt with many similar scenarios with other artists but after careful debate and explanations and assurances the signed contracts kept coming in.

Pink Floyd not surprisingly were represented by one of the UK's best and most professional firms of music business solicitors.

I eventually discovered that by the end of the process there was more than 50 pages of correspondence (but lots of duplication) relating to Pink Floyd.

That tells a tale in itself – imagine going through that process for each artist appearing.

The band's solicitors had highlighted 10 days before that our standard contract was not acceptable, but as I say it is likely that was the initial position taken by many of the artists legal representatives, but then the other artists had eventually understood that the only sensible and realistic approach was for us to treat all artists equally. However, I emphasise the letter of 21st June 2005 made the band's position clear and there was subsequent correspondence before the 12 conditions of July 1st.

I think I was only superficially being kept in the picture until this eve of the concert but now the issue was firmly on my desk. I was sent a two page letter with 12 substantive points. It came across my desk late in the day.

Even if I felt we should engage there simply wasn't the time.

I won't go into the detail of the points but they would have caused us problems on a number of fronts.

You may remember I said that for most of the run-up to the concert we had huge expenses and zero income, and that it was a fact of life and law that we were trading insolvently, and I had written to Bob and Harvey saying that all our homes were at risk. We had resolved our shortfall by entering into commercial contracts including broadcast contracts, a sponsorship contract, and an agreement to release a DVD. We needed certain unconditional rights from every artist that appeared on a Live 8 stage to comply with those contracts.

Again I want to emphasise that the 12 demands would not have been unreasonable in almost any commercial scenario, indeed if I had been representing the artists I might have asked for the same things, but we simply weren't in a position to agree them and of course the fact that it was the day before the concert made it even more difficult.

Of course I felt sick to my stomach. We could not make any substantive changes because of the principles of equality with other artists, but also many of the requests would have the potential to put us in breach of other contracts that we had signed.

It was clear we would not be able to reach agreement in the hours left to the concert, but in any event I had not the slightest doubt that we could not grant exceptional contract terms for any artist, even Pink Floyd – at its most basic level it simply was not fair on the other artists.

The band's lawyers said in the last of their 12 points that if the band performed we were deemed to have accepted their terms – that was clever because it put the horrible onus on me to tell them to not turn up.

EEK!

My stomach kept churning! It would be impossible to overstate how huge the media story was behind this Pink Floyd reunion – it was a major global story and the media focus on this landmark performance was just massive.

I decided I needed a biscuit with my cup of tea as I sat down to think what to do next.

But actually I did not really need to think much because I knew the whole modus operandi of Live 8 worked on the basis of treating everyone equally, and whilst I completely understood that the band's representatives were doing their job, and indeed doing it well, it would be a slap in the face to all the other artists, managers, lawyers and record companies to start giving Pink Floyd exceptional terms.

I felt it would have been an act of bad faith to all the other artists and their representatives.

Indeed the 12 points raised on behalf of the band insisted no one must be given more favourable terms than them even though if I conceded to their wishes I would be giving them more favourable terms than anyone else!

So I sent a message back expressing our immense disappointment that it had come to this and the whole world would be sad to miss out on the much anticipated reunion.

My actual words at 5.58pm were;

"If your clients want to go on stage in the spirit of the event then we would be delighted to accept them on the basis of the artist clearance submitted – if not, 'I understand'!"

GULP.

I had just suggested Pink Floyd should not turn up for maybe the most important concert in history.

There were now only a few hours to go to the concert – less than 24 and virtually zero business hours. I had arranged to meet Bob at the Hyde Park venue for a catch-up and to walk the site.

I cannot tell you how hard Bob had worked to get this reunion to happen. He had played a 'Henry Kissinger' role for weeks until he was able to announce to the world that Pink Floyd would re-form for Live 8, what a story, what a coup, what a musical treat for music fans around the world.

As it happened the decision came too late to help our texting revenues but the kudos and excitement it generated was incredible .

That was the background in which 'GULP' took place.

As it happened if they did not appear it did not affect our revenues but that observation misses the point in so many ways.

Anyhow, with a heavy heart I got in the lift and headed off to Hyde Park. The buzz there was fantastic, the mood was tense and anticipatory and just felt as if history was in the making – AGAIN – 20 YEARS LATER.

I walked the site with Bob who of course was on cloud 9 – even now so many things could go wrong but it felt as if they wouldn't and the weather forecast for tomorrow was beautiful sunshine.

After an hour of absorbing the whole thing I said,

"Bob there is something you need to know."

He looked quizzically and I said,

"Pink Floyd won't be turning up."

I think his words were,

"Kennedy that doesn't get close to being funny."

And I replied, "Maybe it's because it's not a joke!"

Freeze that frame there! The horror of what I had just said – this is a sliding doors moment depending on how Bob reacts. Even as I write this 19 years later my stomach is churning!

Bob went pale and I explained the situation and of course he asked me if I was sure I was doing the right thing. I said I did not have the slightest doubt even with the potential dire consequences – just think of the superstars who had trusted us when we said we could not negotiate our terms for appearing – they trusted us and I wasn't prepared to be in a position where we had lied to them.

In fact it had a real risk of unravelling everything because the different lawyers representing different members of Pink Floyd wanted any changes we gave to apply to all their other clients who were appearing. I could see why that was happening as those same lawyers had told their clients to sign our contract because we would not make changes – if we now made the changes then they would be embarrassed. Our contractual 'house of cards' was in danger of collapsing with the potential for us to be in breach of contracts that we had already signed and for which we had been paid.

That money was being used to put on the 11 concerts around the world for a physical audience of millions, and a broadcast audience of billions, at a cost of about 10 million pounds – money we simply did not have two weeks ago!

Bob looked at me and said, "Well if you are sure."

He didn't mean, 'oh yes, no problem if Pink Floyd don't turn up 'If you are sure.' He was understandably desperate for them to perform but he was being supportive. I knew then it would be OK.

If he had told me, 'just give them what they want to get them on stage' that would have been a bigger problem as I just could not have done it. I know it sounds sanctimonious but it would simply have been wrong having relied on the goodwill of all the other artists who signed following our assurances that we needed the rights we were requesting for the media and the financial ecosystem of the concerts and could not change our contracts.

Again I emphasise that I don't think Pink Floyd or their representatives were behaving badly they were just sticking to their usual modus operandi.

However given Bob's support I felt it would all work out – I was not supremely confident but I was optimistic – this was quite an occasion for the band to miss out on. The media, their fans, and maybe most importantly, their families were looking forward to the big day.

How would they explain their absence? … 'contractual differences'?

It would seem a bit feeble even if they believed they were doing the right thing, and even if they were doing the right thing, which they were from their perspective.

It was a horrible scenario but I assumed they would turn up.

I knew if I didn't respond to their assertion that if they performed they performed on their terms then that might cause us problems later so I had responded in unambiguous terms that we did not accept and could not accept their conditions and if they turned up they should only do so on the basis of our contract.

At 9.40pm I made it clear again (just in case I had been ambiguous) to the band's lawyers, 'we need the artist to accept the obligations before going on stage.'

GULP AGAIN.

All of this was legally important, but in practical terms I felt a catastrophe had been averted. I was fairly certain the band would turn up, but they had been clever enough to make me suggest they shouldn't – not a position I had wanted to be in but in it I was!

I just thought that after the event we would try and find a meeting of minds that was not disrespectful to the other artists. I really did not think that would be difficult – in spite of the brinkmanship, there were great reasonable professionals on both sides.

Why wouldn't common sense prevail?

I am not sure Bob had even asked to be kept informed – he certainly wasn't going to be reading emails – we didn't use text at the time and I rarely phoned him – maybe he was supremely confident that it would all be OK.

When there was a real risk that the band might not perform I tried to console myself that the time that had been allotted to them was now freed up so that helped with our 10.30pm curfew, but I knew I was clutching at straws! Even I wasn't convinced this was a win and I am pretty sure I didn't present it as an upside to Bob to NO PINK FLOYD!

As I said at the start of this chapter I was expecting my main crisis on the eve of the show to be the curfew not Pink Floyd.

This was a very, very, real issue. The park authorities had never wanted this concert but when they were told by the powers above that it was happening then they were very clear there would be a 10.30pm curfew come what may.

At 10.30pm the power would be turned off, no matter who was performing or who was still to perform, even if as was likely that meant that The Who, Robbie Williams, Pink Floyd and Paul McCartney never made it to the stage.

Harvey as the greatest showman on earth had tried to address the situation but Bob would not engage. Harvey had a simple pragmatic solution – start earlier.

Bob would not engage – I think a Gay Pride march was a slight complication, but in any event Bob would not engage.

Harvey was apoplectic.

On the Friday when I was delivering Bob the Pink Floyd news we were supposed to be looking for a solution. We met again with the park authorities who were not for engaging or changing their stance.

They were adamant the plug would be pulled at 10.30pm – they were supported in their stance by the emergency authorities who felt if the concert ended at 10.30pm hundreds of thousands of people could get home, but if it went past then, then they couldn't!

This was a time when the tube finished at 11.00pm and night buses were a rarity. The set list did not just state on stage times to the minute but to the second.

To my mind pulling the plug before Robbie Williams, The Who, Pink Floyd, and Paul McCartney performed was a recipe for trouble and disorder of a much greater magnitude than the problem of people getting transport home.

Well Pink Floyd distracted us on the Friday, but even if it hadn't we did not have any great solution to it so we left it as a problem for another day, the only difficulty with that was that TOMORROW *was* the other day – but who was going to make the call of culling artists from the line-up.

Imagine having to call those artists and saying sorry you won't be performing now – but as you read in the previous chapter we got away with it by the seat of our pants.

Going back to the Pink Floyd situation even though we THOUGHT the band would perform we were still trying to make peace. At 11 minutes past midnight, so now on the actual day of the concert, Richard Bray our solicitor was on my instructions emailing Pink Floyd's lawyers. The message remained very firm on rights but is very conciliatory on creative issues especially the editing, altering or mixing of the performances for the DVD.

But of course the dispute ran out of time – there was simply too many other things to juggle. Of course (easy to say now) Pink Floyd turned up and it was, without meaning any disrespect to any other artist, probably the most important performance of the day – because whilst the whole Live 8 tableau was history in the making, this reunion was a significant piece of music history within a piece of history.

Ironically at half past midnight after the concert I found myself sitting at a table back stage having a beer with Roger Waters – it was as if neither of us had any friends, but with the big difference that he had just performed to billions of adoring 'friends'. We chatted as he told me it was one of the best days of his life – and mine I said as we clinked bottles!

The DVD of the concert was released with creative input from the band.

I thought peace had broken out and we were all friends – but you will be astonished to know that as we approach the 20th anniversary of the Live 8 concerts the dispute is very much alive and kicking!

I had assumed the contractual stand-off was consigned to the past. We had fulfilled our contractual responsibilities and whilst I had little doubt that we were the copyright owners of the performances we would ask their permission if we received a request to use them.

To my mind there was nothing for us to disagree about.

All was quiet on the western front UNTIL …

More than 10 years after Live 8, I was advised that one of the managers of one of the members of the band had asked the BBC for the Live 8 Pink Floyd tapes.

The BBC have been a fantastic partner for Band Aid, Live Aid, and Live 8 over the years. They generously store and look after our intellectual property assets including the footage from Live Aid and Live 8. There are security protocols in place but they did not work on this occasion. The tapes were released.

I was not unduly alarmed, this was a respected industry 'player' – the tapes were in safe hands but I would like to have them returned to the custodianship of the BBC .

I did not at this stage realise that we were about to go back to the battle lines of the 1st July 2005, but we were.

Their assertion was that the copyright in the recordings of the performances were owned by Pink Floyd – I did not see how that could be the case but I had not practiced law for a very long time. I asked them for the rationale for that legal position but I don't believe I got an answer to that.

I cannot begin to tell you how much I did not want a battle – I wanted a quiet life. I discovered that the intention was to use the performances in the Pink Floyd exhibition at the Victoria and Albert Museum. I sort of presumed, but without knowing, that the profits from that went to the museum, another charitable cause, so I was ready to apply a light touch.

Over the years we have developed an impressive body of intellectual property. First there was the Band Aid recording and the song that it contained. At the beginning I had suggested to Bob and Midge that they should give all their rights in the song to the trust – they readily agreed. The song and the recording have made many, many, millions for the trust. Then there are the Live Aid and Live 8 concerts. All in all our intellectual property now earns us £2 million a year which we continue to spend on projects that might be life-changing or even life-saving – this is 39 years after we started on this journey.

We can only do this because Bob and Midge signed their rights to the trust and the various artists who performed at the concerts allow us to monetise these assets. Before we embarked on this monetisation programme some of the recordings were being pirated, so as well as being a money earner our programme protects the assets as well.

At the risk of repeating myself I was not looking for a battle with Pink Floyd but one of our volunteers reminded me it was not fair if Pink Floyd could use what we believed were our assets when their peers paid to do so for the benefit of the charity and the schools and hospitals and water sources that we spent the money on.

I realised I had been suitably told off.

So the conversations of 1st July 2005 were re-opened 12 years later. Again there was some legal 'tennis' and then after I felt I was being fobbed off it was suggested I meet with the band's managers and their legal team. Even during the legal 'tennis' it was clear there was mutual goodwill between the band and the charity.

I went in a sense of optimism all these issues were so easy to resolve or at least I thought so.

It was quite an unpleasant meeting I wasn't expecting that.

I said, "Look these issues are so easy to resolve."

I continued, "If the Victoria and Albert exhibition use was not a commercial venture for the band then we will grant a licence and the fee will be one pound – and I will personally pay that one pound. If it is a commercial venture let's agree a reasonable fee. We won't make any use of the performances without your consent. If you want to use the performances we will licence them to you at our standard rate of £2,000 per minute."

Many artists licensed their footage from us at that rate and didn't complain about the fee. In fact the only person who complained about the fee was Bob, saying it was too low – I said Bob please 'butt out' – the ecosystem works well on that basis – he reluctantly agreed.

I thought that was an easy package for everyone to agree and after all these years we could satisfactorily resolve the long-standing disagreements. I was asked to leave the room whilst my offer was discussed. I was then invited back in. As I went in I expected everyone to say, 'DEAL AGREED.'

BUT NO ... my suggestions were rejected.

The main stumbling block was that they said there would be no deal unless they could use the footage free of charge for whatever purpose without our permission.

No other Live 8 artist had that right so I was not in a position to agree that – I said,

"REALLY guys – when I am offering you a licence at just £2,000 a minute?'

The answer was – YES REALLY.

I was very disappointed, as I was leaving I said,

"We have discovered that Live Aid and Live 8 footage is being pirated on YouTube, so third parties are making money out of it so we intend to put the footage up on YouTube – would you like us to include or not include Pink Floyd performance?"

They were outraged at the suggestion and made it clear they were choosing the 'NOT INCLUDE' option.

I accepted that decision.

So I left the meeting feeling frustrated and disappointed.

I still hoped for a peaceful life as I wasn't going to go to war for the use of the performances at the exhibition at the Victoria and Albert Museum as I presumed – though I didn't know that that was a not-for-profit project for the band.

But then ... Oh no! ... I was told that their Live 8 performances had been put up on YouTube. After I had particularly respected the request not to put the performances on YouTube.

Oh dear, what was I going to do?

I didn't really have the time for this and I didn't want to spend trust money on litigation/legal fees, and of course I didn't want to sue a band (and Bob CERTAINLY didn't) that had contributed so impressively to Live 8 – but again this wasn't fair on the other artists whose performances were now earning the trust hundreds of thousands of euros a year from YouTube venues .

And of course it was possible this was a test to see if we would take action to protect our rights.

I realised that sadly doing nothing was not an option.

I so wanted this to go away.

I engaged with the band's solicitors but wasn't really getting anywhere.

Bob was at times annoyed with me and on other occasions touchingly supportive. He accepted that I could not do nothing and whilst he was disappointed with how things had unfolded, these were his friends who had done him an enormous favour by reuniting to perform at Live 8.

He did not like me taking the legal or moral high ground.

I was totally bemused – I was advised they were probably earning about 30,000 euros or pounds a year – I believed, though they did not, that that money should come to the trust.

I found it difficult to believe that the artists themselves were willing participants in this – their share of revenues, after management commission and the pot was split, were negligible but I did not think they would rather they had the monies than the charity.

So I drafted a legal letter, but Bob felt it was too long, but anyhow understandably he vehemently disagreed with my legal approach, and then asked if I wanted him to engage with the artists on this. I said I had tried to keep him out of it, but yes if he did not like my approach which I understood then yes that was the only thing to do

As always Bob was a powerful advocate – there was immediate progress but in incremental stages.

It was agreed that we could put the performances up on our YouTube channel though they said they would keep on their channel.

Then we received a donation of a sum that seemed like it could be the equivalent of YouTube revenues to the date of the donation – a very nice sum just in excess of £100,000, money we could put to good use.

That was a big step forward.

So very real progress from artist to artist engagement, far more effective than the legal route.

We are not quite there yet but we have made real progress and I am optimistic that by the time this book is published we will have reached a consensus.

Outstanding issues would actually be simply resolved by an agreement that the Live 8 performances will not be used for any new use without both parties agreement – simple?

We for our part have already agreed to that!

Again I emphasise all parties including managers and legal representatives were doing what they thought was right for their clients but we just had a disagreement over what 'right ' looked like.

But I feel a happy ending is around the corner after a 19 year tussle! I think Bob called me stubborn during this – I was not sure if that was a compliment or an insult given who it was coming from!

Even now after all these years I sometimes wake up in a cold sweat as I relive the time I am heading to Hyde Park to try and casually drop into conversation with Bob, 'By the way, Pink Floyd won't be turning up'!

Even with all the detail of this tussle there is one thing in no doubt – the work of art that is the Live 8 concert would have been much depleted by the absence of Pink Floyd.

Today I am going to shout 'PUBLISH' on my book and yesterday, more than 19 years after the tussle started, I received an indication that Pink Floyd are generously sending us more monies – I suspect an indication that they will continue to do so over the years – these are monies we will spend well and wisely so pretty well a happy ending – and this further recent development has produced an ironic twist.

I frowned on Pink Floyd putting the Live 8 material up on YouTube but the fact that they did has actually increased revenues to our charity. The tussle has produced more good than bad. One client always advises me to expect the unexpected – THANK YOU PINK FLOYD, you continue to be heroes not villains.

What else could have gone wrong the day before Live 8!

Well in the week before, after it looked like we had earnings to cover our costs and a bit more, I suggested to Harvey we spend some of the surplus on an insurance policy – he didn't think it was necessary and I actually can't remember if we did or we didn't.

Well ... 100 hours after the Hyde Park concerts, four suicide bombers struck London's transport network with of course unbelievably tragic results.

If those bombers had chosen the Thursday before Live 8 rather than the Thursday after Live 8 then it is unlikely that the authorities would have allowed Live 8 London to go ahead – it does not bear thinking about.

Maybe telling Pink Floyd not to turn up was an easy day's work by comparison with what could have unfolded!

The remarkable achievements of IFPI chairman and CEO John Kennedy, promoter Harvey Goldsmith and Sir Bob Geldof as Band Aid trustees were recognised with two honours at Midem. The trio were honoured as personalities of the year by Reed Midem at the event's 40th anniversary dinner, just hours after they also received *Chevalier de l'ordre des arts et des lettres* medals from the French Government. Midem chief executive Paul Silk paid tribute to the three at the lavish dinner, for their work in getting the Live 8 idea off the ground and into millions of homes around the world. The dinner, which followed a firework display over the Cannes bay in honour of Midem's 40th anniversary, also recognised the achievement of the Midem Pioneers – a select band of delegates who have been to all 40 Midems, as well as Midem director Dominique Leguern.

2006 MIDEM Award : Personalities of the Year; John, Harvey and Bob.

The top table at the Personalities Of The Year Award gala dinner. From left: Kevin Wall, Harvey Goldsmith, Bernard Brochand, Caroline Kennedy, Bill Roedy, Bob Geldof, Jeanne Marine, Paul Zilk, Dany Brochand and John Kennedy.

2006 MIDEM Gala Dinner.

The 2007 World Music Awards

We are delighted to support this nineteenth prestigious World Music Awards ceremony.

IFPI represents the recording industry worldwide, an industry that has seen phenomenal changes in the past two decades. These changes have generated amazing opportunities for the music fans and creators, but they have produced great threats as well.

Digital technology means that it has never been easier to bring music to busy consumers on the move. Indeed if you had predicted 19 years ago that by 2007 people would be obtaining a piece of music they liked using a mobile phone sitting in a café, many would not have believed you. Yet record labels have been licensing more than four million tracks to over 500 digital services worldwide.

Unfortunately, this new technology is also being misused to hurt the whole creative community – a community made up of artists, songwriters, musicians and producers. Here is a painful statistic: today, there are 20 illegal music downloads for every legal one. In the long run this means less music in people's lives with reduced revenues from current stars to fund future acts. This is not a problem just for the record industry. This is a problem for culture and for society.

One thing that hasn't changed is the heart and raison d'être of our business. Record labels are still second to none at discovering and nurturing new talent and promoting their music to the public – and it is that great music we are celebrating today.

The World Music Awards honours the best of global talent in front of a worldwide television audience. IFPI and its national groups are delighted to continue to support the awards which bring well deserved acclaim to the nominees and winners and entertain us all globally.

John Kennedy
Chairman and Chief Executive
IFPI

A Limited Company Registered in England No. 1492091. Registered Office as shown.

2007 World Music Awards : IFPI introduction.

CHAPTER 20

GLENEAGLES

AND WAS IT WORTH DONATING AN HOUR OF MY TIME?

The Live 8 concerts had been a spectacular success as entertainment but they were all for nothing if they hadn't put pressure on the G8 leaders to do something dramatic about making poverty history. The summit was taking place at Gleneagles, just a few miles from the Edinburgh Live 8 concert – of course no coincidence. The Edinburgh venue and concert had been planned for the Wednesday following the main Live 8 day and to coincide with the G8 summit.

It was incredibly unusual to have outsiders at such a summit but Tony Blair had invited Bob Geldof and Bono into the inner circle of the summit. On the Sunday after Live 8 I was having lunch at a friend's house and I got a call from Emma Freud, Richard Curtis's long-term partner – she was asking me who I thought should accompany them. It seemed like a strange question because I certainly didn't have any 'Access All Areas' G8 summit pass to hand out, but I realised I was being lobbied and of course she wanted me to say Richard Curtis should be there. She didn't have a difficult job because I agreed Richard should 1000 per cent be there.

In many ways he had been the mastermind not of the concerts but the overall campaign which would come to fruition (or not) on Wednesday July 6th, and in fact Live 8 as an idea would not have got off the starting line but for Richard and Bono persuading Bob it was the right thing to do.

Bob, Bono and Richard Curtis had a private 40 minute meeting with President Bush – he had watched Live 8, 'the most moving moment' he said, 'was when Birhan the child who had appeared at death's door back in 1985 came out on stage 20 years later.' It made him realise very evocatively that there are individuals like her who live or die as a result of decisions by the likes of him.

All three were impressed by his interest in and knowledge of Africa – the three secured personal commitments from him regarding aid and trade. Bob has frequently privately told me what great things President Bush did for Africa – indeed they became friends and if Bob did not have enough great moments in his life he travelled with the President on Air Force One to Africa.

I have heard many celebrity name drops but that plane would beat most name drops.

Bono and Bob were taken by helicopter out of the summit to the Edinburgh concert which had always been planned for the Wednesday after Live 8 to coincide with the summit. Bono went on stage to the 60,000 crowd and told them that 38 million people had signed up to the Live 8 campaign and 157 million to the Global Action against Poverty Campaign – people from 75 countries – Bob followed him and talked of the 3.8 billion people who had watched Live 8.

It is not amateur campaigning to turn up with signatures showing you have a constituency of 195 million people – none of the G8 leaders would have that many supporters.

There are always naysayers about what was, or was not, achieved by particular campaigns and there were certainly enough people prepared to tell the press about the shortcomings of the decisions from Gleneagles, but if they focused on what had been achieved instead of what had not been achieved they would have declared it a huge success.

With everything that was going on in the summit it was very touching that Bob called me – very excited – to say what was being achieved.

There were the pillars of DATA – Debt relief, Aid, Trade. I could tell things were going well, but because Bob was there and in the moment it was quite hard to follow, so I said, 'Bob tell me how many out of 10 for each limb'.

I was then amused to watch him a couple hours later on the news giving a journalist his report from the summit scoring each pillar out of 10. It was a good way of communicating a complex subject – even if I say so myself! Who else is going to!

Aid for the next few years was doubled to $50 billion for Africa …10/10!

Debt cancellation 100 per cent agreed for 14 African countries – this was a big deal in the context of the Sisyphus like statistic that for every $2 given in aid at least $1 is used for debt repayments … a bit less than 8/10. Trade – for every $1 we give in aid we take back $2 through unfair trade! Trade tariffs being the biggest offender – effectively we tax Africa's development whilst subsidising our own food producers at home. The summit agreed to reform world trade to remove the bias against the poor.

50 of the things that the commission for Africa called for had been delivered.

All of these had the potential to be a huge boost for Africa's economy.

Bob was understandably moved, but he realised it was the power of the people.

'Billions of us could force the men in charge to move, we roared on behalf of those who were mute, we moved power for the powerless, we walked that long walk for many who cannot even crawl, and billions of us stood up for the beaten down and put upon.'

That's impressive and moving oratory.

It hadn't been all plain sailing at Gleneagles. The G8 leaders were reluctant to do most of what was being asked of them – Tony Blair as host was trying to marshal progress. Bob and Bono were a formidable combination – it helped that they were so famous and had huge followings, but it also helped that they were passionate, sincere, eloquent and intelligent.

I have experienced both their eloquence one-on-one on many occasions – just me and them. I came home one day and told my wife I had had Bob on the phone for 40 minutes making a point to me, and he was as engaging and as forceful as if he had been on a TV show with an audience of millions – that was not a one-off.

Someone once described the two working together as a wonderful example of well-rehearsed spontaneity. Bono credits much of his work on philanthropy to Bob and even thanked me personally for showing him what could be achieved. Bono also said he learnt from Bob that there was no reason to take 'No' for an answer.

Alistair Campbell reported that Tony Blair was making really good progress with his G8 colleagues, and Tony came out to report to Bob and Bono, and was stunned when Bob started effing and blinding that that wasn't good enough.

Understandably Tony was put out – he said to them,

"I don't think you understand how difficult it is – we are looking at Everest in there!"

Far from being sympathetic Bono said,

"Tony, Everest isn't for looking at – its for climbing!

Get back in there!"

That's true – the next bit may be apocryphal – Bob said to Bono,

"You stole that line from me."

Bono said, "I don't think so, but one thing is for sure, you never caught me trying to steal one of your songs!" OUCH!

Kofi Annan, the UN Secretary General was not a naysayer, he said,

"This has been without doubt, the greatest G8 summit there has ever been for Africa." So Live 8 was a huge success from an entertainment and political achievement perspective.

All of this book is my own perspective and views and tales – not at any stage do I speak for Bob or the trust.

As I write this in 2024, Ethiopia and Sudan are facing terrible, terrible problems. Understandably people ask then did Band Aid achieve anything, did it move the needle, was it worthwhile? In one sense the journey has been a rollercoaster – for years the Ethiopian economy grew and became one of the strongest growing economies in the world, but then in a spectacular own goal the Ethiopian government took the country into a civil war, that not only damaged the economy but was a catastrophe for the Ethiopian people. At the same time that part of the world felt harshly the consequences of climate change as drought and famine returned.

I have no doubt on the subject of whether Band Aid moved the needle, and if you give Bob 15 minutes on the subject he will leave you reeling with the achievements, not least of course those of Gleneagles.

At a speech at a music awards ceremony in 2006, with his usual eloquence, he recited the following achievements:

5 million people alive every year
5 million orphans taken into care instead of being abandoned
21 million kids in school
290 million free of debt slavery
Universal aids treatment to be available by 2010.

Having spent so much of my time on this project do I personally ever feel my time was wasted? No, not for a second.

Bob has often said if one life was saved then it was all worthwhile – I have no doubt that many lives were saved and many lives were improved. When Birhan came on the Live 8 stage in 2005, the young baby from the 'Drive' video in 1985 –Bob introduced her to the crowd with words to the effect, 'Don't let them tell you this stuff doesn't work.' Bob has met Oxford dons and sporting champions who would have died but for aid they received.

The name Band Aid was clever on so many levels. Bob made the point that it was called that because you can't put a sticking plaster on the gaping wound of poverty. As an aside it has become popular to criticise some aid help as being from 'White Saviours'. An observation my younger daughter made when I took her to a workshop for the Live Aid musical. I have to be open to the concept, but I am afraid I fail to understand it. I have seen the footage of the famine of biblical proportions, I have seen the footage where the white Scandinavian nurse had to choose who to feed or not feed, I have stood in the field in Korem where the original footage was filmed. As a father if my child needed food or medicine it would not matter to me what the skin colour was of the person who helped. Maybe that's just too simplistic.

Starvation is a brutal way to die, the body eats itself from the inside out. We know in history people have killed others fighting over food – if you and your family are dying do you care or have the luxury of choosing where help comes from. Of course the aim is to teach people to fish, not give them fish, but first things first!

As a result of Band Aid hundreds of millions have been raised and spent. It would be ridiculous to think not a penny of our expenditure was wasted, but we never received reports of such wastage, even though we monitored and sought and received follow up reporting from projects we funded.

Projects included:

Band Aid ships to save on transport costs not just for us but for other aid agencies.

12 ships operated a constant circular route between Tilbury docks and Port Sudan carrying 100,000 tonnes of aid.

Band Aid trucks to break local cartels – our drivers were bombed and shot and killed as this was done.

Accommodation for medical staff
Agricultural machinery
Airfreight costs
Beekeeping
Blankets
Boreholes
Bridges
Brick manufacturing
Cereal banks
Cleft lip surgery
Club leg surgery
Clothes
Construction of gravity fed pipelines
Control of Guinea worm

Control of locust infestation
Credit schemes
Dams
Dispensaries
Donkey carts
Drilling rigs
Eye surgery
Family reunification projects
Food
Food for work projects
Forestation
Fuel
Goats
Grain
Grinding mills
Health centres
Helicopter airlift costs
Hospitals
Houses
Immunisation
Insecticide for malaria control
Irrigation
Land cruisers
Latrines
Libraries in schools
Literacy programmes
Livestock
Malaria control
Medicine
Micro finance initiatives
Midwifery training
Mosquito nets
Nutrition screening programme
Ophthalmic programmes
Pesticide
Pig farming
Poultry
Port repairs

Plumpy'Nut to treat severely malnourished children

Printers for schools

Protein biscuits

Radio spares

Recruitment and retention of teachers

Research relating to trachoma and glaucoma

Rehabilitation of boreholes

Rice cultivation

Refugee support

Sanitation projects

Seed distribution

Scholarships

Schools

School furniture and equipment

School meals – kids go to school to get a meal and then get a side dish of education

Shelter

Small boats

Soil conservation

Spray planes

Support for those who were HIV positive

Tools

Training programmes

Transport

Tree planting

Tyres

Vaccines

Vegetable oil

Veterinary and poultry

Water pumps

Water reservoirs

Water supplies

Wells

Wheat flour

These projects were followed up on and evaluated.

At all times we were able to respond quickly to emergency situations. We were able to make decisions in 24 hours and implement those decisions immediately – we could transfer money in 24 hours. We were available at weekends – I found a note recently when Bob emailed me on a Saturday at 5.00pm and was complaining at 6.00pm that I hadn't replied!

After Live Aid, Bob had access to presidents and prime ministers and through his political lobbying he at least doubled the monies raised by Live Aid through government commitments.

In some cases he was using his new platform to get that access but he had created followers who would become world leaders. Both Tony Blair and George Bush junior had been moved by and were influenced in future policy by Live Aid.

Live Aid did not just raise consciousness it got into the people's bloodstream! It was a seminal moment for Tony Blair when he met Birhan in Ethiopia. At first he thought he was being politely introduced to a beautiful young agricultural student and then he was told that she was from the '*Cars*' video. It is not the wildest of speculation to suggest that fuelled his passion and determination at Gleneagles all those years later. Even earlier he, as an opposition MP lobbied Maggie Thatcher, to give us back the VAT she had taken from the Band Aid record. Bob saw how moved Tony Blair was by Birhan's survival, and took the opportunity to motivate him further. He said,

"You, we, political leaders have been focused on small things, now you have to do the whole thing, corruption, debt, trade, investment – in one large package."

In those 26 words were the agenda for the G8 at Gleneagles.

Of course there was some reneging on the Gleneagles commitments, but the net delivery from Gleneagles was of huge importance, and is attributable in no small part to Live 8 and the Make Poverty History campaign.

The cancellation of poor countries debt, the doubling of aid and an increase in the level of commitments to the poorest people in the world had a value of billions in what was actually delivered let alone promised.

In the Independent on Sunday newspaper, Paul Vallely said, 'Gleneagles commitments put 40 million more children in school, gave life-saving drugs to 6 million people with HIV/AIDS and halved malaria in eight countries'.

I have a list of more than 250 household names; artists, designers, and celebrities who helped achieve this, including the likes of Nelson Mandela and Bill Gates, but there is simply no room to list them – and without effort I could list 21 different types of professions that supplied their professionals!

And of course Live Aid wasn't just about raising money – it was about raising awareness.

'*The day the music changed the world*' was the branding for the DVD and if pressed Bob can elegantly explain how true that is.

In fact a small snippet from him on the subject;

"*Quite literally the boys and girls with guitars and pianos had written and forced what Kofi Annan, the then general secretary of the United Nations, called the Rubicon crossing moment in the relationship between North and South.*"

Michael Buerk the journalist whose report from Ethiopia triggered all this didn't mince his words, he said Live Aid was 'the greatest shared experience in mankind's history'.

Overseas aid had been nowhere on the political agenda and now it was on the top. I am astonished by what I am about to write but I believe Bob said that in 1986 the United Nations debated Africa for the first time in its history. In his autobiography Bob said Band Aid would be wound up by 1986! In 1991 he made a definitive effort to draw a line in the sand to say Band Aid was over.

A touching pamphlet was created to distribute publicly – of course Band Aid was nothing without the public, and particularly 'Beth of Basildon'. It was a 41 page detailed pamphlet charmingly called, *With Love from Band Aid* and it is a detailed summary of seven years work at a time when Bob believed Band Aid was being wound up.

Bob's messaging is as strong, beautiful, and touching as ever.

As we approach our 40th anniversary it's worth quoting extensively:

"*Seven years! You can count them now in trees, and dams, and fields, and cows, and camels, and trucks, and schools, and health clinics, medicines, tents, blankets, clothes, toys, ships, planes, tools, wheat, sorghum, beans, research grants, workshops... Maybe you should count them in terms of people. There are thousands upon thousands of people in a bitter and blasted part of this planet who were helped.*

We promised that every penny would go there and it did. Every penny that was raised through individual or corporate donations was sent to countries we operated in. Their pain was eased, their burden lifted momentarily.

Perhaps you gave them only an extra few weeks, a year or two, maybe a whole new start. It doesn't really matter.

What matters is that it worked. Not one of these would turn down those few weeks, years, whatever.

The experts will tell you it's hopeless. After seven years I am as expert as anyone, It is not a hopeless thing for one individual to care for another, to extend the hand of sympathy and shared humanity.

Ask those people (who receive help) is it hopeless?

Ask especially the poorest of the poor, the most innocent of all, the victims of both environmental degradation and political ruthlessness.

Ask them as they fall from hunger and tiredness, why they do not just give in, and succumb to what seems to be their inevitable fate?

Because they don't believe in a world without hope.

They think it's worth living.

Humans have an awkward tendency to not give up hope.

It goes on. We never pretended we could stop it.

We wished to do Something. We did.

We wanted to make a point. We made it.

We tried to take an issue nowhere on the political agenda and place it right on the top. We placed it there."

Amazingly the pamphlet said, 'the money has now been spent and the offices are closed.'

I wish I had known that was the end of the road, and that I was done with 'JUST FOR ONE HOUR'.

After that there was Band Aid 20, Band Aid 30, a Live Aid DVD, Live 8, Gleneagles and a Live 8 DVD.

We raised a further £50 million mainly from exploitation of intellectual property, recordings and videos.

Band Aid started as an acorn and grew into an oak tree with offshoots that inspired neighbouring trees. Comic Relief, Data with full engagement and funding from Bill Gates, Bono's philanthropic efforts some with Bob some without, Jubilee, The Africa Commission, One, Make Poverty History, and even Farm Aid, a huge and important movement in the USA.

And then 39 years after the record, and in spite of Bob's efforts to wind things up, there is a musical about Live Aid – maybe our last new fundraising source? I think that has been said before! We have already earned a quarter of a million pounds from it, with £450,000 certainly in the pipeline with the potential for much, much more.

I wasn't even going to mention the musical but every writer needs to bring a chapter to an end.

Bob was nominated for the Nobel Peace Prize, but let me go fully sycophantic and say he could get a nod for a literature prize too.

The previous words for the farewell pamphlet are impressive, but then with 24 hours to go for the print programme for the musical to go to print, he was asked to do a programme note, and he came up with the following on behalf of himself and his fellow trustees:

In the wake of Live Aid and the torrent of cash that ensued, Band Aid ramped up its organisational ability to now deliver on the promise made to its supporters. Penny and Kevin Jenden brought much needed expertise and competence to the structure needed to undertake the vast humanitarian organisation required. Over 600 trucks were required to break the logjam of food and other desperately needed assistance.

12 Band Aid ships operated a constant circular route between Tilbury docks and Port Sudan.

John James was our man on the ground and through working with the government and rebel organisations we were able to negotiate routes through the longest running war of the twentieth century, and across some of the most inhospitable land in order to get to the people we said we would help. All of this despite our drivers being bombed, and shot, and killed – this was done.

None of this was easy and none of us – all people in the entertainment business – had ever had any experience in doing anything similar, or on such a vast scale. But we did it and it worked, 40 years on the six original Band Aid guys are still doing it. None of us particularly want to do it, but none of us feel we should or indeed can stop. Turns out we can do it, so we must. I think we feel it's a personal responsibility even though none of us have ever talked about it. We just get on with it whilst living our other more understandable lives. Occasionally we pinch ourselves and think 'bloody hell' and the sense of satisfaction at what has been achieved makes up for everything.

As the worst ravages of the famine abated and the rebels took the capital our work moved towards establishing schools, sanitation, water, farming, agriculture, hospitals – longer term development. Sport Aid, School Aid, Fashion Aid, Art Aid etc. all followed on from the concerts. But of course besides raising hundreds of millions of dollars, we had also raised a giant political lobby for change in the way that the North – the richer world dealt with the South – the poorer part of the planet. Something needs to change if we were not to be locked into this endless, horrifying, and debilitating cycle of pain and awfulness visited upon the innocent poor of our world. The politics needed to change.

For the next 20 years Band Aid and friends set up the structures and allied with experts in order to develop policy and access to world leaders. This exhausting effort reached its summit in 2005 at Live 8 and the British G8 meeting in Scotland.

1000 of the greatest national and international artists and a million people across each of the nine cities watched by the 3.5 billion television and online audience obliged the leaders of the seven richest economies plus Russia to cancel the debt of Africa's poorest countries. A crippling mortgage type debt which had hitherto checked their economies and then to double the necessary aid to the poorest of the poor.

What had begun with a little Christmas record had over 20 years grown to a vast civil movement for change. One that had corralled the political process and bent it to its desired end. Since then both economies and democracies within the African concert have risen and fallen but always now with the certainty that the circumstances were not immutable, things could change, change for the better, and yes sometimes slip away again. But here finally was the proof that people were neither impotent nor hopeless, that given a fair chance anyone could be as productive as the next.

That a healthy life full of possibility was and should be open to all.

We are often told that Britain can or does lead on this, that, or other issue. It is embarrassing because the truth is it does not. However on this single perhaps greatest issue of all time – empathy and understanding of those who are in pain or who are mute, powerless, subject to the whims of climate change, politics, economics, or plain brute stupidity, Britain has shown and consistently shown that in comparison to other world powers the people of this country once aroused have shown they will not stand for it. We should be very proud of that indeed.

Band Aid is that, it is you. It has always been you. It remains so.

And when we are gone and when it is time, another Band Aid will come. Maybe one of you watching this play tonight will be the one who does it. We hope so.

Lots of Love,
Band Aid
Bob, John, Harvey, Michael, Midge and Chris.

And not surprisingly over the years we had, as we should, our critics – sometimes brutal. If any of us thought even naively at the beginning that there would be a time we could declare victory then that stupid notion was swept away long ago.

So no victory to be declared, but that does not make doing nothing a better option, and I find it difficult to believe we were wasting our time, or that we were busy fools!

"IN 2005 WE MADE GREAT STRIDES IN THE FIGHT AGAINST POVERTY AND I'M PROUD OF EVERY ONE THAT JOINED THE CAMPAIGNS AROUND THE WORLD TO MAKE POVERTY HISTORY.

BECAUSE YOU CAME TOGETHER AND ACTED AS ONE, WORLD LEADERS MADE PROMISES THAT HAVE THE POTENTIAL TO HELP MILLIONS ESCAPE THE PRISON OF POVERTY. THAT IS A GREAT ACHIEVEMENT. BUT NOW WE FACE THE DIFFICULT TASK OF MAKING OUR GOVERNMENTS TURN THEIR PROMISES INTO THE ACTIONS THAT WILL SAVE MILLIONS OF LIVES.

WE CAN KEEP LIVE 8 ALIVE. WE CAN BE THE GREAT GENERATION THAT MAKES POVERTY HISTORY. BUT TO MAKE POVERTY HISTORY WE MUST NOW MAKE PROMISES HAPPEN ONE BY ONE. DON'T GIVE UP NOW - LET YOUR POLITICIANS KNOW YOU ARE WATCHING EVERY STEP THEY TAKE. THEY MADE PROMISES - NOW THEY MUST MAKE THEM GOOD."

NELSON MANDELA

Nelson Mandela – 2005 : Keeping Live 8 alive and the continuing 'Fight Against Poverty'.

29 September 1985

J.P. Kennedy & Co.
Solicitors
54A York Street
London W1H 1FN

Dear parasites,

I defined 'Band Aid' as 'A piece of media sticking plaster applied to the Cancer of world hunger by Bob Geldof'. Live Aid was marginally more promising.

That the money raised is being expropriated for the trivial pursuits (Oh dear, someone else has a monopoly - er - exclusive rights on that one now) of pedantic jerks like you and squandered in the appeasement of your own puerile, pedantic prejudices is proof enough that I am nothing to do with you.

However, should any more small-minded, paranoid creeps count you among their friends or send the letter to you rather than returning it to me with a pound as planned, sorry, envisaged, then you may use this letter as evidence that I am absolutely nothing to do with Band Aid, neither the 'Trust' mismanaged by sharks like you, nor the sticking plaster.

Why not take a real bite of the cherry and take out an injunction, then I could call it BANNED AID.

Are you really representing Bob Geldof, who got so incensed with the clockwork morons around him that he shouted 'Fuck the address!' when interrupted while appealing for donations during the Live Aid appeal on television?

You may represent the 'Trust' but you misrepresent the man if I'm any judge of character.

Yours most sincerely,

Harry Alderslade
Freelance Ecologist

cc. Bob Geldof

P.S.   Should you not make it clear on your letters that you are n nothing to do with the John Kennedy?

P.P.S. Who is Philip Rusted or was that a statement?

Back in 1985 – a less than enthusiastic supporter of our project.

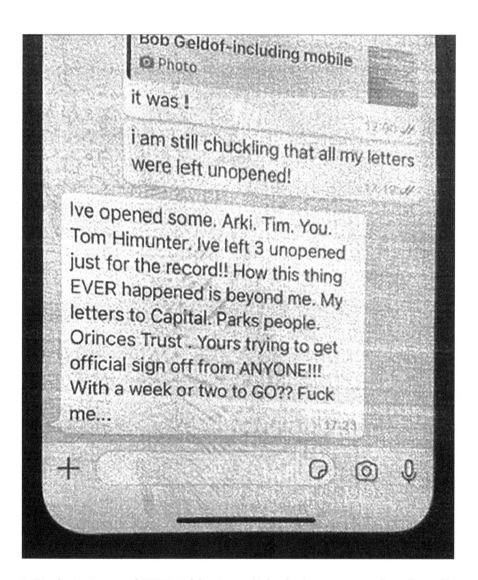

Bob Geldof-including mobile
📷 Photo

it was !

i am still chuckling that all my letters were left unopened!

Ive opened some. Arki. Tim. You. Tom Himunter. Ive left 3 unopened just for the record!! How this thing EVER happened is beyond me. My letters to Capital. Parks people. Orinces Trust . Yours trying to get official sign off from ANYONE!!! With a week or two to GO?? Fuck me...

In March 2021, because of COVID, Bob has time on his hands – he starts opening letters he would not open in the weeks before Live 8 and concludes, 'How this thing EVER happened is beyond me'.

His Holiness the 14th Dalai Lama

Bill Clinton

Tony Blair

Luciano Pavarotti

CHAPTER 21

THE DALAI LAMA, BILL CLINTON, TONY BLAIR
THE MAESTRO PAVAROTTI AND PETER BLAKE

And now we near that final curtain of this book. I feel I have had many fantastic 'pinch me' moments. I have been privileged to meet and work with just extraordinary characters and legends, so as we reach the end I wanted to touch on four particular meetings which were not where I expected to be when I begged to be let into the music industry, and a tale about the great artist Peter Blake.

THE DALAI LAMA

A number of years ago I was tracked down by the representative of the Dalai Lama in London – he told me that his 'boss' wanted to put on a charity concert and he wanted my help given my experience with Universal Music, and Band Aid, and Live Aid.

I agreed to have some conversations and think about the feasibility of such a project. After a few meetings I was sceptical as to whether this idea had actually come from the man himself or indeed if he actually knew anything about it. One thing was sure if he was not one hundred per cent behind it, it would not get off the ground.

We reached a crossroads in terms of strategising and I said the next step was for me to meet with his holiness to discuss what he was looking for from this project.

This request caused a great deal of consternation and basically I was told it was not possible. I said I am not entirely surprised by that answer but I can't carry on without knowing what his holiness was seeking to achieve. I was immovable on the subject but really thought that was the end of the story.

But about four weeks later I got a call to say that the Dalai Lama was going to be in Dublin in a couple of weeks and a meeting had been arranged. I was both surprised and excited.

So I headed off to Dublin with my wife Caroline not knowing what to expect. When I got there I was told, to my astonishment, I had a 45 minute slot. When the great moment arrived Caroline and I were ushered into his room where there was only His Holiness, Caroline and I, and his assistant. I have met many superstars but here was the biggest of all – maybe the pope is bigger, but who needs to quibble. It was for us a remarkable but incredibly simple experience. He personally served us green tea and just chatted with us about our children, Ireland (Caroline is Irish), the weather, and one overriding thing came through – he had the most astonishing sense of humour and just the best and most enthusiastic laugh you have ever heard. I have never been in a meeting where anyone laughed so much – not because of our gay wit and repartee, but he made himself and us laugh throughout.

And then as our time was running out, he said,

"And John, why do you want to put on this concert?"

I said, "Well actually that was my question to you.

He replied, "I am not sure it's a good idea."

And I said, "Well frankly I agree."

He laughed even louder than before.

The meeting was coming to an end but he stood and gave me a beautiful shawl, which of course I still treasure, and he asked if he could have a photo. Now that is true style – he knows everyone who meets him wants that photo, but I could never have asked so he pretends he wants one.

Sadly I can't find that photo, but I think it is on some device that I still have, so I haven't given up looking.

This was one hero I was very pleased to have met – what humility, what style, but most of all what a laugh!

BILL CLINTON

In December 2004, when the Band Aid 20 record was moving up the charts, I got one of Bob's cryptic calls - can I be at the Metropolitan Hotel tomorrow for a breakfast meeting.

No idea with who or what about – Bob worked on the assumption everyone else's diary was completely empty, but if by chance you had something in it, it was moveable. On this occasion I could move my prior appointment.

So I turned up at the Metropolitan Hotel as arranged at 9.00 am – Bob arrived pretty well on time. I gave him a quizzical look – he says,

"We are having breakfast with someone who wants to give Band Aid a big donation."

"Fair enough," I say, "Worth bumping my other appointment for."

Apparently the guy in question had had lunch with Richard Curtis a couple of days earlier and Richard had set up the meeting.

"Anyone I know?" I say.

He says, "A guy called Tom Hunter – a bit of a philanthropist."

Again – fair enough.

We are sent up to the penthouse where we are greeted by Tom and his lovely wife Marion. I don't think I am imagining it, but I suspect Tom at least, had had a late party night.

Anyhow they were both charming and fun, and they had a chef who offered us breakfast. I didn't get the impression Bob and Tom had met before. Tom explained he had made a lot of money in fashion and he had put a lot of that money into the The Hunter Charitable Foundation which had a particular interest in charitable projects in Africa.

Earlier that year he had made an announcement that he would give £100 million of his fortune to charity. Subsequently that sum would be increased to a promise that during his lifetime he would donate a billion pounds to charity.

He knew of Band Aid of course and the Band Aid 20 record had caused a new surge in publicity for us.

He was ready to donate £6 million pounds to us – fair enough – that felt like a good morning's work – so I had two poached eggs instead of one.

I asked whether there was to be secrecy or publicity around the donation. Tom didn't mind either way. I had an idea – the Band Aid 20 record was selling well, but not fantastically. I said why don't we announce you will pay band aid £4 for every Band Aid single purchased and £10 for every Live Aid DVD purchased, subject to a 'cap' of £6 million. I said that's the sort of story that drives sales.

Everyone liked the idea and I was charged with the responsibility of sorting out a press release.

I left with Bob and as I did I asked Bob how much he knew about Tom – not a lot – so I said I ought to make some enquiries before we put our names to this press release. I only needed to make two calls to Harvey Goldsmith our co-trustee and to Richard Caring the famous restauranteur. I think both were amused that I didn't know who Tom was, but both gave glowing references – he was clearly a diamond geezer!

The £6 million looked good and apparently Tom was also going to donate £1 million to Make Poverty History. So I worked on the press release with our wonderful PR guru Bernard Doherty and Tom's office.

After Xmas I contacted Tom's office – they explained they wanted to spend the money on mutually agreed projects rather than just hand the money over to us. They would keep the money until the projects were agreed as they could invest the money in the meantime, thus earning more money for their charitable foundation. They favoured educational projects which was fine, but they had two specific countries in mind, Uganda and Mozambique. We had funded projects in Uganda, but it was a bit of a stretch for us to include Mozambique in the scope of our work, as it was a bit further than our geographical brief.

This was feeling less and less like our money, and less and less like our projects, but in big picture terms the money was going to be spent in Africa on what looked like good projects, so no need for us to resist, but it certainly felt like our role was more passive than usual.

So over the first few months of 2005 this all got more complex, but in some ways more interesting.

It became clear that Tom wanted to fund the designated projects in partnership with the Clinton Foundation and now the UK department for overseas development also wanted to be involved!

So now it really felt as if we were the outsider – if we were a partner we were very much the junior partner, number four out of four partners.

Again these felt like two good projects now endorsed by the UK government and the Clinton Foundation, with us having a lesser or non role as each day went by, but no need to create a fuss, this was not costing us anything and there would be real beneficiaries in Africa and having Bill Clinton and the UK government associated with the projects should put the wind in their sails. In fact there wasn't really anything for us to do.

Some of my dearest friends and clients have often described me as paranoid. Undoubtedly they mean it as a gentle insult – I take it as meaning I am careful, cautious, and try to look out for unwanted and/or unintended developments!

The department for overseas development were clearly very excited understandably about Bill Clinton's involvement and planned major publicity for the signing ceremony. They sent me a five page agreement which the Band Aid Trust was expected to sign unamended.

I explained there was really no need for us to be a party to the agreement as we really had no role in this anymore. However, I was told everyone involved wanted Band Aid to get some of the kudos from these projects because of the original conversations back in December 2004.

OK – I suppose – just about OK. So I read the agreement – there was a major flaw in the agreement – it said Band Aid was donating £6 million to the projects. Well I suppose we would but only when we received the money from The Hunter Foundation.

The civil servants were at first irritated with me and then furious with me – they said I was being pedantic. Anyhow it was an easy thing to address, but each time I amended the agreement it came back with the same incorrect provision.

The day of Bill Clinton's arrival approached and still the agreement was incorrect. They sent me across signature copies for the trust to sign in advance.

I have some of the worst handwriting known to man – some say I should have been a doctor! As well as paranoid, some friends, even family, call me stubborn. I corrected the agreements with my spidery writing.

A very senior civil servant called me and rather patronisingly explained to me that they could not possibly ask their minister or ex-President Clinton to initial spidery amendments on such important documents. I completely agreed, I said please redo with my amendments incorporated, or I can if you prefer. I won't say the phone was slammed down on me but it was clear my name was mud.

Of course I was not being pedantic. When we received the money we would pass it on to the projects, but we were not going to be primary funders for projects we had not chosen, and for which we had no real role.

I had no problem if the money went direct, it did not need to come to us at all, but the £6 million must not be a Band Aid obligation until the money was received by Band Aid – it wasn't a complex concept.

I wouldn't budge but the civil servants assumed I would not create a fuss on the day.

The great day came – Bob and I went to the Ministry for Overseas Development. The press was out in force to witness Bill's arrival – in the seating plan Bob and I were either side of Bill. We sat and waited for his arrival – I heard the click of cameras – Bill bounded up the stairs demonstrating great energy.

We all sat and chatted and then it was time to sign. I immediately put my versions in front of the ex-President. All concerned; Bill, Bob, Tom and the minister Douglas Alexander were surprised they had to initial a number of amendments but they did. Bill even said, 'it's a long time John since I have had to do this!'

It was great to meet Bill (though actually I had met him once before in St. Petersburg – but that's another story). His famous charisma and charm were on full display and were very impressive – it was an enjoyable experience.

As I have said there was not much of a role for us to play in the projects that were the subject of the agreement, but I was informed that there were some complications with the projects, but I believe the complications were resolved, and I understand that the projects were fully funded. As I heard that there were complications I was relieved that the simple phrase *'the Band Aid trust will pay the funding for the projects'* had been deleted, and the deletion initialled even if President Clinton had to borrow my black Bic pen to initial the spidery amendments – fortunately the pen did not choose that moment to leak!

I was relieved that because I was paranoid and pedantic the obligation to fund was not with Band Aid.
SOMETIMES PARANOIA CAN BE A VIRTUE RATHER THAN A VICE !

THE FINANCIAL TIMES / TONY BLAIR AND PETER GABRIEL

One of my varied roles in the music industry was that I was, for a number of years, chairman and CEO of the IFPI (International Federation of the Phonographic Industry) – a lobbying organisation that represents the music industry globally.

I would travel the world trying to persuade governments to introduce new laws to enhance intellectual property rights, especially in the fight against piracy. During my tenure one of my main ambitions was to persuade the European Union to extend the copyright period from 50 to 70 years.

At the time, copyright was not something that was as revered as it had been in the past, and the new guys in town like Google and Facebook thought it should be shortened rather than lengthened, and interestingly enough even journalists advocated more liberal copyright laws, even though copyright protection was fundamental to their business model.

I found it very odd that journalists did not understand the importance of copyright protection. They took great pleasure in attacking the music industry, and indeed blaming the music industry for the fact that a whole new generation was taking our music for free instead of paying for it.

The Financial Times were particularly guilty in this arena, and I often asked to meet with Lionel Barber, it's editor, to explain the situation and to debate it – he refused to meet.

In frustration I wrote to the Financial Times.

I asked them to co-operate in an experiment.

I said let's assume your newspaper is ready to be printed at 10.00 pm at night. At 10.01pm either you give me a copy of your publication, or if you are not co-operating in the experiment – I will hack into your systems and steal your paper.

The following morning, wherever you sell, I will have distributors on the opposite pavement giving the paper away free, but I will have sold my advertising instead of yours – I will have had none of the costs of operation, my costs will only be the print cost and the cost of the people who give the paper away free.

'Free' I said is a powerful marketing tool – so I will have a greater circulation than you and soon even your most moral and loyal readers will wonder why they are paying for the paper.

My circulation numbers will increase and yours will decrease, your revenue from sales and adverts will not only decrease but will fall through the floor – my revenue from adverts will soar as my distribution numbers increase.

I asked whether they thought my conduct was fair, and I asked whether in those circumstances they could survive.

This was a thinly veiled description of the woes of the music industry for which the Financial Times had no sympathy.

They never answered my questions, but to be fair they did publish my letter, but no meeting with Mr Barber.

It would not be long before the public could get all the newspaper stories they wanted for free on the internet. The music industry has rallied with a subscription model – the newspaper industry has not had the same level of success.

In the meantime UK politicians were being heavily courted by the very strong lobbying teams of Google, Facebook and others, and it was by no means certain that even though there was a very strong UK music industry, and even though it punched above its weight around the world generating impressive export revenues, it was by no means certain that the UK government would support copyright extension.

So I thought it was time to lobby the Prime Minister for his support. I realised he was not likely to see me on my own.

I had already had conversations with Bob Geldof on the subject, as a recording artist he was of course in favour of an extended period.

I knew Bob had a great relationship with Tony Blair but I felt we needed another heavyweight. Peter Gabriel was someone I had great respect for as a musician, businessman and human being, a man who has championed many great causes. However I wasn't sure if he would be in favour of copyright extension, as he was generally a quite liberal soul, but when I spoke to him he was a big believer in intellectual copyright protection, less in his own interest, more so that more people could earn a proper living as musicians, and he had a great interest in so-called 'world music' being protected around the world.

Peter agreed to come to Downing Street if we could get a slot. By a lot of co-ordination of Tony's, Bob's and Peter's diary we found a slot. Peter, Bob and I knocked at the famous door of number 10 and were shown to an anteroom. Tony bounded in – he just seemed to have so much energy. I was impressed by his demeanour. There was fun banter between Tony and Bob – it was clear they had a shared friendship and had respect for each other. Tony led us into his office where tea and biscuits were laid out for us. Understandably, I had been told by a private secretary that we had 40 minutes and it was my job to make sure we did not overstay our welcome.

It would be difficult to find a more unassuming or modest man than Peter, but for Tony Blair he was the only person in the room. Famously Tony had been in a band at university, and fortuitously he was a huge fan of Genesis and Peter.

I introduced the subject and told the Prime Minister we wanted the UK government to support our campaign, and the conversation just flowed and flowed. It was simply fun with jokes and banter, but a solid discussion of the topic we were here for – then our 40 minutes was up and I gave the PM a chance to bring matters to a conclusion. He saw my cue but ignored it and just chatted on – at one hour a private secretary put his head around the door but got waved away, and then at one hour 15 minutes, Bob said,

"Well Prime Minister you clearly have all the time in the world but I am a busy man."

Tony laughed and said,

"I might have known Bob that you were the exception, but it is very rare in my role as Prime Minister that someone else brings a meeting to an end."

We all laughed.

As we left the Prime Minister's office Gordon Brown was outside – he was taken aback to see Bob and Peter leaving. Gordon called me over – his well known rivalry with Tony meant he was anxious to know what the meeting was about – I explained.

'Ah," he snorted, "the campaign to make rich musicians even richer!" I offered to explain to him now, or at a later date, the financial benefits to the UK economy in particular of copyright extension but he had moved on.

The meeting had been a success. The UK government agreed to support our campaign – Bob helped out elsewhere – particularly persuading the Prime Minister of Portugal to switch from being against the campaign to supporting the campaign. Not for the first time Bob's influence and persuasiveness with prime ministers, presidents and statesmen and women around the world was very impressive.

By the time my tenure at the IFPI was over we were only one vote away from procuring the copyright extension and that vote was procured within weeks of my departure with the actual extension following soon after.

That extension simply would not have happened if the UK had been non-supporters, or if indeed Gordon Brown had been prime minister at the time of the decision. The extension was of incalculable value to the music industry and artists and many economies, in particular the UK economy.

PAVAROTTI – THE MAESTRO!

Luciano Pavarotti became one of the most acclaimed tenors of all time and sold more than 100 million albums, a rare combination in the world of opera of critical acknowledgment of his creative talent and commercial success.

In my 'pinch me moments' I have met many great stars but the maestro stood out as a king in his field. Of course he had an imposing physical presence, and when he opened his mouth to sing it was an extraordinary experience, even or maybe more so because I was a philistine in this area. This very cultured man could have been very dismissive of me when he found out that I was chairman of his company, but he wasn't because he was a man of style and grace and because he was wily.

He was feted the world over by kings and queens and by prime ministers and presidents. Female opera singers would say that when he sang to them on stage it was as if he was making love to them and that he was, in that role, the best lover in the world.

With this adoration and fame it would have been surprising if he was completely untouched by his status. His first wife said that he had so many people around him to indulge him that if he said he wanted donkey's eggs then in ten minutes there would be a bowl of eggs in front of him, with the absolute assurance they were donkey's eggs.

I had the privilege of spending a lot of time with him, but more importantly I saw many of his magnificent performances – even to my untrained ear these were magical experiences.

One Sunday night I had just witnessed one such spectacular performance at the Royal Opera House and I was then hosting a dinner for him after the show!

This was a time when the critics could be tough, the standards he had set were so high that if on any occasion he did not quite make the high C's then they could be brutal. However on this occasion even the most mean spirited critics were describing it as one of the greatest performances of all time. The maestro did not need to hear that acclaim from them, he knew himself and from his audience what he had done!

I sat at dinner opposite him at a long table in a beautiful room at a 5 star hotel. There was a printed menu for the sumptuous meal ahead. The finest wines had been chosen, of course not by me.

It was shaping up to be a wonderful evening ahead.

In accordance with the printed menu the waiter brought in the starter, a sophisticated salad. The maestro looked in disgust at the salad and nearly threw it back at the waiter. Everyone at the table was taken aback, but pretending nothing had happened, he realised he may have gone too far – but was unrepentant, he looked at me gently accusing, after all I was hosting the dinner and should know better, using the full power of his operatic voice he bellowed;

"THE GREAT PAVAROTTI DOES NOT EAT SALAD,
JOHN, I AM HUNGRY, BRING ME PASTA!"

For a moment I think he expected me to go into the kitchen and get the pasta, which I would have happily done, but miraculously a huge bowl of pasta was put in front of him, and he looked at it as adoringly as he had been looking at his wife-to-be Nicoletta!

Apart from this salad faux pas, he and I had carved out a good working relationship. He was as I have said wily, I think he liked me but he had had many different chairmen over the years. He had learnt they come and go.

Early in our relationship he bought me a beautiful Italian briefcase, I still take it with me to meetings and on my travels.

I live in hope that someone will say, 'that is a magnificent briefcase', and

I will then say, 'Oh yes thank you, the maestro gave it to me'.
PRETENTIOUS … MOI?
That exchange hasn't happened so far.

Pavarotti was not only one of the greatest musical talents of all time he was also a great philanthropist.

Each year in his home town, Modena, he would put on a concert, 'Pavarotti and Friends' to raise funds for his charitable endeavours.

He was very persuasive and his Friends included;
U2
Celine Dion
Stevie Wonder
Sting
Bob Geldof
Bryan Adams
Andrea Bocelli
Meat Loaf
Michael Bolton
Dolores from the Cranberries
Simon Le Bon
Elton John
Sheryl Crow
Eric Clapton
Liza Minnelli
Jon Bon Jovi
The Spice Girls
Mariah Carey
Lionel Richie
B.B. King
George Michael
Eurythmics
Enrique Iglesias
James Brown
Queen

Astonishingly, some of the elite from the world of opera did not approve of the maestro singing pop songs, with pop stars.

His response according to Wikipedia was to say;

"Some say the word 'pop' is a derogatory word to say 'not important' – I do not accept that. If the word 'classic' is the word to say 'boring,' I do not accept. There is good and bad music."

As you can imagine it was expensive to put these concerts on. At first the TV broadcasts, the albums, and the DVDs made it a successful commercial project for all concerned – but after a while it was becoming an expensive venture for us as his record company.

In the years before I became chairman, my predecessors had tried to push back on funding the expenses only to find the wily maestro very persuasive. I believe there was a general view that I was the one to stand up to him and I do remember thinking this really must stop, but then my briefcase arrived with a hand written note;

'I can't tell you how much I value our wonderful working relationship and your personal support and belief it means a lot to me, Luciano.'

The classical team and my financial director were surprised, maybe incredulous, by my new-found belief in the commercial potential for the 'Pavarotti and Friends' project.

ME, A SUCKER? ... NON!

At the rehearsals for that year's event I stood in a beautiful opera house in Bologna – not ten people in the room, Andrea Bocelli on stage, and me standing next to Pavarotti, listening to the most beautiful sound of Andrea rehearsing – certainly a 'pinch me moment' beyond all 'pinch me moments'.

I was mesmerised by the beauty of Andrea's voice.

Midway through the rehearsal, the maestro whispered in my ear and said 'as you can hear he can't sing'!

I didn't flinch, I looked straight ahead, acknowledged I had heard what had been whispered, and listened to the astonishing sounds coming from the stage – and of course I nodded in agreement as I thought for someone who cannot sing to me he sounds like an angel and certainly sells millions and millions of albums.

Of course what the maestro meant was that this young upstart, who may be after my mantle as the greatest singer in this genre, was not as good as the great maestro Pavarotti, but then WHO WAS!

PETER BLAKE

I have met Peter but it was in a crowd at a dinner table. This short tale is not about meeting him.

Peter, is one of this country's finest and most famous artists.

He is most famous for designing the album cover for Sgt. Pepper's Lonely Heart Club Band. He has been a big supporter of Band Aid, designing the artwork for the original single and the Live 8 poster.

Of course he never got paid for his astonishing contribution but there was something worse than that.

Over the years, tens of thousands of people have volunteered their time and skills for Band Aid, Live Aid, and Live 8, and all the numerous offshoots.

Everything happens so fast that often people's contributions can be invaluable, absolutely invaluable, but they get no recognition or thanks though Bob is excellent at doing that, but often of course neither he nor the other trustees know of people's good deeds or selflessness!

One day someone told me they had met one of their heroes, Peter Blake, and then I saw them hesitate …

"What ?" I said.

They said, "I don't know whether to say this or not."

"Well," I said, "you have started so you should finish!"

They said,

"Peter is so proud of his association with Band Aid, but he is a bit sad about it because no one said thanks."

I was mortified but I could see how that could have happened. The next day I sent Peter a case of Dom Perignon from all the trustees (not paid for by the trust). I was worried that he would not see it as 'better late than never' – but I got word back that he was absolutely chuffed!

––––––––––––––

And now to all those thousands and thousands who did great things and got no recognition or thanks, a deep heartfelt THANK YOU!

But no point sending me a message that the absence of a thanks before now has made you sad, because I can't afford Dom Perignon for all of you!

You are simply too many!

CHAPTER 22

BITTER SWEET SYMPHONY

One day I got a call from a friend of mine Steve Kutner. Steve had had a very successful career in the music industry but more recently he had been a very successful sports agent including representing the football manager Claudio Ranieri when he won the Premier League, and players like Frank Lampard, Patrick Viera and many others. Clients, friends, family know I am not a great one for phone calls – if I have to have them at all I like them short and sweet. Familiar with this modus operandi Steve rushed through the pleasantries of how was I and said how did I fancy managing Richard Ashcroft with him. That was an easy answer – I didn't. I thought Richard was an immensely talented artist, a truly great songwriter, but I didn't want to manage him or indeed anyone else – I just did not believe that I had the required skill set for such an important role.

What makes an artist great is their creativity and when you manage someone you have to create an environment that nurtures that creativity, and most importantly you have to be there for them, and if that involves regular 50 minute conversations about the artwork for their new release then that's your job. That's simply a job I would not be good at, no matter how much I admired an artist, and indeed I admired and respected Richard Ashcroft a great deal.

So my answer was an emphatic 'thanks but no thanks'.

Steve said, "Richard has asked me to manage him and I will only do it if you do it with me." There was no logic to this. Steve had all the skills to be a great manager; patience, tenacity, love of music, great business acumen.

So I said, "This is nonsense, I don't have the skills to do it but you should." He said, "Will you at least meet Richard?"

I thought lunch with a legend like Richard is always worth a few hours of your life, and even though long ago he had been a client of my law firm – I had never met him, so yes I agreed and looked forward to the lunch.

So lunch was arranged in Knightsbridge. I of course was five minutes early and sat at a nice table by the window with a good view of the street. At 1.00pm Steve rang, he was on time but he was just parking – a normal situation for Steve who has a wonderful collection of classic cars and would never take a cab or be driven. He arrived in the restaurant five minutes later. I was relaxed – I had time and half expected Richard to be late. As I chatted with Steve I kept one eye on the street and after about 15 minutes I saw Richard approaching. It is hard to describe star quality but it's easy to recognise when you see it. He walked up the street like he owned it, as if he was in a video but without trying.

He was accompanied by his wonderful wife Kate. What I noticed most was Richard smiled a lot and his great sense of humour was illustrated by his constant banter with Steve. It was also clear that Richard and Kate had a fabulous relationship. We ordered some food. There was potential for an awkward atmosphere as I didn't think I had the skills to manage Richard, and he didn't want me to manage him, he just wanted Steve. In spite of this it was good fun. Richard was a big fan of The Stone Roses, and he knew I had worked with them, and said he respected what I had done for them, so that gave us common ground. He said, "Maybe I could look at the dispute he had had over his song *Bitter Sweet Symphony*."

I knew there had been a dispute, but I didn't know the detail, but it was one of the most heartbreaking stories for any songwriter. It could be described as one of the great music industry cock-ups, but it's not clear that you could say who was at fault, but it was certainly a travesty of justice with, in theory, a potential villain Allen Klein – but a villain who would describe himself, maybe rightly from one perspective, as the hero – the protector of songwriters.

The Verve had been signed to Virgin Records, a much admired label started by Richard Branson. This band were much respected, but real global success eluded them, and the inter band relationships were, to say the least, tempestuous. The band went through a cycle of breaking up and reforming. When they weren't The Verve, then as Richard was a lead singer and song-writer, he was a solo artist. It was during a non-Verve spell that he wrote his most important song to date 'Bitter Sweet Symphony', along with much of the classic album Urban Hymns, but for various complex reasons it would be released by The Verve.

This masterpiece of a song included a tiny part (three 4 bar loops lasting 10 seconds) of a record by the Andrew Loog Oldham Orchestra – an instrumental recording of the Rolling Stones song 'The Last Time'. You can't go round using bits of other people's songs unless you get their permission. So Virgin were told of the use – technically called a sample – and they got permission from Andrew Loog Oldham.

Incomprehensibly, no one thought at the same time to get permission from the songwriters and publishers who were Mick Jagger and Keith Richards and Abkco music. A fatal error.

Richard would point out that the version he originally listened to was The Staples Singers *'This May Be The Last Time'* which he said was credited as traditional.

Mistakes like this do happen and usually a deal can be worked out.

By the time the error was realised, *'Bitter Sweet Symphony'* was to be released on an album by The Verve called *'Urban Hymns'.* All the Virgin companies around the world were very excited, the commercial promise that The Verve had always shown was about to be delivered.

But there was this spanner in the works – the song was a walking, talking, all singing, copyright infringement until there was permission from Mick, Keith and Abkco to use their song.

An added irony was that it was suggested that Mick and Keith had at least been inspired in their songwriting by The Staple Singers *'This May Be The Last Time'.*

The right thing to do was to hold up the release of the record until permission was granted, and if permission was not given redo the track without the offending bit. I would like to think that is what would have happened if Steve and I were managing, but maybe that is easy with the benefit of hindsight.

Anyhow the album release had momentum, it was going to be released around the world, no one wanted to stop the release. Again in those circumstances I think Steve and I would have insisted a non-offending version was readied to use if permission was a problem.

What happened next is not absolutely certain, and there have been myths and apocryphal stories, but the eventual outcome is clear.

It's fair to say that Ken Berry, President of Virgin Records, would have been confident he could resolve the problem and why not, the Rolling Stones were on Virgin and he knew the notorious Allen Klein, the owner of Abkco publishing. So Ken apparently went off to see Mister Klein in the hope that when he played the song he would love it so much that Allen would melt and a deal would be done.

But Allen Klein was not a man who melts. If you were being fair to him, and why he would have argued he was a hero, he would say he always violently opposed the practice of sampling and would not endorse it by giving licences – particularly after the event, and particularly for his most important songs, which would certainly include all Rolling Stones songs, so the most likely outcome is that Ken got a simple blank 'no' – no licence.

But there is an apocryphal story that did the rounds. As it's apocryphal it doesn't really warrant telling but this is only a book so what harm in taking an interlude.

The story goes that Ken was first hardballed by Klein, but then Klein said Ken because I like you I will grant you a licence on the basis that Abkco owns 50 per cent of the song. Given that the sample was less than five per cent of the music for the song, and none of the lyrics, then this would be a great deal for Abkco, but Ken would also have recognised that it would resolve an otherwise unresolvable impasse. But it was not in Ken's gift to do this deal as it was Richard's song. So as the story goes, Ken reported back to The Verve's manager Jazz Summers. Now Jazz was a very talented, very successful, but short-tempered manager who was not beyond using bullying as his modus operandi.

Again the story goes that Jazz was outraged and asked for Klein's phone number. Ken begged him to accept the deal but Jazz (who sadly is no longer with us) insisted and the following is the APOCRYPHAL story;

Jazz – 'Can I speak to Allen Klein?'

Secretary – 'Who shall I tell Mr Klein is calling?'

Jazz – 'Jazz Summers, manager of The Verve.'

Secretary – 'Putting you through to Mr Klein.'

Klein – 'Mr Klein speaking.'

Jazz – 'Are you the f*cking cu*t who thinks he is taking 50 per cent of my client's song?'

Klein – 'Mr Summers I *was* the f*cking cu*t who was taking 50 per cent of your client's song ... but now after your rude intervention, I am the f*cking cu*t who is taking 100 per cent of your client's song!'

CLICK as Klein puts the phone down.

It's a great story but I understand it didn't happen, though there are still people who tell me the story as if it's a fact, but that's the music industry for you.

Klein was immovable to everyone including Ken Berry and Virgin and Jazz, and there was no plan B.

Klein would insist he was being consistent – he did not give sampling licences, especially when they were being negotiated after the sample had been used. As I say in his version he wasn't a villain, he was a champion of songwriters' rights, a campaigner against intellectual property theft, but whatever hat he was wearing it was a disaster for Richard.

There is no myth, no apocryphal story about the simple outcome – in order to avoid being sued Richard had to give up one hundred per cent of the song for one thousand dollars.

I don't know what publishing stories are worse than this.

The financial cost was immeasurable, though credible publications have estimated MANY lost millions! But what in many ways was even worse was the creative implication that Richard had not written what was to prove to be his most successful song.

Mick and Keith were beneficiaries of Klein's tough stance without ever being involved – they even got a Grammy nomination for a song they hadn't written, certainly not an honour they were looking for.

This sorry saga is best summed up by Klein's own words, according to his biographer Fred Goodman, Klein described what he had done in relation to the song and said; 'I WAS VERY BAD TODAY.'

So that is a very long diversion from Richard's request at our lunch table.

Years of experience told me that if there was anything that could be done for Richard's plight it would have been done a long time ago, so I said, "Richard I will take a look but I doubt if there is anything I can do."

My instincts were correct – many moons ago, not one, but two, barristers had taken a look and decided there was nothing that could be done. Richard had signed an onerous but enforceable agreement.

I did end up co-managing Richard with Steve and enjoyed it, and continue to enjoy it – in fact I consider it a privilege. Steve, as promised, does most of the daily contact with Richard as they are close friends as well as having a professional relationship, but I am there in the background when needed. I am thrilled to be part of the team.

Richard continues to write great songs and has released three, strong, solo albums in the last few years and another one is in the pipeline as I write. His live shows are stunning, his audiences are treated to a great set of songs. When Chris Martin introduced Richard at Live 8 to sing '*Bitter Sweet Symphony*' with Coldplay he said, "Here is probably the best song ever written, to be sung by the best singer in the world."

That's as good an intro as you can get, and night after night on tour Richard lives up to that title. He always 'delivers' for his audience.

But of course the pain of having his song taken away from him has never gone away, and on a regular basis Richard would raise it with Steve, and Steve would raise it with me. Each time my answer would be the same – I feel Richard's pain and I really do but there is nothing we can do.

Steve is like a terrier when he has something to do and eventually he told me he was going to approach Allen Klein's son Jody and appeal to him to do the right thing. I didn't want to discourage this, but I absolutely knew it had zero chance – ZERO – of success, but maybe it would make Richard feel that absolutely everything possible had been tried, and he would be able to move on – maybe, but I doubted it. Steve asked his good friend Lucian Grainge, probably the most important executive in the music industry, to put him in touch with Jody, and Steve called Jody. Jody was perfectly civil, especially as he knew that Steve and Lucian were friends, but left no opening for a renegotiation or handing back of rights, but suggested Steve approach Mick and Keith.

And then I had a left field idea.

By coincidence I was to have lunch with Joyce Smyth, the Rolling Stones manager. This had been arranged by Bernard Doherty the PR legend who seemed to work for everyone and had certainly worked for the Stones for forever. Bernard had done an astonishing job for Band Aid and Live Aid of course – for free. I had known Joyce for at least 30 years, but we wouldn't be in contact much these days so I was very much looking forward to seeing her.

Joyce is one of the most impressive, and most understated, and modest people you could expect to meet. Not many bands have a female manager but Mick and Keith, who would have every manager in the world falling over themselves to manage the Stones, had asked Joyce to manage them. Mick is undoubtedly one of the smartest artists in the history of the music industry, not just a great singer and an astonishing creative force, but has immense business acumen – the fact that he had chosen Joyce to be his representative spoke volumes.

I chuckled at the people who would engage with Joyce and under-estimate her and pay a heavy price for doing so.

So we had a lovely lunch at Le Caprice – Joyce, me and Bernard.

I then asked Joyce if she knew of the 'Bitter Sweet Symphony' story – she said vaguely – Bernard said he did – so I asked Joyce if I could tell her – she said please do. So I told her and she saw the travesty that it was. So I asked Joyce if I could write to Mick and Keith on Richard's behalf, appealing to them to give up their share of income – of course it was very likely that the answer would be 'no' – but I thought it was worth a try.

As a friend I also counselled Joyce to think carefully before getting involved. I said it's not a great thing for a manager to do to go to their clients and ask them to lose an income stream! It's a manager's job to increase income streams, not remove them.

Now at this stage, 999 out of 1000 people would have said I understand how terrible this is but it is political suicide for me to get involved with zero, absolutely zero, upside for Joyce and her clients.

But I was sitting with that person in a thousand, and she said I am making no promises but send me a note of the full story – I could not ask for anything more. My pitch was that Mick and Keith, as songwriters themselves, might think what it was like to be in Richard's shoes and might understand his pain and right a wrong.

What was interesting for me was not just Joyce's sense of right and wrong but she clearly knew her clients were decent human beings who just might be receptive – they might not, but many managers would have known it would be a complete and absolute waste of time to ask their clients to do the right thing when it involved a financial cost to them.

So we parted on the basis I would write down the story!

Which I did.

First I brought Steve up to date, but suggested we did not say anything to Richard as the chances of success in our endeavour remained very slim. Steve and I wrote down the story.

In our note for Joyce;

We explained that many people misunderstand the offending sample. Allen Klein's biographer said, 'the irony was that the segment lifted ... didn't sound a bit like the original Stones song'. The sample is only four seconds long out of a six minute song – only just about three per cent of the song! Actually you could argue it's that percentage of the music, and zero per cent of the lyrics, so it is less than one and a half per cent of the song. None of the lyrics were infringing but Richard was forced to sign those over as well. Richard has paid a heavy price for what he did 20 years ago at 25 years old.

We said;

"So Joyce – a sorry story – without any leverage we are asking Mick and Keith if after 20 years they would 'forgive' the mistake made by 25 year old Richard and those around him. The only possible rationale for such a wonderful gesture would be their respect as songwriters for the writer of what is generally recognised as a magnificent musical work – the future earnings even over a long period will not match the earnings of the past, but that is irrelevant,

it would obviously mean a huge amount emotionally as well as financially to Richard and would be a great and meaningful artistic gesture from two of the greatest of all songwriters.

After 20 years it feels timely to make this appeal. Richard really enjoyed playing as a special guest at a couple of the Stones concerts last year, and at the end of May he is being honoured by his songwriting peers with an Ivor Novello for Outstanding Contribution to British Music – what a great opportunity to announce the generosity of Mick and Keith.

Joyce I hope none of this note comes across as if we presume Mick and Keith will make this gesture – we know in most respects there is simply no need for them to do so but ... we live in hope."

After receiving my note Joyce wrote to me and asked me to bear with her, she would choose her moment to raise it with Mick and Keith during rehearsals for their next live dates – as I read the note I just thought what an amazing woman.

And then many weeks later, I was driving in my car and heard on the news that Mick had suffered a heart incident of some kind during rehearsals. Well, I thought that puts paid to that! Joyce has bigger priorities.

But even I had underestimated Joyce.

This was a problem that had haunted Richard for more than 20 years, but a mere 178 days after our lunch Joyce had performed a miracle. She told me she had raised the 'ghastly issue' – what a great description! – with both Mick and Keith and they were horrified and 100 per cent in agreement that they should forego anything further.

I really couldn't believe it – 'doing the right thing' is not a normal modus operandi for the music industry, but for once Richard had had a bit of luck with this song – three decent human beings had done what was fair.

Steve called Jody to tell him what had happened and I think it is fair to say he was very impressed with this magnificent gesture by Mick and Keith knowing they could simply have done nothing.

As you can imagine Richard was emotional when he was told. I think many people were fairly dismissive when Steve and I explained that the financial aspect of this was secondary but it really was – the implication for 20 years had been that Richard hadn't really written his most important and most successful song. At best a look at the credits would suggest that Richard wrote the lyrics but none of the music – that was a terrible cloud to live under. The timing couldn't have been better – a few weeks after Joyce delivered the good news, Richard received his Ivor Novello for his Outstanding

Contribution to British Music and he was able to use that platform to personally and publicly thank Mick and Keith for what they had done.

In the accompanying press release Richard said;

"It gives me great pleasure to announce that as of last month Mick Jagger and Keith Richards agreed to give me their share of the song *'Bitter Sweet Symphony'*. This remarkable and life affirming turn of events was made possible by a kind and magnanimous gesture from Mick and Keith, who have also agreed that they are happy for the writing credit to exclude their names and all their future royalties derived from the song they will now pass to me."

After 20 years a wrong had been righted because of two great gentlemen songwriters and one truly formidable woman!

The BBC headline said it all;

'ONE OF ROCKS MOST FAMOUS INJUSTICES
HAS FINALLY BEEN RESOLVED.'

During all this process of course I kept in touch with Bernard, one of the greatest PR gurus of his generation, and I did an interview with Billboard magazine about the full story of tragedy to glory.

Bernard then sent me a message that Mick was full of admiration for how the recent events had been handled and I think what gave him most satisfaction, if you will excuse the pun, was the magnificent and heart-warming role that Joyce Smyth had played in all of this.

There are 100 million songs on Spotify and only 600 songs have been streamed a billion times, but *'Bitter Sweet Symphony'* has achieved that! It is a very, very special song and a terrible wrong has been partly righted for one of our greatest artists and songwriters by two legendary artists and songwriters.

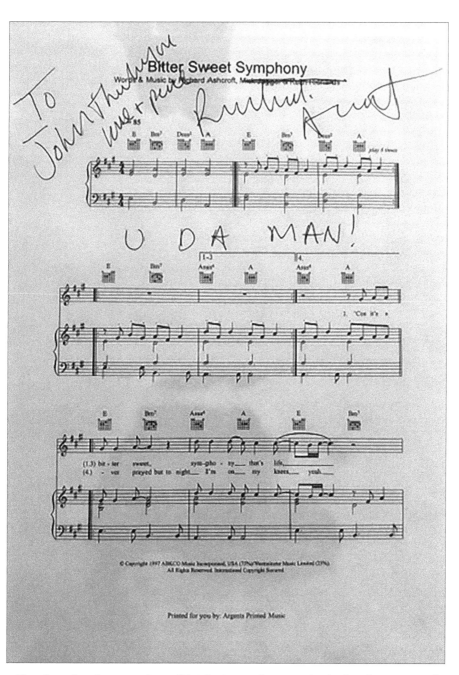

Bitter Sweet Symphony song sheet – "To John, Love and Peace, Richard Ashcroft. U DA MAN!"

CHAPTER 23

THE FINAL CHAPTER

I have watched over the years as recording artists don't know when it is time to say their album is finished. They keep on recording and remixing but someone should tell them to stop. I still have stories I want to tell swirling around my head but there is also a voice there, my own voice, saying 'John Stop'.

And then how do you finish?

Well, I am going to finish with a simple story.

It is 2024. I really wanted to work in the music industry and now I have done so for 46 years – will I make 50?

Well that's for God and good fortune to decide. It's been a fantastic journey, personally and professionally. So many 'pinch me' moments.

I am still working at a top level with many big names and interesting clients, but I am not on the front line, I am no longer a 'player' – but you aren't supposed to get more than 40 years in the music industry.

I may have addressed this before, if I see I have, I will keep repetition to a minimum.

As you will have seen I have had the privilege of working with some household names and over the years I have been asked who is the biggest 'Prima Donna'. I have seen very little bad behaviour. I have always been on their side, whether as their adviser or as chairman of their record company.

If there is a trait I disapproved of then it's that occasionally an artist did not appreciate, I was going to say how lucky they were, but it's not just about luck it's about talent – you have to have luck, talent and a work ethic in equal measures.

Every artist has at one time or other dreamt of being a star and craved fame and fortune. Bob Geldof famously said, he always wanted to get rich, get famous and get laid. He did better than Meat Loaf who said 'two out of three ain't bad' – Bob did the full house.

But sometimes I saw artists who had wanted the success so much subsequently whingeing about the problems it brought. I was never a sympathetic ear on that subject. Over dinner one star's wife told me, 'how terrible it was they had been on a ski trip and fans kept coming up to them'. Of course it's irritating to have that happen but my wife Caroline berated me for saying, 'Rachel the real problems begin when the fans are no longer interested' – and of course I watched as that came to pass as indeed it does for most artists.

Many artists ended up loathing their fellow band members. I tried to counsel that it was worth finding a space in your head where you can find a way of making the relationship work, because I know you will find back to reality out of the public eye even more difficult than difficult colleagues.

But no rudeness to me personally, in fact gratitude oft expressed and sincerely expressed; thank you's in letters, presents, gold discs, from the stage, invites to parties, and on album covers – ALWAYS certainly much appreciated by me.

So now it's 2024 the tail end of a fabulous career.

Caroline's cousins Steven and JP, a wonderful couple, invite us to their wedding, our first gay wedding.

At 2.00am Elton and Kiki's *'Don't Go Breaking My Heart'* is played by the DJ and the dance floor is full of joy. The happy couple tell me how much they adore Elton.

I, now a few drinks in, say I will get you tickets for his tour – they are beside themselves with happiness for their fantastic wedding day now made even better with this wonderful offer from John.

Over my poached eggs and avocado the next day Caroline says, 'do you remember what you promised last night?'

I look a bit hazy and she says, 'you promised Steven and JP tickets for Elton's tour'. What she is really saying is did you forget it's a long time since you were chairman of Elton's record company – where are you getting those tickets from? My stomach is feeling queasy – is it the hangover or the promised tickets?

A few months go by and very graciously Steven and JP never send me a reminder. Occasionally I remember but I move on, but then I hear on the radio that, after a break caused by COVID, Elton is coming to the end of his global record-breaking tour.

OH NO! – I can probably get away with doing nothing but I promised, it might have been better if I didn't, but I promised. I look at the dates – I have already missed the London dates and there is only a handful to go.

One of those is Glasgow. Steven and JP live in Derry, they could easily get to Glasgow. Smart thinking on my part logistically but what about the small issue of tickets?

Then by good fortune on a train I bump into a good friend of mine who used to work with Elton. I say to him, 'how do I get some Elton tickets for Glasgow?' He says, 'you buy them on the friends and family list that Elton's tour manager organises'. I say, 'these days it would be a stretch to describe myself as friends and family'. He says, leave it to me. I hear him call the tour manager and introduce me as the former chairman of Elton's record company. The tour manager says he will email me a link to buy tickets.

Thank you God, my friend Derek, and the said tour manager.

The link arrives and I buy the said tickets, contact Steven and JP as if this was a long-standing planned delivery on my wedding promise.

Can you get yourselves to Glasgow? They certainly can.

We meet up on the Saturday night outside Glasgow Arena and they cannot stop telling me how excited and grateful they are.

We go inside and start walking to our seats, we walk, and we walk, and we walk, until we reach our seats which are clearly the best seats in the house. Elton knows how to look after his friends and family .

The concert starts, Elton's voice sounds stronger than ever and he sings hit after hit.

Steven and JP are besides themselves, giving me regular thumbs up signs signalling how thrilled they are with the seats and the show.

Elton's energy is just astonishing. He then slows things down and tells the audience how much he has enjoyed the tour, and he says he has a few friends in tonight and calls out their names, and then he says, 'there is one dear friend who I haven't seen for a number of years but I am going to play this next song for JOHN KENNEDY' and proceeds to play *'Don't Let The Sun Go Down On Me'.*

It's one of my favourite Elton songs, and by coincidence the song that George Michael had told Caroline at Live Aid that he was going to perform with Elton.

Well I was open-mouthed, but not as open-mouthed as Steven and JP!

What a fantastic thing for Elton to do. The show continued with incredible hit after incredible hit, and then as the last song of the main part of the show is halfway through someone taps me on the shoulder and says, 'Elton wondered whether you would like to watch the encores from the side of the stage'.

I indicate pretty well in sign language that I would love to, but it would be rude to leave my guests, he makes it clear that Caroline and them are welcome too.

We are led right to the very edge of the side of the stage to listen and watch as Elton delivers three mesmerising encores just a few feet away from us. JP a very good looking Brazilian guy says to me, 'I cannot believe how close I am to my hero'.

The encores finish, the crowd go crazy, Elton leaves the stage and the lights go up. We all look at each other as if we can't believe what has just happened.

The same guy who had previously tapped me on the shoulder does so again, I assume he is saying time to move out and I indicate I understand but thank you – but he says, 'Elton was wondering if you have time to say 'hello'!

Well funnily enough I do, but again I gesture to Caroline and our guests, and he says of course all four of you.

Steven and JP cannot speak as we walk back stage.

There are a number of guests there, friends and family, but we are taken straight to Elton's dressing room. His welcome comes with hugs and kisses for me and a genuine chat about what I have been up to. We cover a lot of ground and we continue for ten minutes during which he includes Caroline, JP and Steven.

We are both conscious that he has many people outside waiting to see him including a number of celebrities and so there is a natural break. As we are ready to make our departure walking on air, Elton says 'would you like a photo?' ! WOULD WE?!

We line up and JP manages to get himself behind Elton and we leave. The photo is sent to us, but we are asked not to use it until 9.00am tomorrow.

OH WHAT A NIGHT!

At one second past 9.00am the following morning Steven and JP put the photo on social media. They said the reaction from their friends and family made them feel like they were celebrities.

I finish my story with this story, as I see it as a story of class and style.

I have been in superstars' dressing rooms many times, I have been in Elton's dressing room many times, but those moments were in the past – I had a role to play in the artists' careers, in Elton's career. Even then it was a theoretical role, I was chairman of his record company, but he had been a global superstar for decades, but there was an etiquette in play between a chairman and an artist. But now I could not do anything for Elton, he did not need to acknowledge my presence in the audience, let alone invite the four of us to his dressing room.

It just says so much about the man.

If you have seen the film 'Rocketman' you know of some of his outrageous behaviour from the past. If you want to see 'Prima Donna' behaviour watch Elton in 'Tantrums and Tiaras' – but that was then and this is now.

Now he is married to David and they have two wonderful sons. Elton is a doting father, and as he correctly said in the dressing room, he is now more successful than he has ever been. He attributes that to a significant degree to David's role as his manager. This reference to greater success than ever was not in an immodest way, more a statement of surprise and gratitude. We had just been reminded of how many incredible hits he had recorded and performed.

I mentioned before that when I got my OBE it was the first time for a long time that one had been awarded to a member of the music industry (with the exception of Saint Bob – but I mean mere mortals).

A week after it was announced I was at an event at Claridges and was chatting to Elton and his then manager John Reid. Surreally, John Reid asked me how they could get one of those things for Elton, and I found myself offering advice as to how it could / would / should happen.

Well, now it is Sir Elton, for services to entertainment and charity.

He is one of the greatest recording artists and songwriters of all time – he has won Oscars, Tony Awards for theatrical success, Grammys, and an Emmy, being one of only 19 people to win all four. If you have all four you have, or are, an EGOT.

But arguably none of those are his greatest achievement, that is undoubtedly the Elton John AIDS Foundation. It has saved countless lives and it's work on awareness of AIDS is just extraordinary.

And yet that night in Glasgow he showed class and style that he did not need to, he needed nothing from me, I could do nothing for him – that's a true superstar in every sense of the word.

GOOD NIGHT, GOD BLESS!

Caroline: I really love you.
John: That's wonderful - it's not the champagne talking is it?
Caroline: No, it's me talking to the champagne.

John and Caroline's Christmas card.

ABOUT THE AUTHOR

After begging for a job in the music industry, John Kennedy has spent more than 45 years in the music industry.

The title of this book 'JUST FOR ONE HOUR' is taken from the day Bob Geldof asked him to give one hour of his time for free. That was nearly 40 years ago and probably 20,000 free hours ago!

Including helping to stage Live Aid and co-producing Live 8 and executive producing the Live Aid and Live 8 DVDs.

Along the way, John Kennedy set up a successful music business legal practice representing many of the top artists songwriters and independent labels of the time.

He then went on to be chairman of Polygram films and records before becoming chairman and CEO of the newly created Universal Music UK, the biggest music label in the UK.

He then became president and COO of Universal Music International before becoming chairman of the body representing the whole music industry globally.

In 1994 he was awarded an OBE by the Queen.

In 2006 he was made Chevalier de l' Ordre des Arts et des Lettres by the French government, along with Bob Geldof and Harvey Goldsmith in the same month that all three were given an award as Music Personalities of the Year.

For a number of years John Kennedy led the ultimately successful campaign to extend the European copyright period for recordings from 50 to 70 years. The extended period is of immense tangible economic benefit to the music industry including both labels and artists.

John Kennedy continues to work as a consultant in the music industry and has the honour and pleasure of co-managing Richard Ashcroft who was the leading member of The Verve before becoming a successful solo artist.

In this memoir John Kennedy mulls that it's been such a great journey – meeting and engaging with real royalty; the Queen, Princess Diana, Prince Charles, Presidents and Prime Ministers, but most importantly of all, music business royalty, and even a Saint, not to mention the occasional sinner!

And he hopes the journey is not yet over!

Milton Keynes UK
Ingram Content Group UK Ltd.
UKHW050119131124
2765UKWH00066B/37/J